The Dissenting Opinions
of
Mr. Justice Holmes

OLIVER WENDELL HOLMES

JUSTICE OF THE SUPREME COURT OF THE UNITED STATES

THE
DISSENTING OPINIONS
OF
MR. JUSTICE HOLMES

Arranged with Introductory Notes, by

ALFRED LIEF

With a Foreword by

DR. GEORGE W. KIRCHWEY

Former Dean, Columbia Law School

NEW YORK: THE VANGUARD PRESS

CONTENTS

[v]

CONTENTS

CONTENTS

Foreword

WE come to know a man only as we see him in action and in action that calls out all his powers. Justice Holmes has given varied and eloquent expression to his philosophy of life and of the law in many public addresses and legal papers, and a compilation of elegant extracts from those utterances would give the reader a satisfying picture of a rich and finely-tempered mind. But "after all," as he has himself said, "the place for a man who is complete in all his powers is in the fight," and we may add that the place to see such a man is in the fight. This is not only because we find ourselves caught up in the joy of battle with him, but for another, if not a better, reason, namely that we see the philosophy as well as the mettle of the man tried out in the only arena in which they can be tested. For his is a fighting philosophy, at war with many of the conceptions which have dominated and which still largely dominate legal policy, and, seeing the battle fought over and over again on many fronts, we come to realize that what we are witnessing is not merely the sword-play of rival philosophies but a war between conflicting theories of public and private rights in which those rights are in fact affirmed or denied; that it is, indeed, our war, in which we may yet be called upon to play our part as combatants—at the ballot-box or even on the field of battle.

It was considerations such as these and not a passion for dissent, as such, that have dictated the publication in a single volume of Justice Holmes' dissenting opinions in the Supreme Court of the nation. Certainly it is not intended to picture him as the great dissenter, a description which would grossly misrepresent his position in that august tribunal. He is not a voice crying in the wilderness. While he has not hesitated on occasion to stand alone, this has rarely been his fate—only once, indeed, in the long period covered by this collection. In seventeen of the fifty-five cases here reported the decisions from which he dissented were reached by a bare majority of the court and in twenty others his dissent was shared by two of his colleagues. To make his record for non-conformity complete, it is only necessary to add the fact that the opinions in which he has given expression to the judgment of the court or in which he has concurred in its judgment far out-number, in the ratio of eight or ten to one, those in which he has felt it necessary to record his dissent.

If it should be urged that this collection does not give a fair picture of the fight as a whole and that it exhibits the hero without an antagonist, the answer is that Holmes' warfare was not waged with men but with ideas, and that the views combatted by him were fully and fairly stated by him, were necessarily put at their best in order that the grounds of his dissent might be squarely presented and fully understood. The lawyer and the law student into whose hands this book may come, have at hand the volumes of reports with which to gratify the professional curiosity to explore more fully the issues of law here presented. For the general reader a selection had to be made and it is believed that for his purpose the dissenting opinions, with the corrective supplied by the extracts from Justice Holmes' majority opinions printed in the last section of the book, will be entirely adequate to place the man in his setting in the major activity of his long and useful life.

No apology is needed for putting the main emphasis on the dissenting opinions. It is only at the points where Holmes' philosophy of life and of the law has clashed sharply with that of the majority of his colleagues that he has found it necessary again and again, in many different aspects, in winged words, to expound and justify that philosophy. It is true that these utterances were not intended for us, the readers of the printed word, but for his colleagues and for the members of his profession, but they have only to be read to become the priceless possession of the wider community whose spokesman he was.

But here a grave question obtrudes itself. *Cui bono?* What is the use of arguing, however wisely and persuasively, against a judgment already rendered? Justice Holmes, himself, in his first dissenting opinion, delivered in 1903, declared that he believed it "useless and undesirable, as a rule, to express dissent." Happily he did not refrain in that case nor in the many others in which, as here, he felt "bound to do so." As he said in the first case here reported, "every opinion tends to become a law," a dictum which has been amply verified in the history of the Supreme Court under his tuition and which, we may well believe, will become increasingly manifest in the years to come. It is to the years to come that we must look for the complete vindication of his rôle as a dissenter, to the younger members of the bar, the judges of the future, who have found and will still find inspiration in his example and leadership in his principles of judicial action.

Concededly a great lawyer and a great judge, Holmes is at the same time a great teacher—a teacher of judges and lawyers and of the great community in which these play their indispensable rôle. To judges he has taught the lessons of humility and independence—the negligibility of their private views of public welfare, their freedom from the bonds of tradition. "The present has a right to govern itself as far as it can. . . . Historic continuity with the past is not a duty, it is only a necessity." To the lawyer he has taught the supreme worth and dignity of his profession. The law is not a mere accumulation of precedents and of more or less casual legislative enactments. It is

[xi]

"the witness and external deposit of our moral life." As a special branch of human knowledge "it is more immediately connected with all the highest interests of man than any other which deals with practical affairs." "And what a profession it is! . . . No doubt every calling is great when greatly pursued. But what other gives such scope to realize the spontaneous energy of one's soul? In what other does one plunge so deep in the stream of life—so share its passions, its battles, its despair, its triumphs, both as witness and actor?"

To you and me, whether or not we are lawyers, Holmes teaches the supreme worth of the life of action. "The main part of intellectual education is not the acquisition of facts but learning how to make facts live." It is not only the explorer who, like Nansen in his quest for the pole, "must face the loneliness of original work," who "may wreak himself upon life, may drink the bitter cup of heroism, may wear his heart out after the unattainable." "No man has earned the right to intellectual ambition until he has learned to lay his course by a star which he has never seen, to dig by the divining rod for springs which he may never reach." "We cannot live our dreams. We are lucky enough if we can give a sample of our best and if in our hearts we can feel that it has been nobly done." "Life is action, the use of one's powers. As to use them to their height is our joy and duty, so it is the one end that justifies itself." "Life is an end in itself and the only question as to whether it is worth living is whether you have had enough of it."

If the reader does not find these challenging words of wisdom and passion in the opinions here reported—they are in fact taken from Justice Holmes' other writings—he will not fail to find there the spirit of fire that has lived them and, to our everlasting good, has embodied them in his creative work in the court.

GEORGE W. KIRCHWEY.

Natural Law *

It is not enough for the knight of romance that you agree that his lady is a very nice girl—if you do not admit that she is the best that God ever made or will make, you must fight. There is in all men a demand for the superlative, so much so that the poor devil who has no other way of reaching it attains it by getting drunk. It seems to me that this demand is at the bottom of the philosopher's effort to prove that truth is absolute and of the jurist's search for criteria of universal validity which he collects under the head of natural law.

I used to say, when I was young, that truth was the majority vote of that nation that could lick all others. Certainly we may expect that the received opinion about the present war will depend a good deal upon which side wins (I hope with all my soul it will be mine), and I think that the statement was correct in so far as it implied that our test of truth is a reference to either a present or an imagined future majority in favor of our view. If, as I have suggested elsewhere, the truth may be defined as the system of my (intellectual) limitations, what gives it objectivity is the fact that I find my fellow man to a greater or less extent (never wholly) subject to the same *Can't Helps*. If I think that I am sitting at a table I find that the other persons present agree with me; so if I say that the sum of the angles of a triangle is equal to two right angles. If I am in a minority of one they send for a doctor or lock me up; and

* Reprinted from the *Harvard Law Review*, by courtesy of the author, the editors of that magazine, and Harcourt, Brace and Company, publishers of Mr. Justice Holmes' *Collected Legal Papers*.

[xiii]

I am so far able to transcend the to me convincing testimony of my senses or my reason as to recognize that if I am alone probably something is wrong with my works.

Certitude is not the test of certainty. We have been cocksure of many things that were not so. If I may quote myself again, property, friendship, and truth have a common root in time. One can not be wrenched from the rocky crevices into which one has grown for many years without feeling that one is attacked in one's life. What we most love and revere generally is determined by early associations. I love granite rocks and barberry bushes, no doubt because with them were my earliest joys that reach back through the past eternity of my life. But while one's experience thus makes certain preferences dogmatic for oneself, recognition of how they came to be so leaves one able to see that others, poor souls, may be equally dogmatic about something else. And this again means scepticism. Not that one's belief or love does not remain. Not that we would not fight and die for it if important—we all, whether we know it or not, are fighting to make the kind of a world that we should like—but that we have learned to recognize that others will fight and die to make a different world, with equal sincerity or belief. Deep-seated preferences can not be argued about—you can not argue a man into liking a glass of beer—and therefore, when differences are sufficiently far reaching, we try to kill the other man rather than let him have his way. But that is perfectly consistent with admitting that, so far as appears, his grounds are just as good as ours.

The jurists who believe in natural law seem to me to be in that naïve state of mind that accepts what has been familiar and accepted by them and their neighbors as something that must be accepted by all men everywhere. No doubt it is true that, so far as we can see ahead, some arrangements and the rudiments of familiar institutions seem to be necessary elements in any society that may spring from our own and that would seem to us to be civilized—some form of permanent association between the sexes—some residue of property individually owned—some mode of binding oneself to specified future conduct—at the bottom of all, some protection for the person. But without speculating whether a group is imaginable in which all but the last of these might disappear and the last be subject to qualifications that most of us would abhor, the question remains as to the *Ought* of natural law.

It is true that beliefs and wishes have a transcendental basis in the sense that their foundation is arbitrary. You can not help entertaining and feeling them, and there is an end of it. As an arbitrary fact people wish to live, and we say with various degrees of certainty that they can do so only on certain conditions. To do it they must eat and drink. That necessity is absolute. It is a necessity of less degree but practically general that they should live in society. If they live in society, so far as we can see, there are further conditions. Reason working on experience does tell us, no doubt, that if our wish to live continues, we can do it only on those terms. But that seems to me the whole of the matter. I see no *a priori* duty to live with others and in that way, but simply a statement of what I must do if I wish to remain alive. If I do live with others they tell me that I must do and abstain from doing various things or they will put the screws on to me. I believe that they will, and being of the same mind as to their conduct I not only accept the rules but come in time to accept them with sympathy and emotional affirmation and begin to talk about duties and rights. But for legal purposes a right is only the hypostasis of a prophecy—the imagination of a substance supporting the fact that the public force will be brought to bear upon those who do things said to contravene it—just as we talk of the force of gravitation accounting for the conduct of bodies in space. One phrase adds no more than the other to what we know without it. No doubt behind these legal rights is the fighting will of the subject to maintain them, and the spread of his emotions to the general rules by which they are maintained; but that does not seem to me the same thing as the supposed *a priori* discernment of a duty or the assertion of a preëxisting right. A dog will fight for his bone.

The most fundamental of the supposed preëxisting rights—the right to life—is sacrificed without a scruple not only in war, but whenever the interest of society, that is, of the predominant power in the community, is thought to demand it. Whether that interest is the interest of mankind in the long run no one can tell, and as, in any event, to those who do not think with Kant and Hegel it is only an interest, the sanctity disappears. I remember a very tender-hearted judge being of opinion that closing a hatch to stop a fire and the destruction of a cargo was justified even if it was known that doing so would stifle a man below. It is idle to illustrate further, because to those who agree with me I am uttering commonplaces and to those who disagree I am ignoring the necessary foundations of thought. The *a priori* men generally call the dissentients superficial. But I do agree with them in believing that one's attitude on these matters is closely connected with one's general attitude toward the universe. Proximately, as has been suggested, it is determined largely by early associations and temperament, coupled with the desire to have an absolute guide. Men to a great extent believe what they want to—although I see in that no basis for a philosophy that tells us what we should want to want.

Now when we come to our attitude toward the universe I do not see any rational ground for demanding the superlative—for being dissatisfied unless we are assured that our truth is cosmic truth, if there is such a thing—that the ultimates of a little creature on this little earth are the last word of the unimaginable whole. If a man sees no reason for believing that signficance, consciousness and ideals are more than marks of the finite, that does not justify what has been familiar in French sceptics; getting upon a pedestal and professing to look with haughty scorn upon a world in ruins. The real conclusion is that the part can not swallow the whole—that our categories are not, or may not be, adequate to formulate what we can not know. If we believe that we come out of the universe, not it out of us, we must admit that we do not know what we are talking about when we speak of brute matter. We do know that a certain complex of energies can wag its tail and another can make syllogisms. These are among the powers of the unknown, and if, as maybe, it has still greater powers that we can not understand, as Fabre in his studies of instinct would have us believe, studies that gave Bergson one of the strongest strands for his philosophy and enabled Maeterlinck to make us fancy for a moment that we heard a clang from behind phenomena—if this be true, why should we not be content? Why should we employ the energy that is furnished to us by the cosmos to defy it and shake our fist at the sky? It seems to me silly.

That the universe has in it more than we understand, that the private soldiers have not been told the plan of campaign, or even that there is one, rather than some vaster unthinkable to which every predicate is an impertinence, has no bearing upon our conduct. We still shall fight—all of us because we want to live, some, at least, because we want to realize our spontaneity and prove our powers, for the joy of it, and we may leave to the unknown the supposed final valuation of that which in any event has value to us. It is enough for us that the universe has produced us and has within it, as less than it, all that we believe and love. If we think of our existence not as that of a little god outside, but as that of a ganglion within, we have the infinite behind us. It gives us our only but our adequate significance. A grain of sand has the same, but what competent person supposes that he understands a grain of sand? That is as much beyond our grasp as man. If our imagination is strong enough to accept the vision of ourselves as parts inseverable from the rest, and to extend our final interest beyond the boundary of our skins, it justifies the sacrifice even of our lives for ends outside of ourselves. The motive, to be sure, is the common wants and ideals that we find in man. Philosophy does not furnish motives, but it shows men that they are not fools for doing what they already want to do. It opens to the forlorn hopes on which we throw ourselves away, the vista of the farthest stretch of human thought, the chords of a harmony that breathes from the unknown.

OLIVER WENDELL HOLMES.

August, 1918.

The series of dots that recur in the Opinions indicate the citations of Court decisions. As these are only of technical interest, the editor has thought best to omit them for the sake of smooth reading. Where asterisks occur, they indicate omissions that occur in the original, except in the majority opinions where they denote editorial selection.

I. On Hampering Social Experiments

Long Hours and Liberty

(*Lochner* v. *New York*, 1904)

EMPLOYMENT IN BAKERIES FOR MORE THAN TEN HOURS A DAY WAS prohibited by a New York statute. A baking company in Utica, which had been fined twice for violating the law, contended that the statute contravened the Constitution by being class legislation and denying "equal protection of the laws."

The question was (according to Mr. Justice Peckham) which of two rights should prevail—the police power of the State or freedom of contract. In the majority opinion he called the Act a "meddlesome interference," holding that the right to purchase or sell labor was part of the liberty guaranteed by the Fourteenth Amendment.

Justice Peckham deplored the spread of such laws in the various States and believed that the motive for them was not so much to protect health as to regulate the hours of labor; almost all occupations affect health more or less, he remarked. "Clean and wholesome bread does not depend on whether a baker works but ten hours per day or only sixty hours a week," was the majority view.

Justices Harlan, White, Day and Holmes dissented. In addition to Harlan's opinion Holmes wrote:

"I REGRET sincerely that I am unable to agree with the judgment in this case and that I think it my duty to express my dissent.

"This case is decided upon an economic theory which a large part of the country does not entertain. If it were a question whether I agreed with that theory, I should desire to study it

[3]

further and long before making up my mind. But I do not conceive that to be my duty, because I strongly believe that my agreement or disagreement has nothing to do with the right of a majority to embody their opinions in law.

"It is settled by various decisions of this Court that State constitutions and State laws may regulate life in many ways which we as legislators might think as injudicious or, if you like, as tyrannical as this, and which equally with this interfere with the liberty to contract. Sunday laws and usury laws are ancient examples. A more modern one is the prohibition of lotteries. The liberty of the citizen to do as he likes so long as he does not interfere with the liberty of others to do the same, which has been a shibboleth for some well-known writers, is interfered with by school laws, by the Post Office, by every State or municipal institution which takes his money for purposes thought desirable, whether he likes it or not. The Fourteenth Amendment does not enact Mr. Herbert Spencer's *Social Statics*.

"The other day we sustained the Massachusetts vaccination law. . . . United States and State statutes and decisions cutting down the liberty to contract by way of combination are familiar to this Court. . . . Two years ago we upheld the prohibition of sales of stock on margins or for future delivery in the constitution of California. . . . The decision sustaining an eight-hour law for miners is still recent. . . . Some of these laws embody convictions or prejudices which judges are likely to share. Some may not. But a constitution is not intended to embody a particular economic theory, whether of paternalism and the organic relation of the citizen to the State or of *laissez faire*. It is made for people of fundamentally differing views, and the accident of our finding certain opinions natural and familiar or novel and even shocking ought not to conclude our judgment upon the question whether statutes embodying them conflict with the Constitution of the United States.

[4]

"General propositions do not decide concrete cases. The decision will depend on a judgment or intuition more subtle than any articulate major premise. But I think that the proposition just stated, if it is accepted, will carry us far toward the end. Every opinion tends to become a law.

"I think that the word liberty in the Fourteenth Amendment is perverted when it is held to prevent the natural outcome of a dominant opinion, unless it can be said that a rational and fair man necessarily would admit that the statute proposed would infringe fundamental principles as they have been understood by the traditions of our people and our law. It does not need research to show that no such sweeping condemnation can be passed upon the statute before us. A reasonable man might think it a proper measure on the score of health. Men whom I certainly could not pronounce unreasonable would uphold it as a first instalment of a general regulation of the hours of work. Whether in the latter aspect it would be open to the charge of inequality I think it unnecessary to discuss."

Lochner v. *New York*
198 U. S. 45, 74

Union Members Discharged

(*Adair* v. *United States*, 1907)

AN OUTCOME OF THE CHICAGO RAILROAD STRIKE IN 1894 WAS THE Erdman Act, passed by Congress four years later, providing for arbitration of disputes between unions and interstate carriers. One section of the Act prohibited discrimination against employees who were union members.

The Louisville & Nashville Railroad Co. appealed on the ground that the law was an attempt to regulate the relation of master and servant "hitherto supposed to be entirely within State control." The Government replied that its purpose was to protect commerce by avoiding strikes and lockouts.

"But what possible connection is there between an employee's membership in a labor organization and the carrying on of interstate commerce?" said the majority opinion of Mr. Justice Harlan. Now that the *Lochner Case* had shown the way, the disputed section of the Act was considered an invasion of personal liberty and of the right of property, including the right to make contracts for the purchase of labor. Such legislation, he said, "no government can legally justify in a free land."

The suit brought in behalf of a discharged locomotive fireman was dismissed; the offending section was held invalid and separable from the rest of the Act.

Mr. Justice McKenna dissented. Justice Holmes did likewise:

"I ALSO think that the statute is constitutional, and but for the decision of my brethren I should have felt pretty clear about it.

[6]

"As we all know, there are special labor unions of men engaged in the service of carriers. These unions exercise a direct influence upon the employment of labor in that business, upon the terms of such employment and upon the business itself. Their very existence is directed specifically to the business, and their connection with it is at least as intimate and important as that of safety couplers and, I should think, as the liability of master to servant—matters which it is admitted Congress might regulate so far as they concern commerce among the States. I suppose that it hardly would be denied that some of the regulations of railroads with unions of railroad employees are closely enough connected with commerce to justify legislation by Congress. If so, legislation to prevent the exclusion of such unions from employment is sufficiently near.

"The ground on which this particular law is held bad is not so much that it deals with matters remote from commerce among the States as that it interferes with the paramount individual rights, secured by the Fifth Amendment. The section is, in substance, a very limited interference with freedom of contract, no more. It does not require the carriers to employ anyone. It does not forbid them to refuse to employ anyone, for any reason they deem good, even where the notion of a choice of persons is a fiction and wholesale employment is necessary upon general principles that it might be proper to control. The section simply prohibits the more powerful party to exact certain undertakings or to threaten dismissal or unjustly discriminate on certain grounds against those already employed. I hardly can suppose that the grounds on which a contract lawfully may be made to end are less open to regulation than other terms.

"So I turn to the general question whether the employment can be regulated at all. I confess that I think that the right to make contracts at will that has been derived from the word liberty in the Amendments has been stretched to its extreme by the decisions; but they agree that sometimes the right may be

[7]

restrained. Where there is, or generally is believed to be, an important ground of public policy for restraint, the Constitution does not forbid it, whether this Court agrees or disagrees with the policy pursued.

"It cannot be doubted that to prevent strikes and, so far as possible, to foster its scheme of arbitration, might be deemed by Congress an important point of policy, and I think it impossible to say that Congress might not reasonably think that the provision in question would help a good deal to carry its policy along. But suppose the only effect really were to tend to bring about the complete unionizing of such railroad laborers as Congress can deal with, I think that object alone would justify the Act.

"I quite agree that the question what and how much good labor unions do is one on which intelligent people may differ,— I think that laboring men sometimes attribute to them advantages, as many attribute to combinations of capital disadvantages, that are really due to economic conditions of a far wider and deeper kind—but I could not pronounce it unwarranted if Congress should decide that to foster a strong union was for the best interest, not only of the men, but of the railroads and the country at large."

Adair v. *United States*
208 U. S. 161, 190

Another Curb on Unionism

(*Coppage* v. *Kansas*, 1914)

A SWITCHMAN WAS DISCHARGED BY THE ST. LOUIS & SAN FRANCISCO Railway in 1911 for refusing to give up his union membership. A Kansas statute of two years' standing made it a misdemeanor to discharge a man for this reason.

Mr. Justice Pitney cited the *Adair Case* on the right to buy and sell labor and pointed out that the worker had a free choice: "He has no inherent right to remain in the employ of one who is unwilling to employ a union man, any more than the same individual has a right to join the union without the consent of that organization." *Judgment reversed*.

Mr. Justice Holmes was brief:

"I THINK the judgment should be affirmed. In present conditions a workman not unnaturally may believe that only by belonging to a union can he secure a contract that shall be fair to him. . . . If that belief, whether right or wrong, may be held by a reasonable man, it seems to me that it may be enforced by law in order to establish the equality of position between the parties in which liberty of contract begins.

"Whether in the long run it is wise for the workingmen to enact legislation of this sort is not my concern, but I am strongly of opinion that there is nothing in the Constitution of the United States to prevent it, and that *Adair* v. *United States* and *Lochner* v. *New York* should be overruled. I have stated my

[9]

grounds in those cases and think it unnecessary to add others that I think exist. See further *Vegelahn* v. *Guntner*, 167 Mass. 92, 104, 108. *Plant* v. *Woods*, 176 Mass. 492, 505. I still entertain the opinions expressed by me in Massachusetts."

Coppage v. *Kansas*
236 U. S. 1, 26

Injunctions Against Pickets

(*Truax* v. *Corrigan*, 1921)

A RESTAURANT OWNER IN BISBEE, ARIZONA, WHOSE WAITERS AND cooks were on strike, protested against a State law which prohibited injunctions in labor disputes. He said that the activities of the pickets and their union had diminished his receipts and deprived him of property without due process of law.

The union answered that the business was not a property right. Chief Justice Taft, for the majority, held that it was; that the loss, intended and inflicted, was clear, and the means illegal: "Violence could not have been more effective." If a rival restaurateur conducted a campaign like the union's he could be enjoined, Taft pointed out, but here immunity was granted to one class and denied to another.

"The Constitution was intended, its very purpose was, to prevent experimentation with the fundamental rights of the individual," said the Chief Justice. An injunction could be issued if evidence sustained the averments.

Mr. Justice Holmes wrote the dissenting opinion. Justices Pitney (Clarke concurring) and Brandeis wrote separate ones.

Holmes said:

"THE DANGERS of a delusive exactness in the application of the Fourteenth Amendment have been adverted to before now. . . . Delusive exactness is a source of fallacy throughout the law. By calling a business 'property' you make it seem like land, and lead up to the conclusion that a statute cannot substantially cut down the advantages of ownership existing before the statute was passed. An established business no doubt may have pecuniary value and commonly is protected by law against various unjustified injuries. But you cannot give it definiteness of contour by calling it a thing. It is a course of conduct and like other conduct is subject to substantial modification according to time and circumstances both in itself and in regard to what shall justify doing it a harm. I cannot understand the notion that it would be unconstitutional to authorize boycotts and the like in the aid of the employees' or the employers' interest by statute when the same result has been reached constitutionally without statute by courts with whom I agree. See *The Hamilton,* 207 U. S. 398, 404. In this case it does not even appear that the business was not created under the laws as they now are. . . .

"I think further that the selection of the class of employers and employees for special treatment, dealing with both sides alike, is beyond criticism on principles often asserted by this Court. And especially I think that without legalizing the conduct complained of the extraordinary relief by injunction may be denied to the class. Legislation may begin where an evil begins. If, as many intelligent people believe, there is more danger that the injunction will be abused in labor cases than elsewhere, I can feel no doubt of the power of the legislature to deny it in such cases. I refer to two decisions in which I have stated what I understand to be the law sanctioned by many other decisions. *Carroll* v. *Greenwich Insurance Co.* [See p. 270] and *Quong Wing* v. *Kirkendall,* 223 U. S. 59.

"In a matter like this I dislike to turn attention to anything but the fundamental question of the merits, but *Connolly* v. *Union Sewer Pipe Co.,* 184 U. S. 540, raises at least a doubt in my mind of another sort. The exception and the rule as to granting injunctions are both part of the same code, enacted at the same time. If the exception fails, according to the *Connolly Case* the statute is bad as a whole. It is true that here the excep-

tion came in later than the rule, but after they had been amal-
gamated in a single act I cannot know that the later legislature
would have kept the rule if the exception could not be allowed.
If labor had the ascendancy that the exceptions seem to indicate,
I think that probably it would have declined to allow injunctions
in any case if that was the only way of reaching its end. But
this is a matter upon which the State court has the last word,
and if it takes this view its decision must prevail. I need not
press further the difficulty of requiring a State court to issue an
injunction that it never has been empowered to issue by the
quasi-sovereign that created the court.

"I must add one general consideration. There is nothing I
more deprecate than the use of the Fourteenth Amendment
beyond the absolute compulsion of its words to prevent the
making of social experiments that an important part of the community desires, in the insulated chambers afforded by the several States, even though the experiments may seem futile or even
noxious to me and to those whose judgment I most respect. I
agree with the more elaborate expositions of my brothers Pitney
and Brandeis and in their conclusion that the judgment should
be affirmed."

*Truax et al., copartners, doing business
under the firm name and style of
William Truax, v. Corrigan et al.*
257 U. S. 312, 343

Child Labor Beyond Reach

(*Hammer* v. *Dagenhart*, 1917)

As CONGRESS COULD NOT ENTER A STATE AND FORBID FACTORIES TO employ children under fourteen, it enacted in 1916 a child-labor law to stop the interstate shipment of child-made goods.

An argument employed in opposition to the Act was that it prohibited the creation of goods unless the local conditions of manufacture conformed to the congressional standard. "Has Congress absorbed the police power of the States?" counsel for the manufacturers asked. "In that event, it is difficult to see what is left to the States."

Here the father of two children working in a North Carolina cotton mill sued to enjoin enforcement of the Act. The controlling question, said Mr. Justice Day, was whether Congress had overstepped its authority, and he added: "The Act in its effect does not regulate transportation among the States but aims to standardize the ages at which children may be employed in mining and manufacturing within the States.*** The goods shipped are of themselves harmless.*** In interpreting the Constitution it must never be forgotten that the Nation is made up of States to which are entrusted the powers of local government."

The Court felt that if the Act were not held invalid these powers might finally be eliminated and "our system of government be practically destroyed."

Mr. Justice Holmes was joined in dissent by Justices McKenna, Brandeis and Clarke:

"THE SINGLE question in this case is whether Congress has power to prohibit the shipment in interstate or foreign commerce of any product of a cotton mill situated in the United States, in which within thirty days before the removal of the product children under fourteen have been employed, or children between fourteen and sixteen have been employed more than eight hours in a day, or more than six days in any week, or between seven in the evening and six in the morning.

"The objection urged against the power is that the States have exclusive control over their methods of production and that Congress cannot meddle with them, and taking the proposition in the sense of direct intermeddling I agree to it and suppose that no one denies it. But if an act is within the powers specifically conferred upon Congress, it seems to me that it is not made any less constitutional because of the indirect effects that it may have, however obvious it may be that it will have those effects, and that we are not at liberty upon such grounds to hold it void.

"The first step in my argument is to make plain what no one is likely to dispute—that the statute in question is within the power expressly given to Congress if considered only as to its immediate effects and that if invalid it is so only upon some collateral ground. The statute confines itself to prohibiting the carriage of certain goods in interstate or foreign commerce. Congress is given power to regulate such commerce in unqualified terms.

"It would not be argued today that the power to regulate does not include the power to prohibit. Regulation means the prohibition of something, and when interstate commerce is the matter to be regulated, I cannot doubt that the regulation may prohibit any part of such commerce that Congress sees fit to forbid. At all events it is established by the *Lottery Case* and others that have followed it that a law is not beyond the regulative power of Congress merely because it prohibits certain transportation out and out. . . . So I repeat that this statute

[15]

in its immediate operation is clearly within the Congress's consitutional power.

"The question then is narrowed to whether the exercise of its otherwise constitutional power by Congress can be pronounced unconstitutional because of its possible reaction upon the conduct of the States in a matter upon which I have admitted that they are free from direct control. I should have thought that that matter had been disposed of so fully as to leave no room for doubt. I should have thought that the most conspicuous decisions of this Court had made it clear that the power to regulate commerce and other constitutional powers could not be cut down or qualified by the fact that it might interfere with the carrying out of the domestic policy of any State.

"The manufacture of oleomargarine is as much a matter of State regulation as the manufacture of cotton cloth. Congress levied a tax upon the compound, when colored so as to resemble butter, that was so great as obviously to prohibit the manufacture and sale. In a very elaborate discussion the present Chief Justice [White] excluded any inquiry into the purpose of an act which apart from that purpose was within the power of Congress. . . . Fifty years ago a tax on state banks, the obvious purpose and actual effect of which was to drive them, or at least their circulation, out of existence, was sustained, although the result was one that Congress had no constitutional power to require. The Court made short work of the argument as to the purpose of the act. 'The judicial cannot prescribe to the legislative department of the Government limitations upon the exercise of its acknowledged powers.' . . . So it well might have been argued that the corporation tax was intended under the guise of a revenue measure to secure a control not otherwise belonging to Congress, but the tax was sustained, and the objection so far as noticed was disposed of by citing *McCray* v. *United States, Flint* v. *Stone Tracy Co.,* 220 U. S. 107.

"And to come to cases upon interstate commerce . . . the Sherman Act has been made an instrument for the breaking up of combinations in restraint of trade and monopolies, using the power to regulate commerce as a foothold, but not proceeding because that commerce was the end actually in mind. The objection that the control of the States over production was interfered with was urged again and again but always in vain. . . .

"The Pure Food and Drug Act, which was sustained . . . with the intimation that 'no trade can be carried on between the States to which it [the power of Congress to regulate commerce] does not extend,' applies not merely to articles that the changing opinion of the time condemns as intrinsically harmful but to others innocent in themselves, simply on the ground that the order for them was induced by a preliminary fraud. . . .

"It does not matter whether the supposed evil precedes or follows the transportation. It is enough that in the opinion of Congress the transportation encourages the evil. I may add that in the cases on the so-called White Slave Act it was established that the means adopted by Congress as convenient to the exercise of its power might have the character of police regulations. . . . In *Clark Distilling Co.* v. *Western Maryland Ry. Co.*, 242 U. S. 311, 328, *Leisy* v. *Hardin*, 135 U. S. 100, 108, is quoted with seeming approval to the effect that 'a subject-matter which has been confided exclusively to Congress by the Constitution is not within the jurisdiction of the police power of the State, unless placed there by congressional action.' I see no reason for that proposition not applying here.

"The notion that prohibition is any less prohibition when applied to things now thought evil I do not understand. But if there is any matter upon which civilized countries have agreed—far more unanimously than they have with regard to intoxicants and some other matters over which this country is now emotionally aroused—it is the evil of premature and ex-

[17]

cessive child labor. I should have thought that if we were to introduce our own moral conceptions where in my opinion they do not belong, this was preëminently a case for upholding the exercise of all its powers by the United States.

"But I had thought that the propriety of the exercise of a power admitted to exist in some cases was for the consideration of Congress alone and that this Court always had disavowed the right to intrude its judgment upon questions of policy or morals. It is not for this Court to pronounce when prohibition is necessary to regulation if it ever may be necessary—to say that it is permissible as against strong drink but not as against the product of ruined lives.

"The Act does not meddle with anything belonging to the States. They may regulate their internal affairs and their domestic commerce as they like. But when they seek to send their products across the state line they are no longer within their rights. If there were no Constitution and no Congress their power to cross the line would depend upon their neighbors. Under the Constitution such commerce belongs not to the States but to Congress to regulate. It may carry out its views of public policy whatever indirect effect they may have upon the activities of the States.

"Instead of being encountered by a prohibitive tariff at her boundaries the State encounters the public policy of the United States which it is for Congress to express. The public policy of the United States is shaped with a view to the benefit of the nation as a whole. If, as has been the case within the memory of men still living, a State should take a different view of the propriety of sustaining a lottery from that which generally prevails, I cannot believe that the fact would require a different decision from that reached in *Champion* v. *Ames*, 188 U. S. 321 [the *Lottery Case*]. Yet in that case it would be said with quite as much force as in this that Congress was attempting to intermeddle with the State's domestic affairs. The national welfare as understood by Congress may require a different attitude within its sphere from that of some self-seeking State. It seems to me entirely constitutional for Congress to enforce its understanding by all the means at its command."

Hammer, United States Attorney for
Western District of North Carolina,
v. Dagenhart et al.
247 U. S. 251, 277

Women, Wages, Morals

(Adkins v. Children's Hospital, 1922)

To protect the women of the district of columbia from ill health and immorality an Act of Congress in 1918 provided for a Minimum Wage Board to fix standards. When a hospital objected to the Board's regulations the answer was made that the Act fell within the police power given to Congress by Article I, equivalent to the legislative power of the States; Congress simply followed the example of many States whose similar laws had been uniformly sustained, the Board said. And public charities were engaged in "impotent amelioration rather than prevention."

Mr. Justice Sutherland, for the majority, cited the *Adair, Coppage* and *Lochner* cases on the right to contract for labor. He regarded the Nineteenth Amendment as having "emancipated women from the old doctrine of special protection and restraints."

"To those who practice economy a given sum will afford economy," he continued, "while to those of contrary habit the same sum will be wholly inadequate.*** The relation between earnings and morals is not capable of standardization." The Act shifted the burden of society to the employer's shoulders, ignoring the incompetence of workers and the exigencies of business stress, Justice Sutherland found; it was an arbitrary restraint of liberty.

Chief Justice Taft dissented (Justice Sanford concurring) and asked why the *Lochner* decision was quoted when *Bunting* v. *Oregon* overruled it, when the Adamson Eight-Hour-Day Law had been held valid, and when *Muller* v. *Oregon* (upholding a limit on women workers' hours) was the controlling case. "It is not the function of this Court to hold congressional acts invalid simply because they are passed

[20]

to carry out economic views which the Court believes to be unwise or unsound," he said, stating that he did not agree "with some general observations in the forcible opinion of Mr. Justice Holmes, who follows me."

Holmes wrote:

"THE QUESTION in this case is the broad one, Whether Congress can establish minimum rates of wages for women in the District of Columbia with due provision for special circumstances, or whether we must say that Congress has no power to meddle with the matter at all. To me, notwithstanding the deference due to the prevailing judgment of the Court, the power of Congress seems absolutely free from doubt. The end, to remove conditions leading to ill health, immorality and the deterioration of the race, no one would deny to be within the scope of constitutional legislation. The means are means that have the approval of Congress, of many States, and of those governments from which we have learned our greatest lessons. When so many intelligent persons, who have studied the matter more than any of us can, have thought that the means are effective and are worth the price, it seems to me impossible to deny that the belief reasonably may be held by reasonable men. If the law encountered no other objection than that the means bore no relation to the end or that they cost too much I do not suppose that anyone would venture to say that it was bad. I agree, of course, that a law answering the foregoing requirements might be invalidated by specific provisions of the Constitution. For instance, it might take private property without just compensation. But in the present instance the only objection that can be argued is found within the vague contours of the Fifth Amendment, prohibiting the depriving any person of liberty or property without due process of law. To that I turn.

"The earlier decisions upon the same words in the Fourteenth Amendment began within our memory and went no farther than an unpretentious assertion of the liberty to follow the ordinary callings. Later that innocuous generality was expanded into the dogma, Liberty of Contract. Contract is not specially mentioned in the text that we have to construe. It is merely an example of doing what you want to do, embodied in the word liberty. But pretty much all law consists in forbidding men to do some things they want to do, and contract is no more exempt from law than other acts.

"Without enumerating all the restrictive laws that have been upheld I will mention a few that seem to me to have interfered with liberty of contract quite as seriously and directly as the one before us. Usury laws prohibit contracts by which a man receives more than so much interest for the money that he lends. Statutes of frauds restrict many contracts to certain forms. Some Sunday laws prohibit practically all contracts during one-seventh of our whole life. Insurance rates may be regulated. . . . (I concurred in that decision without regard to the public interest with which insurance was said to be clothed. It seemed to me that the principle was general.) Contracts may be forced upon companies. . . . Employers of miners may be required to pay for coal by weight before screening. . . . Employers generally may be required to redeem in cash store-orders accepted by their employees in payment. . . . Payment of sailors in advance may be forbidden. . . . The size of a loaf of bread may be established. . . . The responsibility of employers to their employees may be profoundly modified. . . . Finally women's hours of labor may be fixed, *Muller* v. *Oregon*, 208 U. S. 412 . . . and the principle was extended to men with the allowance of a limited overtime to be paid for 'at the rate of time and one-half of the regular wage' in *Bunting* v. *Oregon*, 243 U. S. 426.

"I confess that I do not understand the principle on which the power to fix a minimum for the wages of women can be denied by those who admit the power to fix a maximum for their hours of work. I fully assent to the proposition that here as elsewhere the distinctions of the law are distinctions of degree, but I perceive no difference in the kind or degree of interference with liberty, the only matter with which we have any concern, between the one case and the other. The bargain is equally affected whichever half you regulate. *Muller* v. *Oregon*, I take it, is as good law today as it was in 1908. It will need more than the Nineteenth Amendment to convince me that there are no differences between men and women, or that legislation cannot take those differences into account. I should not hesitate to take them into account if I thought it necessary to sustain this Act. . . . But after *Bunting* v. *Oregon* I had supposed that it was not necessary, and that *Lochner* v. *New York* would be allowed a deserved repose.

"This statute does not compel anybody to pay anything. It simply forbids employment at rates below those fixed as the minimum requirement of health and right living. It is safe to assume that women will not be employed at even the lowest wages allowed unless they earn them, or unless the employer's business can sustain the burden. In short, the law in its character and operation is like hundreds of so-called police laws that have been upheld. I see no greater objection to using a Board to apply the standard fixed by the Act than there is to the other commissions with which we have become familiar, or than there is to the requirement of a license in other cases. The fact that the statute warrants classification, which like all classifications may bear hard upon some individuals, or in exceptional cases, notwithstanding the power given to the Board to issue a special license, is no greater infirmity than is incident to all law. But the ground on which the law is held to fail is fundamental and therefore it is unnecessary to consider matters of detail.

"The criterion of constitutionality is not whether we believe

[23]

the law to be for the public good. We certainly cannot be prepared to deny that a reasonable man reasonably might have that belief in view of the legislation of Great Britain, Victoria and a number of States of this Union. The belief is fortified by a very remarkable collection of documents submitted on behalf of the appellants, material here, I conceive, only as showing that the belief reasonably may be held. In Australia the power to fix a minimum for wages in the case of industrial disputes extending beyond the limits of any one State was given to a court, and its President wrote a most interesting account of its operation (29 *Harvard Law Review* 13). If a legislature should adopt what he thinks the doctrine of modern economists of all schools, that 'freedom of contract is a misnomer as applied to a contract between an employer and an ordinary individual employee' (*ibid* 25) I could not pronounce an opinion with which I agree impossible to be entertained by reasonable men. If the same legislature should accept his further opinion that industrial peace was best obtained by the device of a court having the above powers, I should not feel myself able to contradict it, or to deny that the end justified restrictive legislation quite as adequately as beliefs concerning Sunday or exploded theories about usury. I should have my doubts, as I have them about this statute—but they would be whether the bill that has to be paid for every gain, although hidden as interstitial detriments, was not greater than the gain was worth: a matter that it is not for me to decide.

"I am of opinion that the statute is valid and that the decree should be reversed."

Adkins et al., constituting the Minimum Wage
Board of the District of Columbia,
v. *Children's Hospital of the District of Columbia*
261 U. S. 525, 567

One Language at School

(*Bartels* v. *Iowa*, 1922)

ZEAL FOR GOOD CITIZENSHIP, GIVEN IMPETUS BY THE WAR, RE-sulted in State laws forbidding school instruction in any language but English (in Iowa and Nebraska) and specifically prohibiting German below the eighth grade (in Ohio).

Teachers were prosecuted for violating these laws. Their liberty, guaranteed by the Fourteenth Amendment, was invaded by the States, they said. In counter-argument they heard: "It is certainly in the province of the legislature to enact laws protective of patriotism and the war power of the country." Religious liberties are unhampered—"if a parent wishes his child taught Martin Luther's dogma in Martin Luther's language" the child could be taught after school hours.

The Court was unwilling to sanction the punishment of an instructor who taught German to a child of ten in a parochial school in Nebraska. On the authority of this decision, the Court reversed three more judgments. Justice Holmes wrote the dissenting opinion, in which Justice Sutherland concurred.

"WE ALL agree, I take it, that it is desirable that all the citizens of the United States should speak a common tongue, and therefore that the end aimed at by the statute is a lawful and proper one. The only question is whether the means adopted deprive teachers of the liberty secured to them by the Fourteenth Amendment.

"It is with hesitation and unwillingness that I differ from my brethren with regard to a law like this, but I cannot bring

[25]

my mind to believe that in some circumstances, and circumstances existing it is said in Nebraska, the statute might not be regarded as a reasonable or even necessary method of reaching the desired result.

"The part of the Act with which we are concerned deals with the teaching of young children. Youth is the time when familiarity with a language is established and if there are sections in the State where a child would hear only Polish or French or German spoken at home I am not prepared to say that it is unreasonable to provide that in his early years he shall hear and speak only English at school.

"But if it is reasonable it is not an undue restriction of the liberty either of teacher or scholar. No one would doubt that a teacher might be forbidden to teach many things, and the only criterion of his liberty under the Constitution that I can think of is 'whether, considering the end in view, the statute passes the bounds of reason and assumes the character of a merely arbitrary fiat.' . . . I think I appreciate the objection to the law but it appears to me to present a question upon which men reasonably might differ and therefore I am unable to say that the Constitution of the United States prevents the experiment being tried.

"I agree with the Court as to the special proviso against the German language contained in the statute dealt with in *Bohning* v. *Ohio*."

Bartels v. *State of Iowa*
Bohning v. *State of Ohio*
Pohl v. *State of Ohio*
Nebraska District of Evangelical Lutheran Synod
of Missouri, Ohio and other States et al.,
v. *McKelvie et al.*
262 U. S. 404, 412

Liability Badly Phrased

(Employers' Liability Cases, 1907)

WHEN TWO LOCOMOTIVE FIREMEN WERE KILLED NOT LONG AFTER the enactment of the Federal Employers' Liability Act in 1906, the railroads which had employed them asserted that Congress had exceeded its bounds. The statute made every common carrier engaged in the District of Columbia or in any Territory or between the States or with foreign nations liable to any of its employees for damages resulting from the negligence of its officers or other employees or from material defects. Counsel for the railroads argued that there was no authority under the commerce clause of the Constitution to regulate master-and-servant relations.

In the Circuit Court the statute was held repugnant to the Constitution because it embraced subjects both within and without the power of Congress—subjects "so interblended that they were incapable of separation"—and this was the view taken by Mr. Justice White and the majority: the phrase "any of its employees" might apply to a person working wholly within a State, as in a local branch office or a repair shop. Justice White believed Congress had the power to regulate employers' liability, but thought this particular statute was unconstitutional.

Of the four dissenters Mr. Justice Moody urged that the Act could and should be interpreted as affording relief to all common-carrier employees except those wholly within the States; Justices Harlan and McKenna said that the law was meant to apply only to employees engaged in interstate commerce at the time of injury, and Justice Holmes said:

"I MUST admit that I think there are strong reasons in favor of the interpretation of the statute adopted by a majority of the Court. But as it is possible to read the words in such a way as to save the constitutionality of the Act, I think they should be taken in that narrower sense. The phrase 'every common carrier engaged in trade or commerce' may be construed to mean 'while engaged in trade or commerce' without violence to the habits of English speech, and to govern all that follows.

"The statute then will regulate all common carriers while so engaged in the District of Columbia or in any Territory, thus covering the whole ground as to them; and it will regulate carriers elsewhere while engaged in commerce between the States, etc., thus limiting its scope where it is necessary to limit it.

"So construed, I think the Act valid in its main features under the Constitution of the United States. In view of the circumstances I do not discuss details."

The Employers' Liability Cases
207 U. S. .463, 541

Compensation in New York

(Southern Pacific Co. v. Jensen, 1916)

THE EMPLOYERS' LIABILITY ACT WAS RE-ENACTED WITH MORE CARE-
ful phrasing but, as it was limited to railroads, it could not be applied
in a case where a stevedore broke his neck while unloading lumber
from a ship that had come up from Galveston to New York. And the
award made to his family under the New York Workmen's Compensation Law was contested on the grounds that this statute regulated interstate commerce, took property without due process and violated that
section of the Constitution which confers admiralty jurisdiction on the
Federal courts.

"The work of a stevedore is maritime in its nature," said Mr. Justice McReynolds for the majority; hence it was not within the jurisdiction of the State. But he also pointed out that the remedy sought by
the law was unknown to the common law and was incapable of enforcement by the ordinary processes of any court.

Justice McReynolds observed that "if New York can subject
foreign ships coming in to her ports to such obligations as those imposed
by her compensation statute, other States may do likewise. The necessary consequence would be the destruction of the very uniformity in
respect to maritime matters which the Constitution was designed to
establish."

Justice Pitney's dissent followed Justice Holmes', and Justices
Brandeis and Clarke agreed with both. Justice Holmes wrote:

"THE Southern Pacific Company has been held liable under
the statutes of New York for an accidental injury happening

[29]

upon a gangplank between a pier and the company's vessel and causing the death of one of its employees. The company not having insured, as permitted, the statute may be taken as if it simply imposed a limited but absolute liability in such a case. The short question is whether the power of the State to regulate the liability in that place and to enforce it in the State's own courts is taken away by the conferring of exclusive jurisdiction of all civil causes of admiralty and maritime jurisdiction upon the courts of the United States.

"There is no doubt that the saving to suitors of the right of a common-law remedy leaves open the common-law jurisdiction of the State courts, and leaves some power of legislation, at least, to the States. For the latter I need do no more than refer to the State pilotage statutes, and to liens created by State laws in aid of maritime contracts. Nearer to the point it is decided that a statutory remedy for causing death may be enforced by the State courts, although the death was due to a collision upon the high seas. . . . The misgivings of Mr. Justice Bradley were adverted to in *The Hamilton* [majority opinion by Holmes] and held at least insufficient to prevent the admiralty from recognizing such a State-created right in a proper case, if indeed they went to any such extent. . . .

"The statute having been upheld in other respects . . . I should have thought these authorities conclusive. The liability created by the New York Act ends in a money judgment, and the mode in which the amount is ascertained, or is to be paid, being one that the State constitutionally might adopt, cannot matter to the question before us if any liability can be imposed that was not known to the maritime law. And as such a liability can be imposed where it was unknown not only to the maritime but to the common law, I can see no difference between one otherwise constitutionally created for death caused by accident and one for death due to fault. Neither can the statutes limiting the liability of owners affect the case. Those statutes extend to non-maritime torts, which of course are the creation of State law. . . . They are paramount to but not inconsistent with the new cause of action. However, as my opinion stands on grounds that equally would support a judgment for a maritime tort not ending in death, with which admiralty courts have begun to deal, I will state the reasons that satisfy my mind.

"No doubt there sometimes has been an air of benevolent gratuity in the admiralty's attitude about enforcing State laws. But of course there is no gratuity about it. Courts cannot give or withold at pleasure. If the claim is enforced and recognized it is because the claim is a right, and if a claim depending upon a State statute is enforced it is because the State had constitutional power to pass the law.

"Taking it as established that the State has constitutional power to pass laws giving rights and imposing liabilities for acts done upon the high seas when there were no such rights or liabilities before, what is there to hinder its doing so in the case of a maritime tort? Not the existence of an inconsistent law emanating from a superior source, that is, from the United States. There is no such law. The maritime law is not a *corpus juris*—it is a very limited body of customs and ordinances of the sea. The nearest to anything of the sort in question was the rule that a seaman was entitled to recover the expenses necessary for his cure when the master's negligence caused his hurt. The maritime law gave him no more. . . . One may affirm with the sanction of that case that it is an innovation to allow suits in the admiralty by seamen to recover damages for personal injuries caused by the negligence of the master and to apply the common-law principles of tort.

"Now, however, common-law principles have been applied to sustain a libel by a stevedore *in personam* against a master for personal injuries suffered while loading a ship . . . and *The Osceola*, 189 U. S. 158, recognizes that in some cases at least seamen may have similar relief. From what source do these new rights come? The earliest case relies upon 'the analogies of the municipal law' . . . —sufficient evidence of the obvious pattern but inadequate for the specific origin.

"I recognize without hesitation that judges do and must legislate, but they can do so only interstitially; they are confined from molar to molecular motions. A common-law judge could not say, 'I think the doctrine of consideration a bit of historical nonsense and shall not enforce it in my court.' No more could a judge exercising the limited jurisdiction of admiralty say, ' I think well of the common-law rules of master and servant and propose to introduce them here *en bloc.*' Certainly he could not in that way enlarge the exclusive jurisdiction of the District Courts and cut down the power of the States. If admiralty adopts common-law rules without an act of Congress it cannot extend the maritime law as understood by the Constitution. It must take the rights of the parties from a different authority, just as it does when it enforces a lien created by a State. The only authority available is the common law or statutes of a State. For from the often repeated statement that there is no common law of the United States . . . and from the principles recognized in *Atlantic Transport Co.* v. *Imbrovek,* 234 U. S. 52, having been unknown to the maritime law, the natural inference is that in the silence of Congress this Court has believed the very limited law of the sea to be supplemented here as in England by the common law, and that here that means by the common law of the State. . . .

"So far as I know, the State courts have made this assumption without criticism or attempt at revision from the beginning to this day. . . . Even where the admiralty has unquestioned jurisdiction the common law may have concurrent authority and the State courts concurrent power. . . . The invalidity of State attempts to create a remedy for maritime contracts or torts, parallel to that in the admiralty, that was established in such cases as *The Moses Taylor*, 4 Wall. 411, and *The Hine* v. *Trevor*, 4 Wall. 555, is immaterial to the present point.

"The common law is not a brooding omnipresence in the sky but the articulate voice of some sovereign or quasi-sovereign that can be identified; although some decisions with which I have disagreed seem to me to have forgotten the fact. It always is the law of some State, and if the District Courts adopt the common law of torts, as they have shown a tendency to do, they thereby assume that a law not of maritime origin and deriving its authority in that territory only from some particular State of this Union also governs maritime torts in that territory—and if the common law, the statute law has at least equal force, as the discussion in *The Osceola* assumes.

"On the other hand, the refusal of the District Courts to give remedies coextensive with the common law would prove no more than that they regarded their jurisdiction as limited by the ancient lines—not that they doubted the common law might and would be enforced in the courts of the States as it always has been. This Court has recognized that in some cases different principles of liability would be applied as the suit should happen to be brought in a common-law or admiralty court. . . . But hitherto it has not been doubted authoritatively, so far as I know, that even when the admiralty had a rule of its own to which it adhered, as in *Workman* v. *New York City*, 179 U. S. 552, the State law, common or statute, would prevail in the courts of the State. Happily such conflicts are few.

"It might be asked why, if the grant of jurisdiction to the courts of the United States imports a power in Congress to legislate, the saving of a common-law remedy, i.e., in the State courts, did not import a like if subordinate power in the States. But leaving that question on one side, such cases as *Steamboat Co.* v. *Chase*, 16 Wall. 522, *The Hamilton*, 207 U. S. 398, and *Atlantic Transport Co.* v. *Imbrovek*, 234 U. S.

52, show that it is too late to say that the mere silence of Congress excludes the statute or common law of a State from supplementing the wholly inadequate maritime law of the time of the Constitution, in the regulation of personal rights, and I venture to say that it never has been supposed to so do, or had any such effect.

"As to the specter of a lack of uniformity I content myself with referring to *The Hamilton*. The difficulty really is not so great as in the case of interstate carriers by land, which 'in the absence of Federal statute providing a different rule are answerable according to the law of the State for nonfeasance or misfeasance within its limits.' . . . The conclusion that I reach accords with the considered cases . . . as well as with the New York decision in this case, 215 N. Y. 514."

Southern Pacific Co. v. *Jensen*
244 U. S. 205, 218

Employers' Obligations

(Knickerbocker Ice Co. v. *Stewart,* 1919)

MARITIME ACCIDENTS WERE INCLUDED AMONG EMPLOYERS' LIABIL-
ities when Congress amended the Judicial Code in 1917 and afforded
claimants the remedies of their State compensation laws. Shortly thereafter an ice company employee fell into the Hudson River and the
New York State Industrial Commission made an award to his widow.
In the Court of Appeals it was held that the reasons given in the
Southern Pacific decision now no longer held.

But the company argued that Congress could not delegate to the
States the power to make or amend maritime law; that a uniform
system must be enacted by Congress if liability was to be extended to
maritime employments; that this principle of compensation was, moreover, "new and revolutionary."

Mr. Justice McReynolds again delivered the opinion. He overrode
the argument that forty-two States had passed compensation laws making for a greater uniformity than would obtain under the common-
law procedure which the Judicial Code already permitted. He declared that the Constitution took from the States the power of regulating international and interstate relations and reposed it in Congress,
which could not transfer its legislative power. The amendment to the
Code was held invalid.

Justices Pitney, Brandeis and Clarke joined in Justice Holmes' dissent:

"I_N *Southern Pacific Co.* v. *Jensen* the question was whether
there was anything in the Constitution or laws of the United
States to prevent a State from imposing upon an employer a

limited but absolute liability for the death of an employee upon a gangplank between a vessel and a wharf, which the State unquestionably could have imposed had the death occurred on the wharf. A majority of the Court held the State's attempt invalid, and thereupon, by an Act of October 6, 1917 . . . Congress tried to meet the effect of the decision by amending § 24, cl. 3, and § 256, cl. 3, of the Judicial Code. . . . Those sections in similar terms declared the jurisdiction of the District Court and the exclusive jurisdiction of the courts of the United States 'of all civil causes of admiralty and maritime jurisdiction, saving to suitors in all cases the right of a common-law remedy where the common law is competent to give it.' The amendment added, 'and to claimants the rights and remedies under the workmen's compensation law of any State.' I thought that claimants had those rights before. I think that they do now both for the old reasons and for new ones.

"I do not suppose that anyone would say that the words 'The judicial power shall extend *** to all cases of admiralty and maritime jurisdiction' (Const. Article III, § 3) by implication enacted a whole code for master and servant at sea, that could be modified only by constitutional amendment. But somehow or other the ordinary common-law rules of liability as between master and servant have come to be applied to a considerable extent in the admiralty. If my explanation, that the source is the common law of the several States, is not accepted, I can only say I do not know how, unless by the fiat of the judges. But surely the power that imposed the liability can change it, and I suppose that Congress can do as much as the judges who introduced the rules. For we know that they were introduced and cannot have been elicited by logic alone from the mediæval sea laws.

"But if Congress can legislate it has done so. It has adopted statutes that were in force when the Act of October 6, 1917, was passed, and to that extent has acted as definitely as if it had repeated the words used by the several States—a not unfamiliar form of law. . . . An act of Congress, we always say, will be construed so as to sustain it if possible, and therefore if it were necessary, the words 'rights and remedies under the workmen's compensation law of any State' should be taken to refer solely to laws existing at the time, as it certainly does at least include them. . . . Taking the Act as so limited it is to be read as if it set out at length certain rules for New York, certain others more or less different for California, and so on.

"So construed the single objection that I have heard to the law is that it makes different rules for different places, and I see nothing in the Constitution to prevent that. The only matters with regard to which uniformity is provided for in the instrument so far as I now remember, are duties, imposts, excises, naturalization and bankruptcy, in Article I, § 8. As to the purpose of the clause concerning the judicial power in these cases nothing is said in the instrument itself. To read into it a requirement of uniformity more mechanical than is educed from the expressed requirement of equality in the Fourteenth Amendment seems to me extravagant. Indeed it is contrary to the construction of the Constitution in the very clause of the Judiciary Act that is before us. The saving of a common-law remedy adopted the common law of the several States within their several jurisdictions, and, I may add by way of anticipation, included at least some subsequent statutory changes. . . . I cannot doubt that in matters with which Congress is empowered to deal it may make different arrangements for widely different localities with perhaps widely different needs. . . .

"I thought that *Clark Distilling Co.* v. *Western Maryland Ry. Co.*, 242 U. S. 311, went pretty far in justifying the adoption of state legislation in advance, as I cannot for a moment believe that apart from the Eighteenth Amendment special constitutional principles exist against strong drink. The fathers

[37]

of the Constitution, so far as I know, approved it. But I can see no constitutional objection to such an adoption in this case if the Act of Congress be given that effect. I assume that Congress could not delegate to state legislatures the simple power to decide what the law of the United States should be in that district. But when institutions are established for ends within the powers of the States and not for any purpose affecting the law of the United States, I take it to be an admitted power of Congress to provide that the law of the United States shall conform as nearly as may be to what for the time being exists.

"A familiar example is the law directing the common-law practice, etc., in the District Courts to 'conform, as near as may be, to the practice,' etc., 'existing at the time' in State courts. (Revised Statutes, § 914.) This was held by the unanimous Court to be binding. . . . I have mentioned the scope given to the saving of a common-law remedy and have referred to cases on the statutes adopting state pilotage laws. Other instances are to be found in the Acts of Congress, but these are enough. I think that the same principle applies here.

"It should be observed that the objection now dealt with is the only one peculiar to the adoption of local law in advance. That of want of uniformity applies equally to the adoption of the laws in force in 1917. Furthermore we are not called on now to consider the collateral effects of the Act. The only question before us is whether the words in the Constitution, 'The judicial power shall extend to*** all cases of admiralty and maritime jurisdiction,' prohibit Congress from passing a law in the form of the New York Workmen's Compensation Act—if not in its present form, at least in the form in which it stood on October 6, 1917. I am of opinion that the New York law at the time of the trial should be applied and that the judgment should be affirmed."

Knickerbocker Ice Co. v. *Stewart*
253 U. S. 149, 166

[38]

II. On Infringing Upon Freedom

Free Press in Wartime

(*Milwaukee Social Dem. Pub. Co.* v. *Burleson,* 1920)

A FEW MONTHS AFTER THE ESPIONAGE ACT WAS PASSED IN 1917 THE Post Office Department revoked the second-class mail permit of Victor Berger's newspaper, the *Milwaukee Leader,* charging the paper with publishing false reports during the war with intent to promote the success of the enemy and to obstruct recruiting, thus violating the Act and subjecting itself to the provision which made newspapers unmailable.

The newspaper argued that the Act deprived it of a trial in court, of free speech, free press and property. But the validity of the law had been upheld in four espionage cases, and Mr. Justice Clarke swept the contentions aside. In his majority opinion he said that there was substantial evidence to support the Postmaster: editorials denouncing the war, the draft law and the Government.

He thought the *Leader* was giving too broad a definition to freedom of the press: "The Constitution was adopted to preserve our Government, not to serve as a protecting screen for those who while claiming its privileges seek to destroy it," and he pointed out that the paper could have used other classes of mail. "Whatever injury the relator suffered was the result of its own choice," Justice Clarke said.

Peace-time freedom was involved, Mr. Justice Brandeis declared in his dissent; the second-class service was not a privilege but a right; even though the third class was still open "Constitutional rights should not be frittered away by arguments so technical and unsubstantial." The order of the Postmaster was clearly punitive, he said; it effected a fine of $150 a day because 9,000 copies were mailed daily and ordinary postage rates were ten times higher than second-class.

Justice Brandeis pointed out that the *Leader* had not been convicted of violating the Act but that Postmaster General Burleson, solely because he believed the paper violated it, refused to carry the

Leader at second class; the Post Office had no power to prevent future mail as a punishment or preventive, otherwise the Postmaster would be "a universal censor of publications"; second-class mail service had nothing to do with a "bad newspaper."

Brandeis said that the Espionage Act empowered the Postmaster to exclude any piece from the mails but did not confer "the vague and absolute authority" of practically denying circulation to a paper for something it might publish.

"If administrative officers have this power in peace, then in every extension of governmental functions lurks a new danger to civil liberty," Justice Brandeis said.

Justice Holmes followed with another dissenting opinion:

"I HAVE had the advantage of reading the judgment of my brother Brandeis in this case and I agree in substance with his view. At first it seemed to me that if a publisher should announce in terms that he proposed to print treason and should demand a second-class rate it must be that the Postmaster General would have authority to refuse it. But reflection has convinced me that I was wrong.

"The question of the rate has nothing to do with the question whether the matter is mailable, and I am satisfied that the Postmaster cannot determine in advance that a certain newspaper is going to be non-mailable and on that ground deny to it not the use of the mails but the rate of postage that the statute says shall be charged.

"Of course the Postmaster may deny or revoke the second-class rate to a publication that does not comply with the conditions attached to it by statute, but as my brother Brandeis has pointed out, the conditions attached to the second-class rate by the statute cannot be made to justify the Postmaster's action except by a quibble.

"On the other hand the regulation of the right to use the mails by the Espionage Act has no peculiarities as a war measure but is similar to that in earlier cases, such as obscene docu-

ments. Papers that violate the Act are declared non-mailable
and the use of the mails for the transmission of them is made
criminal. But the only power given to the Postmaster is to refrain from forwarding the papers when received and to return
them to the senders. . . .

"He could not issue a general order that a certain newspaper
should not be carried because he thought it likely or certain
that it would contain treasonable or obscene talk. The United
States may give up the Post Office when it sees fit, but while it
carries it on, the use of the mails is almost as much a part of
free speech as the right to use our tongues, and it would take
very strong language to convince me that Congress ever intended to give such a practically despotic power to any one man.
There is no pretense that it has done so. Therefore I do not
consider the limits of its constitutional power.

"To refuse the second-class rate to a newspaper is to make
its circulation impossible and has all the effect of the order that
I have supposed. I repeat: when I observe that the only powers
expressly given to the Postmaster General to prevent the carriage of unlawful matter of the present kind are to stop and
to return papers already existing and posted, when I notice that
the conditions expressly attached to the second-class rate look
only to wholly different matters, and when I consider the ease
with which the power claimed by the Postmaster could be used
to interfere with very sacred rights, I am of opinion that
the refusal to allow the relator the rate to which it was entitled
whenever its newspaper was carried, on the ground that the
paper ought not to have been carried at all, was unjustified by
the statute and was a serious attack upon the liberties that not
even the war induced Congress to infringe."

United States ex rel. Milwaukee Social
Democratic Publishing Co.
v. Burleson, Postmaster
255 U. S. 407, 437

Sedition From a Housetop

(Abrams v. *United States,* 1919)

WHEN AMERICAN TROOPS WERE SENT INTO RUSSIA AFTER THE revolution there in 1917, a group of Russian-born people met in a basement room in New York and printed a few thousand leaflets of protest. Scattered from the roof or distributed secretly, the circulars fell into the hands of the Department of Justice. Four men and a girl were sentenced to prison.

Their defense (that freedom of speech was denied by the Espionage Act) had already been disposed of in the *Schenck, Frohwerk* and *Debs* cases, where Mr. Justice Holmes wrote the majority opinions. (See pp. 231, 236, 242)

Mr. Justice Clarke held here that "this is not an attempt to bring about a change of administration by candid discussion" but a plan to excite "disaffection, sedition, riots, and, as they hoped, revolution in this country for the purpose of embarrassing and if possible defeating the military plans of the Government.*** It will not do to say that the only intent of these defendants was to prevent injury to the Russian cause. Men must be held to have intended and to be accountable for the effects which their acts were likely to produce."

The "defendant alien anarchists" intended to provoke resistance to the United States in the war, the Court said, and evidence was plentiful. Evidence was meager, thought Holmes (Brandeis agreeing):

"THIS INDICTMENT is founded wholly upon the publication of two leaflets which I shall describe in a moment. The first count

[44]

charges a conspiracy pending the war with Germany to publish abusive language about the form of government of the United States, laying the preparation and publishing of the first leaflet as overt acts. The second count charges a conspiracy pending the war to publish language intended to bring the form of government into contempt, laying the preparation and publishing of the two leaflets as overt acts. The third count alleges a conspiracy to encourage resistance to the United States in the same war and to attempt to effectuate the purpose by publishing the same leaflets. The fourth count lays a conspiracy to incite curtailment of production of things necessary to the prosecution of the war and to attempt to accomplish it by publishing the second leaflet to which I have referred.

"The first of these leaflets says that the President's cowardly silence about the intervention in Russia reveals the hypocrisy of the plutocratic gang in Washington. It intimates that 'German militarism combined with Allied capitalism to crush the Russian revolution,' goes on that the tyrants of the world fight each other until they see a common enemy—working-class enlightenment—when they combine to crush it; and that now militarism and capitalism combined, though not openly, to crush the Russian revolution. It says that there is only one enemy of the workers of the world and that is capitalism; that it is a crime for workers of America, &c., to fight the workers' republic of Russia, and ends 'Awake! Awake, you workers of the world!' Signed 'Revolutionists.' A note adds, 'It is absurd to call us pro-German. We hate and despise German militarism more than do you hypocritical tyrants. We have more reasons for denouncing German militarism than has the coward of the White House.'

"The other leaflet, headed 'Workers—Wake Up,' with abusive language says that America together with the Allies will march for Russia to help the Czecho-Slovaks in their struggle against the Bolsheviki, and that this time the hypocrites shall not fool the Russian emigrants and friends of Russia in America. It tells the Russian emigrants that they now must spit in the face of false military propaganda by which their sympathy and help to the prosecution of the war have been called forth and says that with the money they have lent or are going to lend 'they will make bullets not only for the Germans but also for the Workers' Soviets of Russia,' and further, 'Workers in the ammunition factories, you are producing bullets, bayonets, cannon, to murder not only the Germans but also your dearest, best, who are in Russia fighting for freedom.' It then appeals to the same Russian emigrants at some length not to consent to the 'inquisitionary expedition to Russia,' and says that the destruction of the Russian revolution is 'the politics of the march on Russia.' The leaflet winds up by saying 'Workers, our reply to this barbaric intervention has to be a general strike!' and after a few words on the spirit of revolution, exhortations not to be afraid, and some usual tall talk, ends 'Woe unto those who will be in the way of progress. Let solidarity live! The Rebels.'

"No argument seems to me necessary to show that these pronunciamentos in no way attack the form of government of the United States, or that they do not support either of the first two counts. What little I have to say about the third count may be postponed until I have considered the fourth. With regard to that it seems too plain to be denied that the suggestion to workers in ammunition factories that they are producing bullets to murder their dearest, and the further advocacy of a general strike, both in the second leaflet, do urge curtailment of production of things necessary to the prosecution of the war within the meaning of the Act of May 16, 1918 . . . amending § 3 of the earlier Act of 1917. But to make the conduct criminal that statute requires that it should be 'with intent by such curtailment to cripple or hinder the United States in the prosecution of the war.' It seems to me that no such intent is proved.

"I am aware of course that the word intent as vaguely used in ordinary legal discussion means no more than knowledge at the time of the act that the consequences said to be intended will ensue. Even less than that will satisfy the general principle of civil and criminal liability. A man may have to pay damages, may be sent to prison, at common law might be hanged, if at the time of his act he knew facts from which common experience showed that the consequences would follow, whether he individually could foresee them or not. But, when words are used exactly, a deed is not done with intent to produce a consequence unless that consequence is the aim of the deed. It may be obvious, and obvious to the actor, that the consequence will follow, and he may be liable for it even if he forgets it, but he does not do the act with intent to produce it unless the aim to produce it is the proximate motive of the specific act, although there may be some deeper motive behind.

"It seems to me that this statute must be taken to use its words in a strict and accurate sense. They would be absurd in any other. A patriot might think that we were wasting money on aeroplanes, or making more cannon of a certain kind than we needed, and might advocate curtailment with success, yet even if it turned out that the curtailment hindered and was thought by other minds to have been obviously likely to hinder the United States in the prosecution of the war, no one would hold such conduct a crime. I admit that my illustration does not answer all that might be said but it is enough to show what I think and to let me pass to a more important aspect of the case. I refer to the First Amendment to the Constitution that Congress shall make no law abridging the freedom of speech.

"I never have seen any reason to doubt that the questions of law that alone were before this Court in the cases of *Schenck*, *Frohwerk* and *Debs*, were rightly decided. I do not doubt for

[47]

a moment that by the same reasoning that would justify punishing persuasion to murder, the United States constitutionally may punish speech that produces or is intended to produce a clear and imminent danger that it will bring about forthwith certain substantive evils that the United States constitutionally may seek to prevent. The power undoubtedly is greater in time of war than in time of peace because war opens dangers that do not exist at other times.

"But as against dangers peculiar to war, as against others, the principle of the right to free speech is always the same. It is only the present danger of immediate evil or an intent to bring it about that warrants Congress in setting a limit to the expression of opinion where private rights are not concerned. Congress certainly cannot forbid all effort to change the mind of the country. Now nobody can suppose that the surreptitious publishing of a silly leaflet by an unknown man, without more, would present any immediate danger that its opinions would hinder the success of the Government arms or have any appreciable tendency to do so. Publishing these opinions for the very purpose of obstructing, however, might indicate a greater danger and at any rate would have the quality of an attempt. So I assume that the second leaflet, if published for the purpose alleged in the fourth count, might be punishable. But it seems pretty clear to me that nothing less than that would bring these papers within the scope of this law.

"An actual intent in the sense that I have explained is necessary to constitute an attempt, where a further act of the same individual is required to complete the substantive crime, for reasons given in *Swift & Co.* v. *United States*, 196 U. S. 375, 396. It is necessary where the success of the attempt depends upon others, because if that intent is not present the actor's aim may be accomplished without bringing about the evils sought to be checked. An intent to prevent interference with the revolution in Russia might have been satisfied without any hindrance to carrying on the war in which we were engaged.

"I do not see how anyone can find the intent required by the statute in any of the defendants' words. The second leaflet is the only one that affords even a foundation for the charge, and there, without invoking the hatred of German militarism expressed in the former one, it is evident from the beginning to the end that the only object of the paper is to help Russia and stop American intervention there against the popular government—not to impede the United States in the war that it was carrying on. To say that two phrases taken literally might import a suggestion of conduct that would have interference with the war as an indirect and probably undesired effect seems to me by no means enough to show an attempt to produce that effect.

"I return for a moment to the third count. That charges an intent to provoke resistance to the United States in its war with Germany. Taking the clause in the statute that deals with that in connection with the other elaborate provisions of the Act, I think that resistance to the United States means some forcible act of opposition to some proceeding of the United States in pursuance of the war. I think the intent must be the specific intent that I have described and for the reasons that I have given. I think that no such intent was proved or existed in fact. I also think that there is no hint at resistance to the United States as I construe the phrase.

"In this case sentences of twenty years' imprisonment have been imposed for the publishing of two leaflets that I believe the defendants had as much right to publish as the Government has to publish the Constitution of the United States now vainly invoked by them. Even if I am technically wrong and enough can be squeezed from these poor and puny anonymities to turn the color of legal litmus paper—I will add, even if what I think the necessary intent were shown—the most nominal punishment seems to me all that possibly could be inflicted, unless the defendants are to be made to suffer not for what the indictment alleges but for the creed that they avow—a creed that I believe to be the creed of ignorance and immaturity when honestly held, as I see no reason to believe that it was held here, but which, although made the subject of examination at the trial, no one has a right even to consider in dealing with the charges before the Court.

"Persecution for the expression of opinions seems to me perfectly logical. If you have no doubt of your premises or your power and want a certain result with all your heart you naturally express your wishes in law and sweep away all opposition. To allow opposition by speech seems to indicate that you think speech impotent, as when a man says that he has squared the circle, or that you do not care wholeheartedly for the result, or that you doubt either your power or your premises.

"But when men have realized that time has upset many fighting faiths, they may come to believe even more than they believe the very foundations of their own conduct that the ultimate good desired is better reached by free trade in ideas— that the best test of truth is the power of the thought to get itself accepted in the competition of the market, and that truth is the only ground upon which their wishes safely can be carried out. That, at any rate, is the theory of our Constitution. It is an experiment, as all life is an experiment. Every year if not every day we have to wager our salvation upon some prophecy based upon imperfect knowledge. While that experiment is part of our system I think that we should be eternally vigilant against attempts to check the expression of opinions that we loathe and believe to be fraught with death, unless they so imminently threaten immediate interference with the lawful and pressing purposes of the law that an immediate check is required to save the country.

"I wholly disagree with the argument of the Government

that the First Amendment left the common law as to seditious libel in force. History seems to me against the notion. I had conceived that the United States through many years had shown its repentance for the Sedition Act of 1798 by repaying fines that it imposed. Only the emergency that makes it immediately dangerous to leave the correction of evil counsels to time warrants making any exception to the sweeping command, 'Congress shall make no law*** abridging the freedom of speech.' Of course I am speaking only of expressions of opinion and exhortations, which were all that were uttered here, but I regret that I cannot put into more impressive words my belief that in their conviction upon this indictment the defendants were deprived of their rights under the Constitution of the United States."

Abrams et al. v. *United States*
250 U. S. 616, 624

Anarchism: Doctrine and Force

(Gitlow v. *People of New York,* 1924)

BENJAMIN GITLOW WAS CONVICTED OF ADVOCATING CRIMINAL anarchy, defined by a New York statute as the doctrine that organized government should be overthrown by force or violence. He had written a pamphlet, "The Left Wing Manifesto," published by the left wing of the Socialist Party, organized June, 1919, in New York City.

Mr. Justice Sanford stated these facts: the manifesto condemned "moderate socialism" for recognizing the necessity of the democratic parliamentary state; it repudiated the policy of introducing socialism by legislation; advocated "Communist Revolution," class struggle, the mobilizing of "the power of the proletariat," mass industrial revolts, political strikes, "revolutionary mass action" establishing "the revolutionary dictatorship of the proletariat."

In answer to the argument that the State had not proved a definite act of criminal anarchy, Justice Sanford said that the New York law did not "penalize 'abstract doctrine' or academic discussion having no quality of incitement to any concrete action," but he read over the last sentence of the manifesto: "The Communist International calls the proletariat of the world to the final struggle!" and observed, "This is not the expression of philosophical abstraction, the mere prediction of future events; it is the language of direct incitement."

The question was whether the law deprived Gitlow of his liberty of expression in violation of the due process clause of the Fourteenth Amendment. There was peril in "a single revolutionary spark," said Sanford, and the constitutionality of the statute was sustained.

Justice Holmes wrote:

[52]

"Mr. justice brandeis and I are of opinion that this judgment should be reversed. The general principle of free speech, it seems to me, must be taken to be included in the Fourteenth Amendment, in view of the scope that has been given to the word 'liberty' as there used, although perhaps it may be accepted with a somewhat larger latitude of interpretation than is allowed to Congress by the sweeping language that governs or ought to govern the laws of the United States.

"If I am right, then I think that the criterion sanctioned by the full Court in *Schenck* v. *United States* applies, 'The question in every case is whether the words used are used in such circumstances and are of such a nature as to create a clear and present danger that will bring about the substantive evils that [the State] has a right to prevent.'

"It is true that in my opinion this criterion was departed from in *Abrams* v. *United States,* but the convictions that I expressed in that case are too deep for it to be possible for me as yet to believe that it and *Schaefer* v. *United States,* 251 U. S. 466, [another Espionage case] have settled the law. If what I think the correct test is applied, it is manifest that there was no present danger of an attempt to overthrow the Government by force on the part of the admittedly small minority who shared the defendant's views.

"It is said that this manifesto is more than a theory, that it was an incitement. Every idea is an incitement. It offers itself for belief and if believed it is acted on unless some other belief outweighs it or some failure of energy stifles the movement at its birth. The only difference between the expression of an opinion and an incitement in the narrower sense is the speaker's enthusiasm for the result. Eloquence may set fire to reason. But whatever may be thought of the redundant discourse before us it had no chance of starting a present conflagration.

"If in the long run the beliefs expressed in proletarian

[53]

dictatorship are destined to be accepted by the dominant forces of the community, the only meaning of free speech is that they should be given their chance and have their way.

"If the publication of this document had been laid as an attempt to induce an uprising against government at once and not at some indefinite time in the future, it would have presented a different question. The object would have been one with which the law might deal, subject to the doubt whether there was any danger that the publication could produce any result, or in other words, whether it was not futile and too remote from possible consequences. But the indictment alleges the publication and nothing more."

Gitlow v. *People of New York*
268 U. S. 652, 672

The Rosika Schwimmer Case

(*United States* v. *Schwimmer*, 1928)

CITIZENSHIP WAS DENIED TO A WOMAN OF FIFTY WHO STATED IN her application that she would not take up arms for this country. Against her willingness to swear allegiance and do everything (except go to war) that a citizen might be called upon to do, the Naturalization Act of 1906 was quoted. This law required applicants to "support and defend the Constitution and the laws of the United States against all enemies" and to satisfy the court of their attachment to the principles of the Constitution.

The District Court doubted that this person held those principles dear. On the other hand, the Circuit Court of Appeals held that women were considered incapable of bearing arms. But the Department of Justice appealed, arguing that Mrs. Schwimmer's incapacity because of her sex was immaterial; her attitude toward the Government's defense "with its necessary influence on others" was the vital matter: "In time of war she would be a menace to the country. If every citizen believed as she does and acted as she will we would have no Constitution and no Government."

Six Justices of the Supreme Court accepted that view. This self-described uncompromising pacifist, who classed herself with male conscientious objectors and asserted she had no sense of nationalism, was said by Mr. Justice Butler to be lacking in "that attachment to the principles of the Constitution of which the applicant is required to give affirmative evidence by the Naturalization Act." He held it a fundamental duty to defend the Government by force of arms; it was important to find out whether an alien applying for citizenship held beliefs opposed to the discharge of that duty: "The influence of con-

[55]

scientious objectors against the use of military force in defense of the principles of our Government is apt to be more detrimental than their mere refusal to bear arms. The fact that, by reason of sex, age or other cause, they may be unfit to serve does not lessen their purpose or power to influence others."

In dissenting Justice Holmes was supported by Justice Brandeis (Mr. Justice Sanford agreed with the reasoning of the Circuit Court of Appeals):

"T HE APPLICANT seems to be a woman of superior character and intelligence, obviously more than ordinarily desirable as a citizen of the United States. It is agreed that she is qualified for citizenship except so far as the views set forth in a statement of facts 'may show that the applicant is not attached to the principles of the Constitution of the United States and well disposed to the good order and happiness of the same, and except in so far as the same may show that she cannot take the oath of allegiance without a mental reservation.'

"The views referred to are an extreme opinion in favor of pacifism and a statement that she would not bear arms to defend the Constitution. So far as the adequacy of her oath is concerned I hardly can see how it is affected by the statement, inasmuch as she is a woman over fifty years of age, and would not be allowed to bear arms if she wanted to. And as to the opinion, the whole examination of the applicant shows that she holds none of the now-dreaded creeds but thoroughly believes in organized government and prefers that of the United States to any other in the world.

"Surely it cannot show lack of attachment to the principles of the Constitution that she thinks it can be improved. I suppose that most intelligent people think that it might be. Her particular improvement looking to the abolition of war seems to me not materially different in its bearing on this case from a wish to establish cabinet government as in England, or a single house, or one term of seven years for the President. To touch a more burning question, only a judge mad with partisan-ship would exclude because the applicant thought that the Eighteenth Amendment should be repealed.

"Of course the fear is that if a war came the applicant would exert activities such as were dealt with in *Schenck* v. *United States* [see page 231.] But that seems to me unfounded. Her position and motives are wholly different from those of Schenck. She is an optimist and states in strong and, I do not doubt, sin-cere words her belief that war will disappear and that the im-pending destiny of mankind is to unite in peaceful leagues.

"I do not share that optimism nor do I think that a philo-sophic view of the world would regard war as absurd. But most people who have known it regard it with horror, as a last re-sort, and even if not yet ready for cosmopolitan efforts, would welcome any practicable combinations that would increase the power on the side of peace.

"The notion that the applicant's optimistic anticipations would make her a worse citizen is sufficiently answered by her examination, which seems to me a better argument for her ad-mission than any I can offer. Some of her answers might excite popular prejudice, but if there is any principle of the Constitu-tion that more imperatively calls for attachment than any other it is the principle of free thought—not free thought for those who agree with us but freedom for the thought that we hate. I think that we should adhere to that principle with regard to admission into, as well as to life within, this country.

"And recurring to the opinion that bars this applicant's way, I would suggest that the Quakers have done their share to make the country what it is, that many citizens agree with the applicant's belief and that I had not supposed hitherto that we regretted our inability to expel them because they believe more than some of us do in the teachings of the Sermon on the Mount."

United States v. *Schwimmer*
279, U. S. 644, 653

The Leo Frank Case

(*Frank* v. *Mangum*, 1914)

LEO M. FRANK, MANAGER OF HIS UNCLE'S PENCIL FACTORY IN AT-
lanta, was convicted of murdering a girl employee. Frank raised a
Federal issue by alleging that riotous scenes had occurred at his trial
and that the jury had been subject to mob domination. He appealed to
the District Court for release on a writ of habeas corpus, although the
Supreme Court of Georgia had said that the alleged disorders were
merely trivial irregularities.

Another point Frank raised was his enforced absence at the polling
of the jury; he said he did not know of the arrangement made by his
counsel at the judge's suggestion. The Supreme Court of Georgia,
having twice heard and refused motions for a new trial and being
asked to set aside the verdict, held that the point should have been made
before; it was too late.

Was Frank denied due process of law? Doomed to death, had he
been given a fair and impartial trial? The State said it was no time to
review the facts; all legal forms had been observed; the State's
authority over police matters was final. And the District Court held
that the writ of habeas corpus could not be granted—that the case was
in the State's jurisdiction.

Frank's failure on the re-trial motion to raise the objection that he
was barred from the courtroom amounted to a waiver, according to
Mr. Justice Pitney; a State had power to establish its own rule of practice. Considering the complete case in the State courts, the majority
found everything in order; Frank was not being held in custody contrary to the Constitution.

Justice Holmes dissented:

"Mr. justice hughes and I are of opinion that the judgment should be reversed. The only question before us is whether the petition shows on its face that the writ of habeas corpus should be denied or whether the District Court should have proceeded to try the facts.

"The allegations that appear to us material are these. The trial began on July 28, 1913, at Atlanta, and was carried on in a court packed with spectators and surrounded by a crowd outside, all strongly hostile to the petitioner. On Saturday, August 23, this hostility was sufficient to lead the judge to confer in the presence of the jury with the Chief of Police of Atlanta and the Colonel of the Fifth Georgia Regiment stationed in that city, both of whom were known to the jury. On the same day, the evidence seemingly having been closed, the public press, apprehending danger, united in a request to the court that the proceedings should not continue on that evening. Thereupon the court adjourned until Monday morning.

"On that morning when the Solicitor General entered the court he was greeted with applause, stamping of feet and clapping of hands, and the judge before beginning his charge had a private conversation with the petitioner's counsel in which he expressed the opinion that there would be 'probable danger of violence' if there should be an acquittal or disagreement, and that it would be safer for not only the petitioner but his counsel to be absent from court when the verdict was brought in. At the judge's request they agreed that the petitioner and they should be absent, and they kept their word.

"When the verdict was rendered, and before more than one of the jurymen had been polled, there was such a roar of applause that the polling could not go on till order was restored. The noise outside was such that it was difficult for the judge to hear the answers of the jurors although he was only ten feet from them. With these specifications of fact, the petitioner alleges that the trial was dominated by a hostile mob and was nothing but an empty form.

"We lay on one side the question whether the petitioner could or did waive his right to be present at the polling of the jury. That question was apparent in the form of the trial and was raised by the application for a writ of error; and although after application to the full Court we thought that the writ ought to be granted, we never have been impressed by the argument that the presence of the prisoner was required by the Constitution of the United States. But habeas corpus cuts through all forms and goes to the very tissue of the structure. It comes in from the outside, not in subordination to the proceedings, and, although every form may have been preserved, opens the inquiry whether they have been more than an empty shell.

"The argument for the appellee in substance is that the trial was in a court of competent jurisdiction, that it retains jurisdiction although in fact it may be dominated by a mob and that the rulings of the State court as to the fact of such domination cannot be reviewed. But the argument seems to us inconclusive. Whatever disagreement there may be as to the scope of the phrase 'due process of law,' there can be no doubt that it embraces the fundamental conception of a fair trial, with opportunity to be heard. Mob law does not become due process of law by securing the assent of a terrorized jury. We are not speaking of mere disorder, or mere irregularities in procedure, but of a case where the processes of justice are actually subverted. In such a case the Federal court has jurisdiction to issue the writ. The fact that the State court still has its general jurisdiction and is otherwise a competent court does not make it impossible to find that a jury has been subjected to intimidation in a particular case. The loss of jurisdiction is not general but particular, and proceeds from the control of a hostile influence.

"When such a case is presented it cannot be said, in our

view, that the State court decision makes the matter *res judicata*. The State acts when by its agency it finds the prisoner guilty and condemns him. We have held in a civil case that it is no defense to the assertion of a Federal right in the Federal court that the State has corrective procedure of its own—that still less does such a procedure draw to itself the final determination of the Federal question. . . . We see no reason for a less liberal rule in a matter of life and death. When the decision of the question of fact is so interwoven with the decision of the question of constitutional right that the one necessarily involves the other, the Federal court must examine the facts. . . . Otherwise the right will be a barren one.

"It is significant that the argument for the State does not go so far as to say that in no case would it be permissible on application for habeas corpus to override the findings of fact by the State courts. It would indeed be a most serious thing if this Court were so to hold, for we could not but regard it as a removal of what is perhaps the most important guaranty of the Federal Constitution. If, however, the argument stops short of this, the whole structure built upon the State procedure and decisions falls to the ground.

"To put an extreme case and show what we mean, if the trial and the later hearings before the Supreme Court had taken place in the presence of an armed force known to be ready to shoot if the result was not the one desired, we do not suppose that this Court would allow itself to be silenced by the suggestion that the record showed no flaw. To go one step further, suppose that the trial had taken place under such intimidation that the Supreme Court of the State on writ of error had discovered no error in the record, we still imagine that this Court would find a sufficient one outside of the record, and that it would not be disturbed in its conclusion by anything that the Supreme Court of the State might have said. We therefore lay the suggestion that the Supreme Court of the State has disposed of the present question by its judgment on one side along with the question of the appellant's right to be present.

"If the petition discloses facts that amount to a loss of jurisdiction in the trial court, jurisdiction could not be restored by any decision above. And notwithstanding the principle of comity and convenience (for in our opinion it is nothing more . . .) that calls for a resort to the local appellate tribunal before coming to the courts of the United States for a writ of habeas corpus, when as here, that resort has been had in vain, the power to secure fundamental rights that had existed at every stage becomes a duty and must be put forth.

"The single question in our minds is whether a petition alleging that the trial took place in the midst of a mob savagely and manifestly intent on a single result, is shown on its face unwarranted by the specifications which may be presumed to set forth the strongest indications of the fact at the petitioner's command. This is not a matter for polite presumptions; we must look facts in the face. Any judge who has sat with juries knows that in spite of forms they are extremely likely to be impregnated by the environing atmosphere. And when we find the judgment of the expert on the spot, of the judge whose business it was to preserve not only form but substance, to have been that if one juryman yielded to the reasonable doubt that he himself later expressed in court as the result of most anxious deliberation, neither prisoner nor counsel would be safe from the rage of the crowd, we think the presumption overwhelming that the jury responded to the passions of the mob.

"Of course we are speaking only of the case made by the petition, and whether it ought to be heard. Upon allegations of this gravity in our opinion it ought to be heard, whatever the decision of the State court may have been, and it did not need to set forth contradictory evidence or matter of rebuttal, or to explain why the motions for a new trial and to set aside the verdict were overruled by the State court. There is no reason to fear an impairment of the authority of the State to punish the guilty.

"We do not think it impracticable in any part of this country to have trials free from outside control. But to maintain this immunity it may be necessary that the supremacy of the law and of the Federal Constitution should be vindicated in a case like this. It may be that on a hearing a different complexion would be given to the judge's alleged request and expression of fear. But supposing the alleged facts to be true, we are of opinion that if they were before the Supreme Court it sanctioned a situation upon which the courts of the United States should act, and if for any reason they were not before the Supreme Court, it is our duty to act upon them now and to declare lynch law as little valid when practiced by a regularly drawn jury as when administered by one elected by a mob intent on death."

Frank v. *Mangum, Sheriff of Fulton County, Georgia*
237 U. S. 309, 345

Newspaper in Contempt

(Toledo Newspaper Co. v. *United States,* 1917)*

TOLEDO PASSED AN ORDINANCE ESTABLISHING A THREE-CENT TROL-
ley fare at the expiration of the franchises held by the company that
controlled the street-car system of that city. The *News-Bee* challenged
the Federal district judge's right to grant the company relief, and its
managing editor was fined for contempt some time later by the judge
himself.

The newspaper invoked the freedom of the press and argued that
there was no evidence or even allegation that its articles had interfered
with the deliberations of the court or the administration of the law.
Chief Justice White held that the criterion here was the reasonable
tendency of the newspaper's acts. Courts should not be influenced by
newspaper dictation or popular clamor, he said, and the *News-Bee* had
been "vociferous and vituperous," its articles capable of subjecting the
District Court to suspicion, odium, disrespect and disregard. Freedom of the press was not a freedom to do wrong with impunity; a free
press depended on free institutions. Although evidence of obstruction
was admittedly lacking, he believed that the newspaper had attempted
to intimidate the judge.

Once more Brandeis concurred in Holmes' dissent:

"ONE OF THE USUAL controversies between a street railway
and the city that it served had been going on for years and had
culminated in an ordinance establishing three-cent fares that
was to go into effect on March 28, 1914. In January of that
year the people who were operating the road began a suit for

an injunction on the ground that the ordinance was confiscatory. The plaintiffs in error, a newspaper and its editor, had long been on the popular side and had furnished news and comment to sustain it; and when, on March 24, a motion was made for a temporary injunction in the suit, they published a cartoon representing the road as a moribund man in bed with its friends at the bedside and one of them saying, 'Guess we'd better call in Doc Killits.'

"Thereafter pending the controversy they published news, comment and cartoons as before. The injunction was issued on September 12. The judge (Killits) who was referred to took no steps until September 29, when he directed an information to be filed covering publications from March 24 through September 17. This was done on October 28. In December the case was tried summarily without a jury by the judge who thought his authority contemned, and in the following year he imposed a considerable fine. The question is whether he acted within his powers under the statutes of the United States.

"The statute in force at the time of the alleged contempts confined the power of courts in cases of this sort to where there had been 'misbehavior of any person in their presence, or so near thereto as to obstruct the administration of justice.' . . . Before the trial took place an act was passed giving a trial by jury upon demand of the accused in all but the above-mentioned instances, October 14, 1914. . . . In England, I believe, the usual course is to proceed by the regular way by indictment. I mention this fact and the later statute only for their bearing upon the meaning of the exception in our law.

"When it is considered how contrary it is to our practice and ways of thinking for the same person to be accuser and sole judge in a matter which, if he be sensitive, may involve strong personal feeling, I should expect the power to be limited by the necessities of the case 'to insure order and decorum in their presence' as it is stated in *Ex parte Robinson*, 19 Wall. 505.

. . . And when the words of the statute are read it seems to me that the limit is too plain to be construed away. To my mind they point and point only to the present protection of the Court from actual interference and not to postponed retribution for lack of respect for its dignity—not to moving to vindicate its independence after enduring the newspaper's attacks for nearly six months as the court did in this case.

"Without invoking the rule of strict construction I think that 'so near as to obstruct' means so near as actually to obstruct —and not merely near enough to threaten a possible obstruction. 'So near as to' refers to an accomplished fact, and the word 'misbehavior' strengthens the construction I adopt. Misbehavior means something more than adverse comment or disrespect.

"But suppose that an imminent possibility of obstruction is sufficient. Still I think that only immediate and necessary action is contemplated, and that no case for summary proceedings is made out if after the event publications are brought to the attention of the judge that might have led to an obstruction although they did not. So far as appears that is the present case. But I will go a step farther. The order for the information recites that from time to time sundry numbers of the paper have come to the attention of the judge as a daily reader of it, and I will assume, from that and the opinion, that he read them as they came out, and I will assume further that he was entitled to rely upon his private knowledge without a statement in open court.

"But a judge of the United States is expected to be a man of ordinary firmness of character, and I find it impossible to believe that such a judge could have found in anything that was printed even a tendency to prevent his performing his sworn duty. I am not considering whether there was a technical contempt at common law but whether what was done falls within the words of an act intended and admitted to limit the power of the courts.

"The chief thing done was to print statements of a widespread public intent to board the cars and refuse to pay more than three cents, even if the judge condemned the ordinance, statements favoring the course, if you like, and mention of the city officials who intended to back it up. This popular movement was met on the part of the railroad by directing its conductors not to accept three-cent fares, but to carry passengers free who refused to pay more; so that all danger of violence on that score was avoided, even if it was a danger that in any way concerned the court. The newspaper further gave one or two premature but ultimately correct intimations of what the judge was going to do, made one mistaken statement of a ruling which it criticized indirectly, uttered a few expressions that implied that the judge did not have the last word and that no doubt contained innuendoes not flattering to his personality.

"Later there was an account of a local Socialist meeting at which a member, one Quinlivan, spoke in such a way that the judge attached him for contempt and thereupon, on the same day that the decree was entered in the principal case, the paper reported as the grounds for the attachment that Quinlivan had pronounced Judge Killits to have shown from the first that he was favorable to the railroad, had criticized somewhat ignorantly a ruling said to put the burden of the proof on the city, and had said that Killits and his press were unfair to the people, winding up 'impeach Killits.'

"I confess that I cannot find in all this or in the evidence in the case anything that would have affected a mind of reasonable fortitude, and still less can I find there anything that obstructed the administration of justice in any sense that I possibly can give to those words.

"In the elaborate opinion that was delivered by Judge Killits to justify the judgment it is said, 'In this matter the record shows that the court endured the *News-Bee's* attacks upon suitors before it and upon the court itself, and carried all the embarrassment inevitable from these publications, for nearly six months before moving to vindicate its independence.' It appears to me that this statement is enough to show that there was no emergency, that there was nothing that warranted a finding that the administration of justice was obstructed, or a resort to this summary proceeding, but that on the contrary when the matter was over, the judge thought that the 'consistently unfriendly attitude against the court' and the fact that the publications tended 'to arouse distrust and dislike of the court,' were sufficient to justify this information and a heavy fine.

"They may have been, but not, I think, in this form of trial. I would go as far as any man in favor of the sharpest and most summary enforcement of order in court and obedience to its decrees, but when there is no need for immediate action contempts are like any other breach of law and should be dealt with as the law deals with other illegal acts. Action like the present in my opinion is wholly unwarranted by even color of law."

Toledo Newspaper Co. et al. v. *United States*
247 U. S. 402, 422

Publishing a Letter

(*Craig* v. *Hecht*, 1923)

CHARLES L. CRAIG, NEW YORK CITY COMPTROLLER, GAVE TO NEWS-papers copies of a letter he had sent to the Public Service Commission, assailing District Judge Mayer for his conduct of street-car receiver-ship proceedings then pending. The judge offered him an opportunity to retract. Craig did not do so. Judge Mayer then sentenced him, four months after publication, to sixty days in jail for contempt.

At that time Circuit Court Judge Manton was sitting in the Dis-trict Court. Craig petitioned him for a writ of habeas corpus and ob-tained it, as well as a final discharge. But the United States Circuit Court had been abolished years back, and when the case came to the Circuit Court of Appeals it was held that circuit judges, as such, were without power to grant such writs; that Judge Mayer had jurisdiction of both the offense and the person. The order of discharge was re-versed.

This met with the approval of the Supreme Court. Mr. Justice McReynolds pointed out that Craig had not sought an appeal but had asked a single judge to review Judge Mayer and upset the pro-ceedings, so that, having won the favorable order, there could be no appeal to the Circuit Court of Appeals—a course indicating "studied purpose to escape review of either proceeding by an appellate court." McReynolds cited the *Toledo News-Bee Case* to show the power of the District Court over contempt proceedings.

Chief Justice Taft concurred. It was essential that courts and judges be not impeded by publications tending to obstruct, he said; Craig's course now "raised the sole issue whether the trial judge had authority to decide the question, not whether he had rightly decided it"; his short-cut had cost him his opportunity for review.

Justice Holmes dissented:

"I THINK that the petitioner's resort to habeas corpus in this case was right and was the only proper course. Very possibly some of the cases confuse the principles that govern jurisdiction with those that govern merits. . . . But I think that this should be treated as a question of jurisdiction. The statute puts it as a matter of power, 'The said courts shall have power*** to punish*** contempts of their authority. *Provided,* that such power to punish contempts shall not be construed to extend to any cases except the misbehavior of any person in their presence, or so near thereto as to obstruct the administration of justice,' &c., Judicial Code § 268.

"I think that these words should be taken literally and that we do not need a better illustration of the need to treat them as jurisdictional and to confine the jurisdiction very narrowly than the present case. For we must not confound the power to punish this kind of contempts with the power to overcome and punish disobedience to or defiance of the orders of a court, although unfortunately both are called by the same name.

"That of course a court may and should use as fully as needed, but this, especially if it is to be extended by decisions to which I cannot agree, makes a man judge in matters in which he is likely to have keen personal interest and feeling, although neither self-protection nor the duty of going on with the work requires him to take such a part.

"It seems to me that the statute on its face plainly limits the jurisdiction of the judge in this class of cases to those where his personal action is necessary in a strict sense in order to enable him to go on with his work. But wherever the line may be drawn it is a jurisdictional line. 'The jurisdiction attaches only when the suit presents a substantial claim under an Act of Congress.' . . .

"I think that the sentence from which the petitioner seeks relief was more than an abuse of power. I think it should be held wholly void. I think in the first place that there was no matter pending before the court in the sense that it must be to make this kind of contempt possible. It is not enough that somebody may hereafter move to have something done. There was nothing then awaiting decision when the petitioner's letter was published. The English cases show that the law of England at least is in accord with my view. . . . But if there had been, and giving the most unfavorable interpretation to all that the letter says, I do not see how to misstate past matters of fact of the sort charged here could be said to obstruct the administration of justice.

"Suppose the petitioner falsely and unjustly charged the judge with having excluded him from knowledge of the facts, how can it be pretended that the charge obstructed the administration of justice when the judge seemingly was willing to condone it if the petitioner would retract? Unless a judge while sitting can lay hold of anyone who ventures to publish anything that tends to make him unpopular or to belittle him, I cannot see what power Judge Mayer had to touch Mr. Craig.

"Even if feeling was tense there is no such thing as what Keating, J., in *Metzler* v. *Gounod*, 30 Law Times R., N. S. 264, [an English case] calls contingent contempt. A man cannot be summarily laid by the heels because his words may make public feeling more unfavorable in case the judge should be asked to act at some later date, any more than he can for exciting public feeling against a judge for what he already has done." (Brandeis concurred.)

Craig v. *Hecht, United States Marshal*
for the Southern District of New York
263 U. S. 255, 280

[71]

Post Office Tyranny

(Leach v. *Carlile, Postmaster,* 1921)

A PATENT-MEDICINE MAN IN CHICAGO ADVERTISED "ORGANO TABLETS" through the mails. They were "prescribed by leading physicians throughout the civilized world for nervous diseases, general debility, sexual decline or weakened manhood." The Post Office issued a fraud order against him, prohibiting the delivery of mail and the payment of money orders to the advertiser, who in turn sued to enjoin enforcement of the order. He complained that the Postmaster General had decided the question whether the medicine was producing the results advertised; that this was a matter of opinion, and he had evidence to the contrary.

Mr. Justice Clarke said it was a question of fact, committed by the statutes to the decision of the Postmaster; the settled rule of law was not to review his conclusion if fairly arrived at, and the record justified the Circuit Court of Appeals in finding abundant ground for the Postmaster's order; the tablets were so far from being the panacea proclaimed that the appellant was perpetrating a fraud on the public.

Justice Holmes was again joined by Justice Brandeis:

"THE STATUTE under which fraud orders are issued by the Postmaster General has been decided or said to be valid so many times that it may be too late to expect a contrary decision. But there are considerations against it that seem to me never to have been fully weighed and that I think it my duty to state.

"The transmission of letters by any general means other than the Post Office is forbidden by the Criminal Code. . . .

Therefore, if these prohibitions are valid, this form of communication with people at a distance is through the Post Office alone; and notwithstanding all modern inventions letters still are the principal means of speech with those who are not before our face.

"I do not suppose that anyone would say that the freedom of written speech is less protected by the First Amendment than the freedom of spoken words. Therefore I cannot understand by what authority Congress undertakes to authorize anyone to determine in advance, on the grounds before us, that certain words shall not be uttered. Even those who interpret the Amendment most strictly agree that it was intended to prevent previous restraints.

"We have not before us any question as to how far Congress may go for the safety of the Nation. The question is only whether it may make possible irreparable wrongs and the ruin of a business in the hope of preventing some cases of a private wrong that generally is accomplished without the aid of the mail. Usually private swindling does not depend upon the Post Office. If the execution of this law does not abridge freedom of speech I do not quite see what could be said to do so.

"Even if it should be held that the prohibition of other modes of carrying letters was unconstitutional, as suggested in a qualified way in *Ex parte Jackson*, 96 U. S. 727, it would not get rid of the difficulty, to my mind, because the practical dependence of the public upon the Post Office would remain. But the decision in that case admits that possibly at least the prohibition as to letters would be valid. That case was not dealing with sealed letters.

"The decisions thus far have gone largely if not wholly on the ground that if the Government chose to offer a means of transportation which it was not bound to offer it could choose what it would transport; which is well enough when neither law nor the habit that the Government's action has generated has made that means the only one. But when habit and law combine to exclude every other it seems to me that the First Amendment in terms forbids such control of the post as was exercised here.

"I think it abridged freedom of speech on the part of the sender of the letters and that the appellant had such an interest in the exercise of the right that he could avail himself of it in this case."

Leach, doing business as Organo Product Co.
v. Carlile, Postmaster,
258 U. S. 138, 140

The Use of a Patent

(Motion Picture v. Universal Film, 1916)

A PATENTED FEEDER FOR MOVING PICTURE PROJECTION MACHINES, insuring regularity of speed, was sold to a New York theater under a license agreement whereby the feeder was to be used solely to exhibit films leased by the Motion Picture Patents Co. upon terms to be fixed. The theater showed pictures of the Universal Film Manufacturing Co. and failed to arrange for royalty terms.

At the time the case was argued before the Supreme Court 40,000 feeders were in use and this mechanism was the only one by which movie films could be projected properly. Mr. Justice Clarke said that the patent laws did not authorize the restriction of materials to be used in operating the feeder; otherwise, "by the obviously simple expedient of varying its royalty charge," the patentee or his assignee would hold "a power for evil" over the industry.

Justice Holmes dissented, joined by Justices McKenna and Van Devanter:

"I SUPPOSE that a patentee has no less property in his patented machine than any other owner and that in addition to keeping the machine to himself the patent gives him further right to forbid the rest of the world from making others like it. In short, for whatever motive, he may keep his device wholly out of use. . . .

"So much being undisputed, I cannot understand why he may not keep it out of use unless the licensee, or, for the matter of that, the buyer, will use some unpatented thing in connection with it. Generally speaking, the measure of a condition is the

[75]

consequence of a breach, and if that consequence is one that the owner may impose unconditionally, he may impose it conditionally upon a certain event. . . .

"No doubt this principle might be limited or excluded in cases where the condition tends to bring about a state of things that there is a predominant public interest to prevent. But there is no predominant public interest to prevent a patented tea pot or film feeder from being kept from the public, because, as I have said, the patentee may keep them tied up at will while his patent lasts.

"Neither is there any such interest to prevent the purchase of the tea or films that is made the condition of the use of the machine. The supposed contravention of public interest sometimes is stated as an attempt to extend the patent law to unpatented articles, which of course it is not, and more accurately as a possible domination to be established by such means. But the domination is one only to the extent of the desire for the tea pot or the film feeder, and if the owner prefers to keep the pot or the feeder unless you will buy his tea or films, I cannot see in allowing him the right to do so anything more than an ordinary incident of ownership, or at most, a consequence of the *Paper Bag Case*, on which, as it seems to me, this case ought to turn. . . .

Not only do I believe that the rule that I advocate is right under the *Paper Bag Case*, but I think that it has become a rule of property that law and justice require to be retained. For fifteen years . . . the public has been encouraged by this Court to believe that the law is as it was laid down in *Heaton-Peninsular Button-Fastener Co.* v. *Eureka Specialty Co.*, 77 Fed. Rep. 288, 25 C. C. A. 267, and numerous decisions of the lower courts. I believe that many and important transactions have taken place on the faith of those decisions, and for that reason, as well as for the first that I have given, the rule last announced in *Henry* v. *A. B. Dick Co.*, 224, U. S. 1, should be maintained.

"I will add for its bearing upon *Straus* v. *Victor Talking Machine Co.*, [in which Holmes dissented but wrote no opinion] that a conditional sale retaining the title until a future event after delivery has been decided to be lawful again and again by this Court. . . .

"I confine myself to expressing my views upon the general and important questions upon which I have the misfortune to differ from the majority of the Court. I leave on one side the question of the effect of the Clayton Act, as the Court has done, and also what I might think if the *Paper Bag Case* were not upheld, or if the question were upon the effect of a combination of patents such as to be contrary to the policy that I am bound to accept from the Congress of the United States."

Motion Picture Patents Co. v.
Universal Film Mfg. Co.
243 U. S. 502, 519

Jeopardy in the Philippines

(*Kepner* v. *United States*, 1903)

A LAWYER IN MANILA WAS TRIED FOR EMBEZZLING A CLIENT'S funds and was acquitted. Under the Spanish law, then in force, right of appeal in criminal cases was available to both parties, but while the case was being appealed Congress passed the Organic Act giving the Philippines a civil government, providing for due process of law and forbidding double jeopardy.

The Philippine Supreme Court reversed the decision of the trial court, sentenced the lawyer to a short prison term and disfranchised him. When this was contested the Government replied that Congress meant to adhere to the old jurisprudence of the Islands wherein double jeopardy did not begin until there had been a final judgment in the court of last resort. Here the trial was continuous from the lower court to the higher, the latter corresponding to the *audiencia* held in Madrid in former days.

What did Congress mean by the phrase in the Act, "no person for the same offense shall be twice put in jeopardy of punishment"? Mr. Justice Day said it must be construed "with reference to the common law from which it was taken," and he took it to mean double prosecution, not double punishment. He held that Congress had supplanted the system whereby the Philippine Government could appeal after acquittal.

Holmes justified the Spanish custom, Justices White and McKenna concurring, while Justice Brown dissented separately. Holmes wrote:

"I REGRET that I am unable to agree with the decision of the majority of the Court. The case is of great importance, not only in its immediate bearing upon the administration of justice in the Philippines but, since the words used in the Act of Congress are also in the Constitution, even more because the decision necessarily will carry with it an interpretation of the latter instrument.

"If, as is possible, the constitutional prohibition should be extended to misdemeanors . . . we shall have fastened upon the country a doctrine covering the whole criminal law, which, it seems to me, will have serious and evil consequences. At the present time in this country there is more danger that criminals will escape justice than that they will be subjected to tyranny. But I do not stop to consider or to state the consequences in detail, as such considerations are not supposed to be entertained by judges, except as inclining them to one of two interpretations, or as a tacit last resort in case of doubt.

"It is more pertinent to observe that it seems to me that logically and rationally a man cannot be said to be more than once in jeopardy in the same cause, however often he may be tried. The jeopardy is one continuing jeopardy from its beginning to the end of the cause. Everybody agrees that the principle in its origin was a rule forbidding a trial in a new and independent case where a man already had been tried once. But there is no rule that a man may not be tried twice in the same case. It has been decided by this Court that he may be tried a second time, even for his life, if the jury disagree . . . or notwithstanding their agreement and verdict, if the verdict is set aside on the prisoner's exceptions for error in the trial. . . . He even may be tried on a new indictment if the judgment on the first is arrested upon motion. . . .

"If a statute should give the right to take exceptions to the Government, I believe it would be impossible to maintain that the prisoner would be protected by the Constitution from being tried again. He no more would be put in jeopardy a second time when retried because of a mistake of law in his favor than he would be when retried for a mistake that did him harm. It cannot matter that the prisoner procures the second trial. In a capital case . . . a man cannot waive, and certainly will not be taken to waive without meaning it, fundamental and constitutional rights. . . . Usually no such waiver is expressed or thought of. Moreover, it cannot be imagined that the law would deny to a prisoner the correction of a fatal error, unless he should waive other rights so important as to be saved by an express clause in the Constitution of the United States.

"It might be said that when a prisoner takes exceptions he only is trying to get rid of a jeopardy that already exists—that so far as the verdict is in his favor, as when he is found guilty of manslaughter upon an indictment for murder, according to some decisions, he will keep it and can be retried only for the less offense, so that the jeopardy only is continued to the extent that it already has been determined against him, and is continued with a chance of escape.

"I believe the decisions referred to to be wrong, but assuming them to be right we must consider his position at the moment when his exceptions are sustained. The first verdict has been set aside. The jeopardy created by that is at an end, and the question is what shall be done with the prisoner. Since at that moment he no longer is in jeopardy from the first verdict, if the second trial in the same case is a second jeopardy even as to the less offense, he has a right to go free. In view of these difficulties it has been argued that on principle he has that right if a mistake of law is committed at the first trial. . . . But even Mr. Bishop [an authority on criminal law] admits that the decisions are otherwise, and the point is settled in this Court by the cases cited above.

"That fetish happily being destroyed, the necessary alternative is that the Constitution permits a second trial in the same case. The reason, however, is not the fiction that a man is not in jeopardy in a case of misdirection, for it must be admitted that he is in jeopardy even when the error is patent on the face of the record, as when he is tried on a defective indictment, if judgment is not arrested. . . . Moreover, if the fiction were true, it would be equally true when the misdirection was in favor of the prisoner. The reason, I submit, is that there can be but one jeopardy in one case. I have seen no other, except the suggestion of waiver, and that I think cannot stand.

"If what I have said so far is correct, no additional argument is needed to show that a statute may authorize an appeal by the Government from the decision by a magistrate to a higher court, as well as an appeal by the prisoner. The latter is everyday practice, yet there is no doubt that the prisoner is in jeopardy at the trial before the magistrate and that a conviction or acquittal not appealed from would be a bar to a second prosecution. That is what was decided, and it is all that was decided or intimated, relevant to this case, in *Wemyss* v. *Hopkins*, L. R. 10 Q. B. 378 [cited by Mr. Justice Day]. For the reasons which I have stated already, a second trial in the same case must be regarded only a continuation of the jeopardy which began with the trial below."

Kepner v. *United States*
195 U. S. 100, 134

III. On Encroaching Upon the States

Theater Ticket Prices

(*Tyson* v. *Banton*, 1926)

TYSON'S THEATER-TICKET AGENCY CONTENDED THAT A NEW YORK statute limiting re-sale profit to fifty cents a ticket was unconstitutional in that it violated the Fourteenth Amendment. Tickets are property—the argument ran—and it was unreasonable to say that the theater or tickets were "affected with a public interest," as the law declared. The State insisted that with congested population, shorter workdays and greater need of recreation, the theater had become more essential to the people.

But Mr. Justice Sutherland observed that for the statute to say that the price of admission was a matter "affected with a public interest" did not make it so. He said he was impressed by the historical place of the theater: "It may be true, as asserted, that among the Greeks amusement and instruction of the people through the drama was one of the duties of goverment. But certainly no such duty devolves upon any American government." And he said that the history of the theater revealed no price-fixing background.

This was price-fixing, Justice Sutherland reminded; the broker was a mere appendage of the theater; the printed price plus the advance made up the total price. "Is every public exhibition clothed with a public interest so as to authorize legislation to fix the maximum amount of charge?" he asked. Let the evils of fraud, extortion and collusive agreements between theater managers and brokers be prevented by legislation that comports with the Constitution, not by such as invades the essential rights of private property.

Justices Holmes and Brandeis concurred in Justice Stone's dissenting opinion that the question was not one of price-fixing but of throttling free competition among buyers and sellers. Here was a situation where the brokers of Manhattan sold two million tickets annually, obtaining

[85]

the best seats (first fifteen rows) with an arrangement for returning twenty-five percent of the unsold tickets; and "it appears the business is profitable" under the fifty-cent restriction. Justice Sanford, dissenting separately, pointed out that a public interest existed by the fact that brokers obtained absolute control of the most desirable seats and deprived the public of the opportunity to buy at regular prices.

Holmes (Brandeis concurring) wrote:

"WE FEAR to grant power and are unwilling to recognize it when it exists. The States very generally have stripped jury trials of one of their most important characteristics by forbidding judges to advise the jury upon the facts . . . and when legislatures are held to be authorized to do anything considerably affecting public welfare it is covered by apologetic phrases like the police power, or the statement that the business concerned has been dedicated to a public use.

"The former expression is convenient, to be sure, to conciliate the mind to something that needs explanation: the fact that the constitutional requirement of compensation when property is taken cannot be pressed to its grammatical extreme; that property rights may be taken for public purposes without pay if you do not take too much; that some play must be allowed to the joints if the machine is to work. But police power often is used in a wide sense to cover and, as I said, apologize for the general power of the legislature to make a part of the community uncomfortable by a change.

"I do not believe in such apologies. I think the proper course is to recognize that a State legislature can do whatever it sees fit to do unless it is restrained by some express prohibition in the Constitution of the United States or of the State, and that courts should be careful not to extend such prohibitions beyond their obvious meaning by reading into them conceptions of public policy that the particular court may happen to entertain.

"Coming down to the case before us I think, as I intimated in *Adkins* v. *Children's Hospital*, that the notion that a business is clothed with a public interest and has been devoted to the public use is little more than a fiction intended to beautify what is disagreeable to the sufferers. The truth seems to me to be that, subject to compensation when compensation is due, the legislature may forbid or restrict any business when it has a sufficient force of public opinion behind it.

"Lotteries were thought useful adjuncts of the State a century or so ago; now they are believed to be immoral and they have been stopped. Wine has been thought good for man from the time of the Apostles until recent years. But when public opinion changed it did not need the Eighteenth Amendment, notwithstanding the Fourteenth, to enable a State to say that the business should end. . . . What has happened to lotteries and wine might happen to theaters in some moral storm of the future, not because theaters were devoted to a public use, but because people had come to think that way.

"But if we are to yield to fashionable conventions, it seems to me that theaters are as much devoted to public use as anything well can be. We have not that respect for art that is one of the glories of France. But to many people the superfluous is the necessary, and it seems to me that government does not go beyond its sphere in attempting to make life livable for them. I am far from saying that I think this particular law a wise and rational provision. That is not my affair. If the people of the State of New York speaking by the authorized voice say that they want it, I see nothing in the Constitution of the United States to prevent their having their will."

Tyson & Bro.-United Theater Ticket Offices, Inc.,
v. Banton, District Attorney, et al.
273 U. S. 418, 445

[87]

Who May Control Land

(*Madisonville Traction Co.* v. *St. Bernard Co.*, 1904)

A RAILROAD WANTED NINE ACRES IN KENTUCKY BELONGING TO A mining company incorporated in Delaware. In accordance with the Kentucky statutes the railroad started condemnation proceedings in a county court; and the county commissioners fixed $100 as the sum to be paid to the landowners. When the owners tried to remove the case to a Federal court as an interstate matter, the county court refused to recognize any right of removal.

The owners then filed a transcript of the case with the Circuit Court, declared that the property was worth more than $2,000 and alleged a prejudiced assessment. The railroad was enjoined from further prosecuting its suit in the county court.

Mr. Justice Harlan said that the fundamental question was whether the case was a removable one in view of the constitutional provision that controversies between citizens of different States fall under the judicial power of the Federal courts. "It is said, however, that when it is proposed to take private property for public purposes the question of appropriation is primarily and exclusively for the State to determine," Harlan noted, but held that this was an interstate controversy.

Holmes dissented:

"I REGRET that I am unable to agree with the decision of the Court. The question on which I differ is whether a proceeding for the taking of land by eminent domain, authorized by the State of Kentucky to be begun in the courts of Kentucky, can be begun in the Circuit Court of the United States, whenever one of the parties is a citizen of another State. Of course I am speaking of the proceeding for the taking of the land, not of that for compensation, to which I shall refer later. The argument which does not command my assent, stated in a few words, is that such a proceeding in such a case is a controversy between citizens of different States, and therefore by the very words of the Constitution must be within the jurisdiction of the United States courts. It seems to me that this is rather too literal a reading, and, on the whole, is a sacrifice of substance to form.

"The fundamental fact is that eminent domain is a prerogative of the State, which on the one hand may be exercised in any way that the State thinks fit, and on the other may not be exercised except by an authority which the State confers. The taking may be direct, by an act of the legislature. It may be delegated to a railroad company, with a certain latitude of choice with regard to the land to be appropriated. It may be delegated subject to the approval of a legislative committee or of a board other than a court.

"When a State makes use of a court, instead for instance of a railroad commission, the character of the proceeding is not changed. The matter still is wholly within sovereign control. The State may intervene after the proceedings have begun and take the land. It may direct the entry of a decree of condemnation. An illustration of its continuing power may be seen in *In re Northampton*, 158 Mass. 299. The matter of grade crossings had been referred by the Legislature of Massachusetts to the courts, and a petition was pending for the abolition of certain grade crossings in Northampton. The case had been sent to commissioners, and they had reported. Pending a motion to confirm their report the Legislature passed an act forbidding a change in that case without the consent of the city council. It was held that, as the whole subject was originally within the control of the Legislature, it did not cease to be so by being referred to the courts, and the act was sustained.

"A further illustration, and one in which substance has prevailed over form, is to be found in the case of suits by citizens of another State against officers of a State. In form such suits are controversies between citizens of different States and within the jurisdiction of the United States courts. But if in substance they have the effect of suits against a State, the jurisdiction is denied. And the decisions do not stop there, but when the State has waived its immunity, as it may, and has given permission to a suit against the officer in a State court, it still is held that, although there is a controversy between citizens of different States which thus has become subject to litigation, that litigation must be confined to the courts which the State has named. Yet, there is no doubt that, with the State's consent, its officers or the State itself could be sued in the courts of the United States. . . .

"It seems to me that if a State authorizes a taking to be accomplished by certain machinery, the United States has no constitutional right to intervene and substitute other machinery because the State has chosen to use its law courts rather than a legislative committee and thus to give to the exercise of its sovereign power the external form of a suit at law. It seems to me plain that the exercise of that power depends wholly on the State, may be limited as the State chooses, and cannot be carried further than the State has authorized in terms.

"Suppose that a proceeding for taking land is removed to the United States court contrary to the legislation of the State, by whose authority—I ask myself—is a subsequent taking to be decreed? It is open to anyone who can think it to say that the attempt to use the State courts to the exclusion of the United States courts makes the taking void; but I cannot understand how a taking unauthorized by the State can be good. If I am right in supposing that the State has an absolute right to limit the exercise of eminent domain as it sees fit, then, so far as the construction of the Kentucky statute is concerned, I need only invoke the cases last cited to show that the statute imports that the State meant to confine the proceedings to its own courts. Certainly it does not purport to authorize them elsewhere, and that is enough. . . .

"The difference between myself and the majority is not merely on the construction of the Kentucky statutes. If that were all I should not express my dissent. But the difference as to construction is a consequence and incident of a difference on the far more important question of power. Of course, what I have said is without prejudice to the possibility that in case a question of rights under the Constitution of the United States should arise and be carried to the highest court of the State, it might be brought here by writ of error, as was said by Mr. Justice Harlan. . . . I do not go into that, as it is immaterial now.

"It is said that the question which I am discussing has been settled by the adjudications of this Court. I do not think so. The only cases that have any bearing are *Boom Co.* v. *Patterson*, 98 U. S. 403, and *Searl* v. *School District No. 2*, 124 U. S. 197. In the former of these cases Mr. Justice Field states in the most explicit way that at the stage the case had reached when it was removed from the State court, the compensation to be paid the owner of the land was the only question open. I have no criticism to make on that case. It seems to me to favor my views throughout. I think it very possible that after the title to property has been taken, if the question of compensation is still unsettled, that may be a controversy within the meaning of the Constitution. The sovereign power of the State is at an end, and the former owner has a right under the Fourteenth Amendment of the Constitution of the United States to get his pay.

"*Boom Co.* v. *Patterson* was followed by *Searl* v. *School District No. 2* seemingly without noticing the distinction that in the latter case the property had not yet been appropriated. There was no serious reasoning in the case, and I should think it a most inadequate justification for trenching upon the powers of the States, even if it were strictly in point. It arose, however, under the former statute as to removals, which did not limit them to cases which could have been begun in the United States courts.

"Whether I should think that a sufficient distinction if that case were before me now I shall not consider—but I feel warranted in believing that no one who took part in that decision imagined that he was establishing the doctrine now laid down or any principle broad enough to cover the present case. I cannot think that even Mr. Justice Matthews [quoted by the majority] would have denied that the day after removal the State could have withdrawn the power to condemn the land, and left the Court in the air, or could have condemned the land pending the proceedings, without paying them the slightest regard. If the State did retain those powers, I think it no less retained the *delectus personarum* and the right to confine its authority, while it left it outstanding, to the persons of its choice.

"I wish to add only that I am not aware of any limitations in the Constitution of the United States upon a State's power to condemn land within its borders, except the requirements as to compensation. All that was decided in *Loan Association* v. *Topeka*, 20 Wall. 655, and *Cole* v. *La Grange*, 113 U. S. 1, was that the constitutions of certain States did not authorize the taking of private property for private use. But if those decisions had been rested on the Fourteenth Amendment, which they were not, and in my opinion could not have been, I do not perceive that they had any bearing upon what I have said or upon the case at bar.

"I am authorized to say that the Chief Justice [Fuller], Mr. Justice Brewer and Mr. Justice Peckham concur in this dissent."

Madisonville Traction Co. v. *Saint Bernard Mining Co.*
196 U. S. 239, 257

A Connecticut Divorce

(*Haddock* v. *Haddock*, 1905)

A COUPLE, MARRIED IN NEW YORK IN 1868, PARTED ON THEIR WED-
ding day. The husband settled in Connecticut and obtained a divorce
there in 1881, remarrying the next year and inheriting property in
1891. The first wife, still in New York, started a divorce action in
1899. Did the New York court refuse full faith and credit to Connecticut when it gave her a decree of divorce by personal service after
her husband had obtained his without personal service?

The husband's contention was that Connecticut had dissolved their
marriage. The wife maintained that his grounds, desertion, were false.
The New York courts sustained her judgment for separation and ali-
mony, and Mr. Justice White held this to be no violation of the Constitution as the Connecticut decree was not based on personal service;
the Connecticut court was without personal jurisdiction over the wife
and was not entitled to compel enforcement in New York.

Mr. Justice Brown dissented (joined by Justices Harlan, Brewer
and Holmes). He regretted that the Court was taking "a step back-
ward in American jurisprudence" and returning to "the old doctrine
of comity, which it was the very object of the full faith and credit
clause of the Constitution to supersede."

Justice Holmes wrote a separate opinion, the other dissenters concurring:

"I DO NOT suppose that civilization will come to an end whichever way this case is decided. But as the reasoning which prevails in the mind of the majority does not convince me, and
as I think that the decision not only reverses a previous well-

[93]

considered decision of this Court but is likely to cause considerable disaster to innocent persons and to bastardize children hitherto supposed to be the offspring of lawful marriage, I think it proper to express my views.

"Generally stated, the issue is whether, when a husband sues in the court of his domicile for divorce from an absent wife on the ground of her desertion, the jurisdiction of the court, if there is no personal service, depends upon the merits of the case. If the wife did desert her husband in fact, or if she was served with process, I understand it not to be disputed that a decree of divorce in the case supposed would be conclusive, and so I understand it to be admitted that if the court of another State on a retrial of the merits finds them to have been decided rightly, its duty will be to declare the decree a bar to its inquiry. The first form of the question is whether it has a right to inquire into the merits at all. But I think that it will appear directly that the issue is narrower even than that.

"In *Atherton* v. *Atherton*, 181 U. S. 155 [cited by the majority] a divorce was granted on the ground of desertion to a husband in Kentucky against a wife who had established herself in New York. She did not appear in the suit and the only notice to her was by mail. Before the decree was made she sued in New York for a divorce from bed and board, but pending the latter proceedings the Kentucky suit was brought to its end.

"The husband appeared in New York and set up the Kentucky decree. The New York court found that the wife left her husband because of his cruel and abusive treatment, without fault on her part; held that the Kentucky decree was no bar and granted the wife her divorce from bed and board. The New York decree, after being affirmed by the Court of Appeals, was reversed by this Court on the ground that it did not give the Kentucky decree the faith and credit which it had by law in Kentucky. Of course, if the wife left her husband because of his cruelty and without fault on her part, as found by the New York court, she was not guilty of desertion. Yet this Court held that the question of her desertion was not open but was conclusively settled by the Kentucky decree.

"There is no difference, so far as I can see, between *Atherton* v. *Atherton* and the present case, except that in *Atherton* v. *Atherton* the forum of the first decree was that of the matrimonial domicile, whereas in this the court was that of a domicile afterwards acquired. After that decision any general objection to the effect of the Connecticut decree on the ground of the wife's absence from the State comes too late. So does any general objection on the ground that to give it effect invites a race of diligence. I therefore pass such arguments without discussion, although they seem to me easy to answer. Moreover, *Atherton* v. *Atherton* decides that the jurisdiction of the matrimonial domicile at least, to grant a divorce for the wife's desertion without personal service, does not depend upon the fact of desertion but continues even if her husband's cruelty has driven her out of the State and she has acquired a separate domicile elsewhere upon the principles which we all agree are recognized by this Court.

"I can see no ground for giving a less effect to the decree when the husband changes his domicile after the separation has taken place. The question whether such a decree should have a less effect is the only question open, and the issue is narrowed to that. No one denies that the husband may sue for divorce in his new domicile, or, as I have said, that if he gets a decree when he really has been deserted, it will be binding everywhere. . . .

"The only reason which I have heard suggested for holding the decree not binding as to the fact that he was deserted is that if he is deserted his power over the matrimonial domicile remains so that the domicile of the wife accompanies him wherever he goes, whereas if he is the deserter he has no such power. Of course this is a pure fiction, and fiction always is a poor ground for changing substantial rights. It seems to me also an inadequate fiction, since by the same principle if he deserts her in the matrimonial domicile he is equally powerless to keep her domicile there if she moves into another State. The truth is that jurisdiction no more depends upon both parties having their domicile within the State than it does upon the presence of the defendant there, as is shown not only by *Atherton* v. *Atherton* but by the rights of the wife in the matrimonial domicile when the husband deserts.

"There is no question that a husband may establish a new domicile for himself even if he has deserted his wife. Yet in these days of equality I do not suppose that it would be doubted that the jurisdiction of the court of the matrimonial domicile to grant a divorce for the desertion remained for her, as it would for him in the converse case. . . . Indeed, in *Ditson* v. *Ditson*, 4 R. I. 87, which, after a quotation of Judge Cooley's praise of it, is stated and relied upon as one of the pillars for the decision of *Atherton* v. *Atherton*, a wife was granted a divorce, without personal service, in the State of a domicile acquired by her after separation, on the sole ground that in the opinion of the Court its decree would be binding everywhere. If that is the law it disposes of the case of a husband under similar circumstances, that is to say of the present case, *a fortiori;* for I suppose that the notion that a wife can have a separate domicile from her husband is a modern idea.

"At least *Ditson* v. *Ditson* confirms the assumption that jurisdiction is not dependent on the wife's actually residing in the same State as her husband, which has been established by this Court. . . . When that assumption is out of the way, I repeat that I cannot see any ground for distinguishing between the extent of the jurisdiction in the matrimonial domicile and that, admitted to exist to some extent, in the domicile later acquired. I also repeat and emphasize that if the finding of a second court, contrary to the decree, that the husband was the deserter, destroys the jurisdiction in the later acquired domicile because the domicile of the wife does not follow his, the same fact ought to destroy the jurisdiction in the matrimonial domicile if in consequence of her husband's conduct the wife has left the State. But *Atherton* v. *Atherton* decides that it does not.

"It is important to bear in mind that the present decision purports to respect and not to overrule *Atherton* v. *Atherton*. For that reason among others, I spend no time in justifying that case. And yet it appears to me that the whole argument which prevails with the majority of the Court is simply an argument that *Atherton* v. *Atherton* is wrong. I have tried in vain to discover anything tending to show a distinction between that case and this.

"It is true that in *Atherton* v. *Atherton* Mr. Justice Gray confined the decision to the case before the Court. Evidently, I should say, from the internal evidence, in deference to scruples which he did not share. But a court by announcing that its decision is confined to the facts before it does not decide in advance that logic will not drive it further when new facts arise. New facts have arisen. I state what logic seems to me to require if that case is to stand, and I think it reasonable to ask for an articulate indication of how it is to be distinguished.

"I have heard it suggested that the difference is one of degree. I am the last man in the world to quarrel with a distinction simply because it is one of degree. Most distinctions, in my opinion, are of that sort, and are none the worse for it. But the line which is drawn must be justified by the fact that it is a little nearer than the nearest opposing case to one pole of an admitted antithesis.

"When a crime is made burglary by the fact that it was committed thirty seconds after one hour after sunset, ascertained according to mean time in the place of the act, to take an example from Massachusetts . . . the act is a little nearer to midnight than if it had been committed one minute earlier, and no one denies that there is a difference between night and day. The fixing of a point when day ends is made inevitable by the admission of that difference. But I can find no basis for giving a greater jurisdiction to the courts of the husband's domicile when the married pair happens to have resided there for a month, even if with intent to make it a permanent abode, than if they had not lived there at all.

"I may add, as a consideration distinct from those which I have urged, that I am unable to reconcile with the requirements of the Constitution, Article IV, § 1, the notion of a judgment being valid and binding in the State where it was rendered, and yet depending for recognition to the same extent in other States of the Union upon the comity of those States. No doubt some color for such a notion may be found in State decisions. State courts do not always have the Constitution of the United States vividly present to their minds.

"I am responsible for language treating what seems to me the fallacy as open, in *Blackinton* v. *Blackinton*, 141 Mass. 432, 436. But there is no exception in the words of the Constitution. 'If the judgment is conclusive in the State where it was pronounced it is equally conclusive everywhere.' . . . I find no qualification of the rule in *Wisconsin* v. *Pelican Ins. Co.*, 127 U. S. 265. That merely decided with regard to a case not within the words of the Constitution, that a State judgment could not be sued upon when the facts which it established were not a cause of action outside the State. It did not decide or even remotely suggest that the judgment would not be conclusive as to the facts if in any way those facts came in question.

"It is decided, as well as admitted, that a decree like that rendered in Connecticut in favor of a deserting husband is binding in the State where it is rendered. . . . I think it enough to read that case in order to be convinced that at that time the

Court had no thought of the divorce being confined in its effects to the Territory where it was granted, and enough to read *Atherton* v. *Atherton* to see that its whole drift and tendency now are reversed and its necessary consequences denied."

Haddock v. *Haddock*
201 U. S. 562, 628

"Independent Judgment"

(*Kuhn* v. *Fairmont Coal Co.*, 1909)

AN OHIO CITIZEN CONVEYED ALL THE COAL IN A WEST VIRGINIA
tract of land to a mining company, which began operations and failed
to leave blocks or pillars of coal as supports. After the overlying surface
cracked and fell in, he brought an action of trespass against the company. The defendant cited as precedent its victory in a similar case
where the Supreme Court of West Virginia held that the contract with
the landowner did not obligate the company to leave enough coal to
support the surface.

The question sent up by the Circuit Court of Appeals was whether
it were bound by the West Virginia decision. Mr. Justice Harlan, for
the majority, said that this decision was a rule of law settled after the
rights of the parties to the contract had become fixed; so it was the
duty of the Circuit Court to use its own judgment. Without expressing
an opinion as to what were the rights, he answered the question: No,
not bound.

Justice Holmes was joined by Justices White and McKenna in the
dissent:

"THIS is a question of the title to real estate. It does not
matter in what form of action it arises; the decision must be the
same in an action of tort that it would be in a writ of right.
The title to real estate in general depends upon the statutes and
decisions of the State within which it lies. I think it a thing to
be regretted if, while in the great mass of cases the State courts
finally determine who is the owner of land, how much he owns

and what he conveys by his deed, the courts of the United States, when by accident and exception the same question comes before them, do not follow what for all ordinary purposes is the law.

"I admit that plenty of language can be found in the earlier cases to support the present decision. That is not surprising in view of the uncertainty and vacillation of the theory upon which *Swift* v. *Tyson,* 16 Pet. 1, and the later extensions of its doctrine have proceeded. But I suppose it will be admitted on the other side that even the independent jurisdiction of the Circuit Courts of the United States is a jurisdiction only to declare the law, at least in a case like the present, and only to declare the law of the State. It is not an authority to make it.

"*Swift* v. *Tyson* was justified on the ground that that was all that the State courts did. But as has been pointed out by a recent accomplished and able writer, that fiction had to be abandoned and was abandoned when this Court came to decide the municipal bond cases, beginning with *Gelpcke* v. *Dubuque,* 1 Wall. 175. . . . In those cases the Court followed Chief Justice Taney . . . in recognizing the fact that decisions of State courts of last resort make law for the State. The principle is that a change of judicial decision after a contract has been made on the faith of an earlier one the other way is a change of law.

"The cases of the class to which I refer have not stood on the ground that this Court agreed with the first decision, but on the ground that the State decision made the law for the State, and therefore should be given only a prospective operation when contracts had been entered into under the law as earlier declared. . . . In various instances this Court has changed its decision or rendered different decisions on similar facts arising in different States in order to conform to what is recognized as the local law. . . .

"Whether *Swift* v. *Tyson* can be reconciled with *Gelpcke*

[101]

v. *Dubuque,* I do not care to inquire. I assume both cases to represent settled doctrines, whether reconcilable or not. But the moment you leave those principles which it is desirable to make uniform throughout the United States and which the decisions of this Court tend to make uniform, obviously it is most undesirable for the courts of the United States to appear as interjecting an occasional arbitrary exception to a rule that in every other case prevails. I never yet have heard a statement of any reason justifying the power, and I find it hard to imagine one. The rule in *Gelpcke* v. *Dubuque* gives no help when the contract of grant in question has not been made on the faith of a previous declaration of law.

"I know of no authority in this Court to say that in general State decisions shall make law only for the future. Judicial decisions have had retrospective operation for near a thousand years. There were enough difficulties in the way, even in cases like *Gelpcke* v. *Dubuque,* but in them there was a suggestion or smack of constitutional right. Here there is nothing of that sort.

"It is said that we must exercise our independent judgment —but as to what? Surely as to the law of the States. Whence does that law issue? Certainly not from us. But it does issue and has been recognized by this Court as issuing from the State courts as well as from the State legislatures. When we know what the source of the law has said that it shall be, our authority is at an end. The law of a State does not become something outside of the State court and independent of it by being called the common law. Whatever it is called it is the law as declared by the State judges and nothing else.

"If, as I believe, my reasoning is correct, it justifies our stopping when we come to a kind of case that by nature and necessity is peculiarly local, and one as to which the latest intimations and indeed decisions of this Court are wholly in accord with what I think to be sound law. I refer to the language of the Court speaking through Mr. Justice Miller. . . .

To administer a different law is 'to introduce into the jurisprudence of the State of Illinois the discordant elements of a
substantial right which is protected in one set of courts and
denied in the other, with no superior to decide which is right.' I
refer also to the unanimous decision in *East Central Eureka
Mining Co.* v. *Central Eureka Mining Co.*, 204 U. S. 266,
272. It is admitted that we are bound by a settled course of decisions irrespective of contract because they make the law. I see
no reason why we are less bound by a single one."

Kuhn v. *Fairmont Coal Co.*
215 U. S. 349, 370

Fee for Local Business

(*Western Union* v. *Kansas*, 1909)

KANSAS CONCEIVED A PLAN FOR ENRICHING HER SCHOOL FUND. SHE required a charter fee from all outside corporations (a percentage of each company's entire capitalization as a condition to doing business in the State) and called on the Western Union Telegraph Co. to pay $20,100. But the fee was not paid and the company was restrained from accepting and delivering messages wholly within the State. Interstate telegrams were not forbidden, but since the percentage was taken on the company's capital stock the Western Union attacked as unconstitutional the statute imposing the fee.

The majority opinion of Mr. Justice Harlan cited cases wherein the Court had guarded the freedom of interstate commerce against hostile State action. The Kansas fee was not simply a tax for the privilege of doing local business in the State but a burden on the company's interstate business by taxing property located or used outside the State, Harlan said; such a condition would make the Western Union surrender rights guaranteed by the Constitution; the statute must be adjudged invalid. Justice White added that Kansas had admitted the company into her territory and could not oust it by unconstitutional conditions.

On the minority side were Chief Justice Fuller, the late Justice Peckham and Justices Holmes and McKenna. Holmes wrote the dissenting opinion:

"I THINK that the judgment of the Supreme Court of Kansas was right, and it will not take me long to give my reasons. I assume that a State cannot tax a corporation on commerce carried on by it with another State, or on property outside the jurisdiction of the taxing State, and I assume further that for that reason a tax on or measured by the value of the total stock of a corporation like the Western Union Telegraph Company is void. But I also assume that it is not intended to deny or overrule what has been regarded as unquestionable since *Bank of Augusta* v. *Earle,* 13 Pet. 519, that as to foreign corporations seeking to do business wholly within a State, that State is the master and may prohibit or tax such business at will. . . . I make the same assumption as to what has been decided twice at least since I have sat on this bench, that the right to prohibit, regulate or tax foreign corporations in respect of business done wholly within a State is not taken away by the fact that they also are engaged there in commerce among the States. . . .

"If it should be said that the corporation had a right to enter the State for commerce with other States, and being there had the same right to use its property as others, I reply that this begs the question, if the premises be granted. If the corporation has the right to enter for one purpose and the State has a right to exclude its entry for another, the two rights can co-exist. To say that the disappearance of the latter is an incident of ownership of the property there is to declare that what is allowed only for a limited purpose must have general results. I think it more logical and more true to the scheme of the Union to recognize that what comes in only for a special purpose can claim constitutional protection only in its use for that purpose and for nothing else. That, at all events, has been decided in the cases to which I have referred.

"Now what has Kansas done? She has not undertaken to tax the Western Union. She has not attempted to impose an absolute liability for a single dollar. She simply has said to the company that if it wants to do local business it must pay a certain sum of money, just as Mississippi said to the Pullman

Company that if it wanted to carry on local traffic it must pay a certain sum. It does not matter if the sum is extravagant. Even in the law the whole generally includes its parts. If the State may prohibit, it may prohibit with the privilege of avoiding the prohibition in a certain way.

"I hardly can suppose that the provision is made any the worse by giving a bad reason for it or by calling it by a bad name. I quite agree that we must look through form to substance. The whole matter is left in the Western Union's hands. If the license fee is more than the local business will bear, it can stop that business and avoid the fee. Whether economically wise or not, I am far from thinking that the charge is inherently vicious or bad.— If the imposition were absolute or if the attempt were to oust the corporation from the State if it did not pay, the arguments that prevail would be apposite. But the State seeks only to oust the corporation from that part of its business that the corporation has no right to do unless the State gives leave.

"Of course the suggestion on the other side is that this is an attempt by indirection to break the taboo on the Telegraph Company's business with other States. The local and the interstate business may be necessary each to the other to make the whole pay. Or the Telegraph Company might carry on the local business at a loss for the sake of popularity or other indirect sources of gain. In the last case the fee would come out of earnings that the State has no right to touch. But these considerations do not reach their aim. To deny the right of Kansas to do as it chooses with the local business is to require the local business to help sustain that between the States. If the latter does not pay alone there is no reason for cutting down powers that up to this time the States always have possessed. If the Telegraph Company chooses to pay the fee out of its other earnings that is its affair. It is master of the situation and it can stop if it sees fit. Exactly this argument was pressed in *Pullman*

Co. v. *Adams,* 189 U. S. 420, 421, and was rejected without dissent. . . .

"What I have said shows, I think, the fallacy involved in talking about unconstitutional conditions. Of course, if the condition was the making of a contract contrary to the policy of the Constitution of the United States the contract would be void. That was all that was decided in *Southern Pacific Co.* v. *Denton,* 146 U. S. 202. But it does not follow that, if the keeping of the contract was made a condition of staying in the State, the condition would be void. I confess my inability to understand how a condition can be unconstitutional when attached to a matter over which a State has absolute arbitrary power. This Court was equally unable to understand it in *Horn Silver Mining Co.* v. *New York,* 143 U. S. 305, 315. In that case it was said, 'Having the absolute power of excluding the foreign corporation the State may, of course, impose such conditions upon permitting the corporation to do business within its limits as it may judge expedient; and it may make the grant or privilege dependent upon the payment of a specific license tax, or a sum proportioned to the amount of its capital.'

"The consequence is the measure of the condition. When the only consequence of a breach is a result that the State may bring about directly in the first place, the condition cannot be unconstitutional. If after this decision the State of Kansas, without giving any reason, sees fit simply to prohibit the Western Union Telegraph Company from doing any more local business there or from doing local business until it has paid $20,100, I shall be curious to see upon what ground the legislation will be assailed. I am aware that the battle has raged with varying fortunes over this matter of unconstitutional conditions, but it appears to me ground for regret that the Court so soon should abandon its latest decision, *Security Mut. Life Ins. Co.* v. *Prewitt,* 202 U. S. 246.

"Finally, in the absence of contract, the power of the State is not affected by the fact that the corporation concerned already is in the State or even has been there for some time. . . . Whatever the corporation may do or acquire there is infected with the original weakness of dependence upon the will of the State. This is a general principle, illustrated by many cases. Thus a water company cannot take away the power of a city to establish rates by making contracts with its customers. . . . Private individuals cannot cut down the police power by their arrangements together. . . . A city cannot limit the power of the legislature over property by making a lease. . . . Or, to pass at once to the most recent and most conspicuous example, the power of Congress to regulate commerce among the States cannot be affected by the acquisition of property or growth of values dependent upon the continuance of its assent. . . . In that case an enormous amount of property had been built up under direct encouragement from the States in which it was situated, and was saved from destruction only by the restricted meaning given to the Act of Congress. The unrestricted power of Congress was affirmed in strong terms.

"In *Horn Silver Mining Co.* v. *New York*, 143 U. S. 305, the corporation showed by its answer that it had employed part of its capital in manufacturing in New York. It had got into the State and was at work there, yet it was held liable to pay a percentage of its entire capital, although the greater part was outside the State.—But furthermore it is a short answer to this part of the argument that in the present case, according to the decisions relied upon by the majority, the State could not have prevented the entry of the corporation because it entered for the purpose of commerce with other States."

Western Union Telegraph Co. v. *State of Kansas*
216 U. S. 1, 52

Burdens on Interstate Commerce

(*Pullman Co.* v. *Kansas*, 1909)

THE PULLMAN CO. WAS FORBIDDEN TO DO BUSINESS WHOLLY WITHIN Kansas because of its failure to pay the percentage fee levied on its capitalization. No charges for berths or meals could be made in the State. But the *Western Union* decision was now law, and on its authority Mr. Justice Harlan held that the Pullman Co. was not required to ask Kansas for permission to do interstate business. The fee, conditional to local commerce, was in effect a tax on the company's interstate business and a waiver of constitutional guaranties, he said.

While Justice McKenna dissented separately, Chief Justice Fuller agreed with Holmes:

"As THIS case has received some further discussion beyond that in *Western Union Telegraph Co.* v. *Kansas*, I will contribute my mite. I do not care to add to what I said the other day as to the supposed accession of rights to a corporation because it already has property in the State. . . . The question whether there is any necessary parallelism between liability to taxation elsewhere and immunity at home still is an open question. . . . In the present case it is alleged that the cars are taxed in other States as well as Kansas, and that the property represented by the capital of the company has no *situs* in Kansas.

"If I thought it material I should say that on the declaration the cars were taxable at the Pullman Company's domicile more certainly than anywhere else. But I think it immaterial, for the reasons that I gave last week; and, furthermore, the argument drawn from the presence in the State of cars that can be and are rolled out of it at will cannot, I should think, be meant to be pressed.

"I will add a few words on the broader proposition put forward that the Constitution forbids this charge, whether the corporation was established previously in the State or not. I do not see how or why the right of a State to exclude a corporation from internal traffic is complicated or affected in any way by the fact that the corporation has a right to come in for another purpose. It is said that in such a case the power of the State is only relative, and in the sense that it is confined to the local business, I agree. But in the sense that it is not absolute over that local business the statement seems to me merely to beg the question that is to be discussed. I do not understand why the power is less absolute over that because it does not extend to something else.

"So again, the proposition that a State may not subject all corporations that enter the State for commerce with other States to such conditions as it sees fit to impose upon local business, no matter how offensive the terms, seems to me a proposition not to be assumed but to be proved; or again, that the arbitrary prohibition of local business is a burden on commerce among the States. I am quite unable to believe that an otherwise lawful exclusion from doing business within a State becomes an unlawful or unconstitutional burden on commerce among States because if it were let in it would help to pay the bills. Such an exclusion is not a burden on the foreign commerce at all, it simply is the denial of a collateral benefit. If foreign commerce does not pay its way by itself I see no right to demand an entrance for domestic business to help it out.

"The distinction that I believe exists is sanctioned by many cases earlier than those referred to in my former dissent. That the local business of the telegraph and railroad companies may be taxed by the States has been held over and over again, with full acceptance of the doctrine that *quoad hoc,* 'the power to tax involves the power to destroy,' *M'Culloch* v. *Maryland,* 4 Wheat. 316, 431, essentially the doctrine on which the power of the States to tax interstate commerce was denied. . . . Thus in *Western Union Telegraph Co.* v. *Alabama,* 132 U. S. 472, it was held that the telegraph company could be taxed upon all messages carried and delivered wholly within the State, and the principle was stated by Mr. Justice Miller to be that this 'class are elements of internal commerce solely within the limits and the jurisdiction of the State, and therefore subject to its taxing power.' This was by a unanimous Court and followed the intimations and decisions of earlier cases.

"The above passage was cited and followed in *Postal Telegraph Co.* v. *Charleston City Council,* 153 U. S. 692, when a license fee or tax was exacted in respect of local business, and the previous decisions were cited and commented upon by Mr. Justice Shiras. One of the arguments repudiated was that the tax was a burden upon commerce among the States. I do not see how the reasoning that denies the power to tax one kind of commerce and asserts it with regard to the other can be reconciled with the denial of the power of the State to exclude the latter altogether, or to tax it for whatever sum it likes. The right to tax 'in its nature acknowledges no limits.' . . .

"I think that the tax in question, for I am perfectly willing to call it a tax, was lawful under all the decisions of this Court until last week. From other points of view, if I were at liberty to take them, I should agree that it deserved the reprobation it receives from the majority. But I have not heard and have not been able to frame any reason that I honestly can say seems to me to justify the judgment of the Court in point of law."

Pullman Co. v. *State of Kansas*
216 U. S. 56, 75

Vested Rights in Streets

(Muhlker v. N. Y. & Harlem R.R., 1904)

A BUILDING WAS ERECTED ON PARK AVENUE AT 115TH STREET, NEW York City, when railroad tracks were on the surface of the avenue. Later, when the tracks were elevated, light and air were cut off. As no compensation was provided and as rentals diminished, the owner sued. He won a $3,000 verdict. But the New York Court of Appeals held that the State was empowered to pass the law; the damage was merely consequential, hence not actionable; the walls had been removed, and what the owner of the building lost in injury to his easements of light and air he recovered by an increase in his easement of access.

"There is something of a mockery," said Mr. Justice McKenna for the majority, "to give one access to property which may be unfit to live on when one gets there. Because the plaintiff can cross the railroad at more places on the street, the State, it is contended, can authorize dirt, cinders and smoke from two hundred trains a day to be poured into the upper windows of his house."

The two constitutional grounds of the case were: No State may pass any law which impairs the obligation of contracts; no State may take property without due process of law. The plaintiff argued that the deeds which conveyed the strip of land to the city in trust as a public street constituted a contract precluding the erection of an elevated railroad. He also contended that easements were property, as the Court of Appeals had held in the so-called *Elevated Railroad Cases*, and that they could not be taken without compensation.

"And this is the ground of our decision," said McKenna for the majority.

Holmes denied both conclusions:

[112]

"I REGRET that I am unable to agree with the judgment of the Court, and as it seems to me to involve important principles I think it advisable to express my disagreement and to give my reasons for it.

"The plaintiff owns no soil within the limits of the avenue. The New York & Harlem Railroad Co. at the time of the change was and long had been the owner, and the other defendant was the lessee, of a railroad with four tracks along the middle of Park avenue in front of the plaintiff's land, at the south end being at the surface of the avenue and at the north in a trench about four feet and a half deep, the railroad being bounded on both sides by a masonry wall three feet high, which prevented crossing or access to the tracks.

"This is the finding of the court of first instance and I take it to be binding upon us. We have nothing to do with the evidence. I take it to mean the same thing as the finding in *Fries* v. *New York & Harlem R. R.*, 169 N. Y. 270, that the defendants had 'acquired the right without liability to the plaintiff to have, maintain, and use their railroad and railroad structures as the same were maintained and used prior to February 16, 1897.' The material portion of the decision of the Court of Appeals is that on this state of facts, as was held in the similar case of *Fries* v. *New York & Harlem R. R.*, the plaintiff had no property right which was infringed in such a way as to be anything more than *damnum absque injuria*. The finding that the railroad had the right to maintain the former structures was held to distinguish the case from the *Elevated Railroad Cases*, where pillars were planted in the street without right as against the plaintiff. . . . The other so-called finding, that the new structure infringes the plaintiff's right, is merely a ruling of law that, notwithstanding the facts specifically found, the plaintiff has a cause of action by reason of his being an abutter upon a public street.

"The plaintiff's rights, whether expressed in terms of property or of contract, are all a construction of the courts, deduced by way of consequence from dedication to and trusts for the purposes of a public street. They never were granted to him or his predecessors in express words or, probably, by any conscious implication. If at the outset the New York courts had decided that apart from statute or express grant the abutters on a street had only the rights of the public and no private easement of any kind, it would have been in no way amazing. It would have been very possible to distinguish between the practical commercial advantage of the expectation that a street would remain open and a right *in rem* that it should remain so. . . .

"Again, more narrowly, if the New York courts had held that an easement of light and air could be created only by express words, and that the laying out or dedication of a street, or the grant of a house bounding upon one, gave no such easement to abutters, they would not have been alone in the world of common law. . . . The doctrine that abutters upon a highway have an easement of light and air is stated as a novelty in point of authority in *Barnett* v. *Johnson*, 15 N. J. Eq. 481, 489, and that case was decided in a State where it was held that a like right might be acquired by prescription. . . .

"If the decisions, which I say conceivably might have been made, had been made as to the common law, they would have infringed no rights under the Constitution of the United States. So much, I presume, would be admitted by everyone. But if that be admitted, I ask myself what happened to cut down the power of the same courts as against the same Constitution at the present day.

"So far as I know the only thing which has happened is that they have decided the *Elevated Railroad Cases*, to which I have referred. It is on that ground alone that we are asked to review the decision of the Court of Appeals upon what otherwise would be purely a matter of local law. In other words, we are asked to extend to the present case the principle of *Gelpcke* v. *Dubuque*, 1 Wall. 175, and *Louisiana* v. *Pilsbury*, 105 U. S. 278, as to public bonds bought on the faith of a decision that they were constitutionally issued. That seems to me a great, unwarranted and undesirable extension of a doctrine which it took this Court a good while to explain. The doctrine now is explained, however, not to mean that a change in the decision impairs the obligation of contracts . . . and certainly never has been supposed to mean that all property owners in a State have a vested right that no general proposition of law shall be reversed, changed, or modified by the courts if the consequence to them will be more or less pecuniary loss. I know of no constitutional principle to prevent the complete reversal of the *Elevated Railroad Cases* tomorrow, if it should seem proper to the Court of Appeals. . . .

"But I conceive that the plaintiff in error must go much further than to say that my last proposition is wrong. I think he must say that he has a constitutional right not only that the State courts shall not reverse their earlier decisions upon a matter of property rights, but that they shall not distinguish them unless the distinction is so fortunate as to strike a majority of this Court as sound. For the Court of Appeals has not purported to overrule the *Elevated Railroad Cases*. It has simply decided that the import and the intent of those cases does not extend to the case at bar. In those cases the defendants had impaired the plaintiff's access to the street. It is entirely possible and consistent with all that they decided to say now that access is the foundation of the whole matter; that the right to light and air is a parasitic right incident to the right to have the street kept open for purposes of travel, and that when, as here, the latter right does not exist the basis of the claim to light and air is gone.

"But again, if the plaintiff had an easement over the whole street he got it as a tacit incident of an appropriation of the street to the uses of the public. The Legislature and the Court of Appeals of New York have said that the statute assailed was passed for the benefit of the public using the street, and I accept their view. The most obvious aspect of the change is that the whole street now is open to travel, and that an impassable barrier along its width has been removed; in other words, that the convenience of travelers on the highway has been considered and enhanced. Now still considering distinctions which might be taken between this and the earlier cases, it was possible for the New York courts to hold, as they seem to have held, that the easement which they had declared to exist is subject to the fullest exercise of the primary right out of which it sprang, and that any change in the street for the benefit of public travel is a matter of public right, as against what I have called the parasitic right which the plaintiff claims. . . .

"The foregoing distinctions seem to me not wanting in good sense. Certainly I should have been inclined to adopt one or both of them, or in some way to avoid the earlier decisions. But I am not discussing the question whether they are sound. If my disagreement was confined to that I should be silent. I am considering what there is in the Constitution of the United States forbidding the Court of Appeals to hold them sound. I think there is nothing; and there being nothing, and the New York decision obviously not having been given its form for the purpose of evading this Court, I think we should respect and affirm it, if we do not dismiss the case.

"What the plaintiff claims is really property, a right *in rem*. It is called contract merely to bring it within the contract clause of the Constitution. It seems to me a considerable extension of the power to determine for ourselves what the contract is, which we have assumed when it is alleged that the obligation of a contract has been impaired, to say that we will make the same independent determination when it is alleged that property is taken without due compensation. But it seems to me that it does not help the argument.

"The rule adopted as to contract is simply a rule to prevent an evasion of the constitutional limit to the power of the States, and, it seems to me, should not be extended to a case like this. Bearing in mind that, as I have said, the plaintiff's rights, however expressed, are wholly a construction of the courts, I cannot believe that whenever the Fourteenth Amendment or Article I, § 10, is set up we are free to go behind the local decisions on a matter of land law, and, on the ground that we decided what a contract is, declare rights to exist which we think ought to be implied from a dedication or location if we were the local courts.

"I cannot believe that we are at liberty to create rights over the streets of Massachusetts, for instance, that never have been recognized there. If we properly may do that, then I am wrong in my assumption that, if the New York courts originally had declared that the laying out of a public way conferred no private rights, we should have had nothing to say. But if I am right, if we are bound by local decisions as to local rights in real estate, then we equally are bound by the distinctions and the limitations of those rights declared by the local courts. If an exception were established in the case of a decision which obviously was intended to evade constitutional limits, I suppose I may assume that such an evasion would not be imputed to a judgment which four Justices of this Court think right.

"As I necessarily have dealt with the merits of the case for the purpose of presenting my point, I will add one other consideration. Suppose that the plaintiff has an easement and that it has been impaired, bearing in mind that his damage is in respect of light and air, not access, and is inflicted for the benefit of public travel. I should hesitate to say that in inflicting it the Legislature went beyond the constitutional exercise of the police power. To a certain and to an appreciable extent the

Legislature may alter the law of nuisance, although property is affected. To a certain and to an appreciable extent the use of particular property may be limited without compensation. Not every such limitation, restriction, or diminution of value amounts to a taking in the constitutional sense. I have a good deal of doubt whether it has been made to appear that any right of the plaintiff has been taken or destroyed for which compensation is necessary under the Constitution of the United States. . . .

"I am authorized to say that the Chief Justice [Fuller], Mr. Justice White and Mr. Justice Peckham concur in the foregoing dissent."

Muhlker v. *New York & Harlem Railroad Co.*
197 U. S. 544, 571

What Price Water?

(*Denver* v. *Denver Water Co.*, 1917)

THE SOLE WATER COMPANY IN DENVER COMPLAINED THAT THE rate fixed by city ordinance did not afford fair compensation and hence amounted to a taking of private property without due process of law. Net earnings would be only 3.64 percent of the reasonable value of the water-works, according to a special master's report. Taking exceptions, the city also pointed out that if it built its own water system the company's property would be worth merely its "junk value."

"We are unable to regard the case as capable of being thus disposed of upon the basis of 'junk value,' " said Mr. Justice Pitney for the majority. He itemized these facts: the company owned its plant; the franchise expired in 1910, the city did not renew but offered to purchase the plant for $7,000,000; the company rejected the offer but continued to supply the city at the old rates; the State gave the city authority to spend $8,000,000 to build a municipal system but the city was advised that the cost would be $12,750,000; in 1914 the inhabitants of Denver voted against buying out the company, and a week later the City Council rushed through an ordinance lowering the rates.

The company argued that it was being compelled to serve at a confiscatory rate; to stop would mean great suffering in this "semi-arid city." Denver asserted its right to exclude the company from its streets and therefore the right to set terms of continuance.

Justice Pitney ruled that the new rates were inadequate and that the ordinance should be construed as the grant of a new franchise of indefinite duration. The case was sent back to the District Court with orders to overrule and not strike out exceptions taken by the city, thus making the decree for the company foolproof. Holmes (joined by Justices Brandeis and Clarke) wanted a complete reversal:

"T HIS IS a bill to restrain the enforcement of an ordinance of the City and County of Denver, passed on March 3, 1914, fixing the rates for water permitted to be charged thereafter to the City and its inhabitants. After the coming in of the answer the case was referred to a special master, there was an investigation of the usual kind, a report and afterwards a final decree for the Water Company, vitiated by the judge's assumption that he was bound by the master's findings of fact. But I need not dwell upon this mistake, because in my opinion the decision ought to be reversed upon a more important ground. In some instances it would seem proper to send the case back for further consideration . . . but that is unnecessary when there is disclosed a fundamental bar to the bill, and I may add that if this be the fact no omission to raise the point in technical form would induce this Court to enter a decree contrary to the manifest equities of the case. . . .

"The Water Company occupied the streets of Denver with its pipes under an ordinance of April 10, 1890, and it is not denied that the franchise granted by that ordinance had expired. . . . I am of opinion that the ordinance complained of does not grant a new term. Perhaps an instrument could be framed that granted while it said that it did not. But this ordinance qualifies all that follows by a preamble that recites that the Water Company is 'without a franchise and a mere tenant by sufferance of the streets of the City and County of Denver' and then, 'without in any manner recognizing said The Denver Union Water Company's right to occupy the streets of the City and County of Denver, or to continue its service as a water carrier, but for the purpose of regulating and reducing the charges made by it during the time it shall further act as a water carrier and tenant by sufferance of said streets,' goes on to fix the rates.

"It seems to me plain that the rates subsequently established, even though purporting to be monthly or semi-annual, are established subject to the preliminary declaration, and to the chance of the practically improbable earlier termination of the license or tenancy at sufferance. The ordinance does not attempt to require the Company to furnish water but simply fixes a limit to its charges while it does furnish it as such tenant at sufferance. While the service continues it is charged with a public interest and is subject to regulation by law. The question at the bottom of the case is, what elements, if any, the Company has a constitutional right to have taken into account in determining whether the rates ordained are confiscatory, and, more generally, whether it has any constitutional rights at all in the matter of rates.

"We must assume that the Water Company may be required, within a reasonable time, to remove its pipes from the streets. . . . And, to illustrate the problem, it may be asked how a company in that situation can assert a constitutional right to a return upon the value that those pipes would have if there under a permanent right of occupation, as against a city that is legally entitled to reduce them to their value as old iron by ordering them to be removed at once. In view of that right of the City, which, if exercised, would make the Company's whole plant valueless as such, the question recurs whether the fixing of any rate by the City could be said to confiscate property on the ground that the return was too low.

"I understand that the Water Company has a right to stop furnishing water, corresponding to the right of the City to order out the pipes. It is hard to see how property could be confiscated by the establishment of almost any rate when whatever value it would have over and above that dependent upon the use of the pipes would remain to the Company if it stopped using them and therefore was in the Company's hands to preserve. The ordinance of the City could mean no more than that the Company must accept the City's rates or stop—and as it could be stopped by the City out and out, the general principle is that it could be stopped unless a certain price should be paid. . . . It is true that this principle has not been applied in cases where the condition tended to bring about a state of things that there was a predominant public interest to prevent, but I see no ground for the application here of anything to be deduced from *Western Union Telegraph Co.* v. *Kansas; Pullman Co.* v. *Kansas,* or *Motion Picture Patents Co.* v. *Universal Film Mfg. Co.* [For the last, see page 75.]

"It may be said that to argue from such abstract rights is to discuss the case *in vacuo*—that practically the Company cannot stop furnishing water without being ruined, or the City stop receiving it without being destroyed. And no doubt this is true —but it is also true and not quite as tautologous as it seems, that the laws know nothing but legal rights. Something more than the strong probability that an enjoyment will continue must be shown in order to make an otherwise lawful uncompensated interference with it a wrong. . . . Or conversely, if a legal title is taken it must be paid for in full notwithstanding a strong probability that the enjoyment of the property will continue long undisturbed. . . . So here the mutual dependence of the parties upon each other in fact does not affect the consequences of their independence of each other in law.

"The question before us is not what would be a fair compensation as between a necessary customer and a necessary seller, but simply whether the property of the Company is taken without due process of law by the City's fixing rates for a service, while it continues, that the Company may discontinue at will and the City may order tomorrow to stop. I am of opinion that it is not. . . . Whatever may be the duty of the City toward its inhabitants, that cannot enlarge its obligations to the Company or of the Company to it after the franchise of the latter has expired, or change the meaning of an ordinance that to my mind is plain upon its face. I presume that if it be necessary the City or the Legislature can take the water works by eminent domain.

"The question is different from that which would arise upon a franchise having but a short time to run but still in force. It might be argued that the short life was a fact to be considered, as no doubt it would be in some connections. . . . Or it well may be that while a limited franchise is in force the very fact that the Company has to rely upon the returns during the life of the franchise to reimburse its outlay and give it whatever profit it can make, entitles it to returns during that period unaffected by the approach of the end. There is no such question here."

City and County of Denver et al.
v. Denver Union Water Co.
246 U. S. 178, 195

Gas Across the Borders

(*Pennsylvania* v. *West Virginia*, 1922)

WEST VIRGINIA ENACTED A STATUTE IN 1919 REQUIRING HER NATural gas corporations to fill local needs before all others. At that time a flourishing business was being done in piping natural gas across state lines as far as Pittsburgh, Cleveland, Cincinnati and Toledo. When the law was passed, Pennsylvania and Ohio protested that it was a regulation of interstate commerce, which belonged within the province of Congress.

West Virginia replied that her supply of natural gas was waning: she must conserve it. In 1918 her pipe-line companies had supplied 157 billion cubic feet to consumers outside the State and only 70 billion within. But Mr. Justice Van Devanter, for the majority, called the law unjustified and unconstitutional: "A State law which by its necessary operation prevents, obstructs or burdens such transmission is a regulation of interstate commerce," impliedly forbidden to the States in Article I of the Constitution.

Justice Holmes dissented, insisting upon States' rights. Justice McReynolds in a separate dissent said it was premature to make a case on the prospect that enforcement would not permit other States to get enough gas for their imperative needs. Justice Brandeis likewise thought that the bill should be dismissed without passing on its constitutionality.

Holmes wrote:

"THE STATUTE seeks to reach natural gas before it has begun to move in commerce of any kind. It addresses itself to gas hereafter to be collected and states to what use it first must be

[124]

applied. The gas is collected under and subject to the law, if valid, and at that moment it is not yet matter of commerce among the States.

"I think that the products of a State until they are actually started to a point outside it may be regulated by the State notwithstanding the commerce clause. In *Oliver Iron Mining Co. v. Lord*, 262 U. S. 172, it was held that the State might levy an occupation tax upon the mining of iron ore equal to six percent of the value of the ore produced during the previous year, although substantially all the ore left the State and was put upon cars for that purpose by the same single movement by which it was severed from its bed. There could not be a case of a State's product more certainly destined to interstate commerce. It was put upon the cars by the same act by which it was produced. But as it was not yet in interstate commerce the tax was sustained. I know of no relevant distinctions between taxing and regulating in other ways. . . .

"But the States have been held authorized to regulate in other ways more closely resembling the present. In *Sligh* v. *Kirkwood*, 237 U. S. 52, a State law was sustained that made it criminal to sell or offer for shipment citrus fruits that were immature or otherwise unfit for consumption. That, upon the grounds of local policy, intercepted before it got into the stream what would have been an object of interstate commerce.

"The local interest in the present case is greater and more obvious than in that of green oranges. Again, the power of the State to preserve a food supply for its people by game laws notwithstanding an indirect interference with interstate commerce is established. . . . If there is any difference between the property rights of the State in game and in gas still in the ground it does not concern the plaintiffs and it is plain from the decisions cited that they do not depend upon a speculative view as to title. . . . The right of the State so to regulate the use of natural gas as to prevent waste was sustained as against the Fourteenth Amendment in *Walls* v. *Midland Carbon Co.*, 254 U. S. 300, and I do not suppose that the plaintiffs would have fared any better had they invoked the commerce clause.

"I need do no more than refer to prohibition of manufacture of articles intended for export, such as colored oleomargarine . . . or spirits. The result of that and other cases has been expressed by this Court more than once in the form of a general recognition of the right of a State to make 'reasonable provisions for local needs.' . . . And the right has been recognized even when the interference with interstate commerce is direct, as when an interstate train is required to stop to accommodate passengers who do not leave the State. . . .

"I see nothing in the commerce clause to prevent a State from giving a preference to its inhabitants in the enjoyment of its natural advantages. If the gas were used only by private persons for their own purposes I know of no power in Congress to require them to devote it to public use or to transport it across state lines.

"It is the law of West Virginia and of West Virginia alone that makes the West Virginia gas what is called a public utility, and how far it shall be such is a matter that that law alone decides. I am aware that there is some general language in *Oklahoma* v. *Kansas Natural Gas Co.*, 221 U. S. 229, 255, a decision that I thought wrong, implying that Pennsylvania might not keep its coal, or the Northwest its timber, &c. But I confess I do not see what is to hinder. Certainly if the owners of the mines or the forests saw fit not to export their products the Constitution would not make them do it. I see nothing in that instrument that would produce a different result if the State gave the owners motive for their conduct, as by offering a bonus.

"However far the decision in the case referred to goes it cannot outweigh the consensus of the other decisions to which I have referred and that seem to me to confirm what I should think plain without them, that the Constitution does not prohibit a State from securing a reasonable preference for its own inhabitants in the enjoyment of its products even when the effect of its law is to keep property within its boundaries that would otherwise have passed outside. . . .

"I agree substantially with my brothers McReynolds and Brandeis, but think that there is jurisdiction in such a sense as to justify a statement of my opinion upon the merits of the case. I think that the bill should be dismissed."

Commonwealth of Pennsylvania v. *State of West Virginia;*
State of Ohio v. *State of West Virginia*
262 U. S. 553, 600

Bars Lifted on Shoddy

(Weaver v. *Palmer Bros. Co.,* 1925)

PENNSYLVANIA PROHIBITED THE USE OF SHODDY IN MATTRESSES TO protect the public from unsanitary conditions in the bedding industry. Then she included in the prohibition all stuffed and filled bedding: covers, quilts, and comfortables. In 1923, when the law was enacted, a Connecticut company made 750,000 shoddy-filled comfortables and sold $180,000 worth in Pennsylvania. The manufacturer's excuse for using reclaimed wool and cotton fiber was: "The world's supply of new wool is insufficient to clothe the people of the temperate zones and to meet other demands."

Mr. Justice Butler said that there was no evidence of sickness or disease caused by using shoddy, that comfortables filled with it were much in demand. "The record shows that, for the sterilization of secondhand materials from which it makes shoddy, appellee uses effective steam sterilizers," he said.

The Court held that the prohibition of shoddy was arbitrary, violated the due process clause of the Fourteenth Amendment, and exceeded the State's police power.

Justices Brandeis and Stone stood with Justice Holmes:

"IF THE Legislature of Pennsylvania was of opinion that disease is likely to be spread by the use of unsterilized shoddy in comfortables I do not suppose that this Court would pronounce the opinion so manifestly absurd that it could not be acted upon. If we should not, then I think that we ought to assume the opinion to be right for the purpose of testing the law.

"The Legislature may have been of opinion further that the actual practice of filling comfortables with unsterilized shoddy gathered from filthy floors was widespread, and this again we must assume to be true. It is admitted to be impossible to distinguish the innocent from the infected product in any practicable way when it is made up into comfortables.

"On these premises, if the Legislature regarded the danger as very great and inspection and tagging as inadequate remedies, it seems to me that in order to prevent the spread of disease it constitutionally could forbid any use of shoddy for bedding and upholstery. Notwithstanding the broad statement in *Schlesinger* v. *Wisconsin* the other day [cited by the majority; Holmes' dissent on page 203] I do not suppose that it was intended to overrule the cases to which I referred there.

"It is said that there was unjustifiable discrimination. A classification is not to be pronounced arbitrary because it goes on practical grounds and attacks only those objects that exhibit or foster an evil on a large scale. It is not required to be mathematically precise and to embrace every case that theoretically is capable of doing the same harm. 'If the law presumably hits the evil where it is most felt, it is not to be overthrown because there are other instances to which it might have been applied.' . . . In this case, as in *Schlesinger* v. *Wisconsin*, I think we are pressing the Fourteenth Amendment too far."

Weaver v. *Palmer Bros. Co.*
270 U. S. 402, 415

Auto Traffic at Large

(*Frost* v. *California*, 1925)

CALIFORNIA DECREED THAT A CERTIFICATE OF PUBLIC NECESSITY
and convenience must be obtained from the State Railroad Commission
by trucking companies. One such firm, ordered to suspend operations
until it procured the certificate, argued that it was a private carrier, as
much entitled to the use of the highways as a man who transports his
own goods.

The State relied on its power to impose regulations on users of its
highways and said that the growth of auto transportation had thrown
many short-line railroads into bankruptcy. Railroads had petitioned the
Supreme Court of California, which ordered the Commission to assume jurisdiction over automotive carriers; the railroads had again
petitioned, and the Legislature passed the Auto Stage and Truck
Transportation Act (1917, amended 1919) bringing private carriers
under regulation.

Mr. Justice Sutherland held that the primary purpose of the Act
was "to protect the business of those who are common carriers in fact
by controlling competitive conditions. Protection or conservation of the
highways is not involved." He made clear that he was not challenging
the power of the State to regulate common carriers posing as private
carriers, but was preventing that power from reaching unconstitutional
results. Judgment sustaining the Act was reversed.

Holmes wrote the dissenting opinion, concurred in by Brandeis, and
McReynolds said separately that this was solely an intrastate matter and
"we should certainly refrain from interference."

Holmes wrote:

"THE QUESTION is whether a State may require all corporations or persons, with immaterial exceptions, who operate automobiles, etc., for the transportation of persons or property over a regular route and between fixed termini on the public highways of the State, for compensation, to obtain a certificate from the Railroad Commission that public necessity and convenience require such operation.

"A fee has to be paid for this certificate and transportation companies are made subject to the power of the Railroad Commission to regulate their rates, accounts and service. The provisions on this last point are immaterial here, as the case arises upon an order of the Commission under § 5 that the plaintiffs in error desist from transportation of property as above unless and until they obtain the certificate required, and by the terms of the statute every section and clause in it is independent of the validity of all the rest. § 10. Whatever the Supreme Court of California may have intimated, the only point that is decided, because that was the only question before it, was that the order of the Commission should stand.

"This portion of the Act is to be considered with reference to the reasons that may have induced the Legislature to pass it, for if a warrant can be found in such reasons they must be presumed to have been the ground. I agree, of course, with the cases cited by my brother Sutherland, to which may be added *American Bank & Trust Co.* v. *Federal Reserve Bank,* 256 U. S. 350, 358, that even generally lawful acts or conditions may become unlawful when done or imposed to accomplish an unlawful end. But that is only the converse of the proposition that acts in other circumstances unlawful may be justified by the purpose for which they are done.

"This applies to acts of legislature as well as to the doings of private parties. The only valuable significance of the much-abused phrase 'police power' is this power of the State to limit what otherwise would be rights having a pecuniary value, when a predominant public interest requires the restraint. The power of the State is limited in its turn by the constitutional guaranties of private rights, and it often is a delicate matter to decide which interest preponderates and how far the State may go without making compensation. The line cannot be drawn by generalities, but successive points in it must be fixed by weighing the particular facts. Extreme cases on the one side and on the other are *Edgar A. Levy Leasing Co.* v. *Siegel*, 258 U. S. 242, and *Pennsylvania Coal Co.* v. *Mahon*, 260 U. S. 393.

"The point before us seems to me well within the legislative power. We all know what serious problems the automobile has introduced. The difficulties of keeping the streets reasonably clear for travel and for traffic are very great. If a State speaking through its legislature should think that, in order to make its highways most useful, the business traffic upon them must be controlled, I suppose that no one would doubt that it constitutionally could, as, I presume, most States or cities do, exercise some such control. The only question is how far it can go.

"I see nothing to prevent its going to the point of requiring a license and bringing the whole business under the control of a railroad commission so far as to determine the number, character and conduct of transportation companies and so to prevent the streets from being made useless and dangerous by the number and lawlessness of those who seek to use them.

"I see nothing in this Act that would require private carriers to become common carriers, but if there were such requirement, it, like the provisions concerning rates and accounts, would not be before us now, since, as I have said, the statute makes every section independent and declares that if valid it shall stand even if all the others fall.

"As to what is before us, I see no great difference between requiring a certificate and requiring a bond . . . and, although, as I have said, I do not get much help from general propositions in a case of this sort, I cannot forbear quoting what seems to me applicable here. Distinguishing between activities that may be engaged in as a matter of right and those like the use of the streets that are carried on by government permission, it is said: 'In the latter case the power to exclude altogether generally includes the lesser power to condition and may justify a degree of regulation not admissible in the former.' 264 U. S. 145. I think that the judgment should be affirmed."

Frost & Frost Trucking Co. v. *Railroad Commission of California*
271 U. S. 583, 600

Taxis and the Common Law

(Black & White v. *Brown & Yellow*, 1927)

THE LOUISVILLE & NASHVILLE RAILROAD CO. HAD ASSIGNED A PLOT OF ground at one of its Kentucky stations to the Brown & Yellow Taxi Company in 1925. Cabs of the Black & White sought business there, and the Brown & Yellow sued to prevent interference with the contract. The defendants said that the contract was contrary to the Kentucky Constitution and that the Brown & Yellow had incorporated in Tennessee for the fraudulent purpose of evading Kentucky laws.

Mr. Justice Butler held, for the majority, that the validity of the contract involved no local law but depended on the question of general law. Federal courts are not bound to follow the courts of the State in which a controversy arises, he said, but to exercise their independent judgment.

Justice Butler observed that the Kentucky Constitution prohibited railroads from making exclusive or preferential arrangements for the conduct of any business as a common carrier, but held that the contract did not relate to the railroad's business as a common carrier and was valid.

Justices Brandeis and Stone concurred in Holmes' opinion:

"THIS IS a suit brought by the respondent, the Brown and Yellow Taxicab and Transfer Company, as plaintiff to prevent the petitioner, the Black and White Taxicab and Transfer Company, from interfering with the carrying out of a contract between the plaintiff and the other defendant, the Louisville and Nashville Railroad Company.

"The plaintiff is a corporation of Tennessee. It had a predecessor of the same name which was a corporation of Kentucky. Knowing that the courts of Kentucky held contracts of the kind in question invalid and that the courts of the United States maintained them as valid, a family that owned the Kentucky corporation procured the incorporation of the plaintiff and caused the other to be dissolved after conveying all the corporate property to the plaintiff.

"The new Tennessee corporation then proceeded to make with the Louisville and Nashville Railroad Company the contract above-mentioned, by which the railroad company gave to it exclusive privileges in the station grounds, and two months later the Tennessee corporation brought this suit. The Circuit Court of Appeals, affirming a decree of the District Court, granted an injunction and upheld this contract. It expressly recognized that the decisions of the Kentucky courts held that in Kentucky a railroad company could not grant such rights, but this being a question of general law, it went its own way regardless of the courts of the State. . . .

"The Circuit Court of Appeals had so considerable a tradition behind it in deciding as it did, that if I did not regard the case as exceptional I should not feel warranted in presenting my own convictions again after having stated them in *Kuhn* v. *Fairmont Coal Co.* But the question is important and in my opinion the prevailing doctrine has been accepted upon a subtle fallacy that never has been analyzed. If I am right the fallacy has resulted in an unconstitutional assumption of powers by the courts of the United States which no lapse of time or respectable array of opinion should make us hesitate to correct.

"Therefore I think it proper to state what I think the fallacy is.—The often repeated proposition of this and the lower courts is that the parties are entitled to independent judgment on matters of general law. By that phrase is meant matters that are not governed by any law of the United States or by any statute of the State—matters that in States other than Louisiana are governed in most respects by what is called the common law. It is through this phrase that what I think the fallacy comes in.

"Books written about any branch of the common law treat it as a unit, cite cases from this Court, from the Circuit Court of Appeals, from the State courts, from England and the Colonies of England indiscriminately, and criticize them as right or wrong according to the writer's notions of a single theory. It is very hard to resist the impression that there is one august corpus, to understand which clearly is the only task of any court concerned. If there were such a transcendental body of law outside of any particular State but obligatory within it unless and until changed by statute, the courts of the United States might be right in using their independent judgment as to what it was. But there is no such body of law.

"The fallacy and illusion that I think exist consist in supposing that there is this outside thing to be found. Law is a word used with different meanings, but law in the sense in which courts speak of it today does not exist without some definite authority behind it. The common law so far as it is enforced in a State, whether called common law or not, is not the common law generally but the law of that State existing by the authority of that State without regard to what it may have been in England or anywhere else. It may be adopted by statute in place of another system previously in force. . . . But a general adoption of it does not prevent the State courts from refusing to follow the English decisions upon a matter where local conditions are different. . . . It may be changed by statute . . . as is done every day. It may be departed from deliberately by judicial decisions, as with regard to water rights, in States where the common law generally prevails. Louisiana is a living proof that it need not be adopted at all. (I do not know whether under the prevailing doctrine we should regard ourselves as authorities upon the general law of Louisiana superior to those trained in the system.) Whether and how far and in what sense a rule shall be adopted whether called common law or Kentucky law is for the State alone to decide.

"If within the limits of the Constitution a State should declare one of the disputed rules of general law by statute there would be no doubt of the duty of all courts to bow, whatever their private opinions might be. . . . I see no reason why it should have less effect when it speaks by its other voice. . . . If a State constitution should declare that on all matters of general law the decisions of the highest court should establish the law until modified by statute or by a later decision of the same court, I do not perceive how it would be possible for a court of the United States to refuse to follow what the State court decided in that domain. But when the constitution of a State establishes a Supreme Court it by implication does make that declaration as clearly as if it had said it in express words, so far as it is not interfered with by the superior power of the United States.

"The Supreme Court of a State does something more than make a scientific inquiry into a fact outside of and independent of it. It says with an authority that no one denies, except when a citizen of another State is able to invoke an exceptional jurisdiction, that thus the law is and shall be. Whether it be said to make or to declare the law, it deals with the law of the State with equal authority however its function may be described.

"Mr. Justice Story in *Swift* v. *Tyson*, 16 Peters 1, evidently under the tacit domination of the fallacy to which I have referred, devotes some energy to showing that § 34 of the Judiciary Act of 1789, c.20, refers only to statutes when it provides that except as excepted the laws of the several States shall be regarded as rules of decision in trials at common law in courts of the United States. An examination of the original document by

[137]

a most competent hand has shown that Mr. Justice Story probably was wrong if anyone is interested to inquire what the framers of the instrument meant. (37 *Harvard Law Review*, 49 at pp. 81-88.) But this question is deeper than that; it is a question of the authority by which certain particular acts, here the grant of exclusive privileges in a railroad station, are governed. In my opinion the authority and the only authority is the State, and if that be so, the voice adopted by the State as its own should utter the last word. I should leave *Swift* v. *Tyson* undisturbed, as I indicated in *Kuhn* v. *Fairmont Coal Co.*, but I would not allow it to spread the assumed dominion into new fields.

"In view of what I have said it is not necessary for me to give subordinate or narrower reasons for my opinion that the decision below should be reversed. But there are adequate reasons short of what I think should be recognized. This is a question concerning the lawful use of land in Kentucky by a corporation chartered by Kentucky. The policy of Kentucky with regard to it has been settled in Kentucky for more than thirty-five years . . . (1892). Even under the rule that I combat it has been recognized that a settled line of State decisions was conclusive to establish a rule of property or the public policy of the State. . . . I should have supposed that what arrangements could or could not be made for the use of a piece of land was a purely local question, on which, if on anything, the State should have its own way and the State courts should be taken to declare what the State wills." . . .

Black & White Taxicab & Transfer Co.
v. *Brown & Yellow Taxicab & Transfer Co.*
276 U. S. 518, 532

Drawing the Tax Line

(Louisville Gas Co. v. *Coleman,* 1927)*

THE CLAUSE OF THE FOURTEENTH AMENDMENT AFFORDING EQUAL protection of the laws is not capable of exact definition so as to solve questions automatically, Mr. Justice Sutherland observed, but he held that it was applicable to a Kentucky law taxing mortgages which matured after five years and exempting others. The burden was borne by one class of borrowers.

The State argued that the uniformity prescribed by the Constitution commanded only that the statutes apply alike to all of a class under the same circumstances; here was no discrimination or any great hardship; the tax on a deed securing thirty-year bonds amounted to one-fifth of one percent a year, whereas short-term notes commonly carried the highest legal rate of interest.

But Justice Sutherland reasoned that if the State had reversed the classification the inequality "probably would be readily conceded but the constitutional infirmity would have been the same."

Justice Brandeis dissented, joined by Justices Holmes and Stone. Justices Brandeis, Sanford and Stone concurred in Holmes' separate opinion:

"WHEN a legal distinction is determined, as no one doubts that it may be, between night and day, childhood and maturity, or any other extremes, a point has to be fixed or a line has to be drawn, or gradually picked out by successive decisions, to mark where the change takes place. Looked at by itself without regard to the necessity behind it, the line or point seems arbitrary. It might as well or might nearly as well be a little more to the one side or the other. But when it is seen that a line or point there must be, and that there is no mathematical or logical way of fixing it precisely, the decision of the legislature must be accepted unless we can say that it is very wide of any reasonable mark.

"There is a plain distinction between large loans secured by negotiable bonds and mortgages that easily escape taxation, and small ones to needy borrowers for which they give their personal note for a short term and a mortgage of their house. I hardly think it would be denied that the large transactions of the money market reasonably may be subjected to a tax from which small ones for private need are exempted. The Legislature of Kentucky after careful consideration has decided that the distinction is clearly marked when the loan is for so long a term as five years. Whatever doubt I may feel, I certainly cannot say that it is wrong. If it is right as to the run of cases a possible exception here and there would not make the law bad. All taxes have to be laid by general rules."

Louisville Gas & Electric Co. v. *Coleman, Auditor*
277 U. S. 32, 41

Discouraging Corporations

(Quaker City Cab Co. v. *Pennsylvania,* 1927)

A PENNSYLVANIA LAW TAXING THE GROSS RECEIPTS OF PASSENGER transportation companies (from their operations within the State) did not apply to the receipts of individuals engaged in the same business. A taxicab corporation protested.

Mr. Justice Butler declared that the Constitution intended that laws should be applied equally to all in the same situation; if there were a real difference a classification might be made, but when it was arbitrary it amounted to requiring a corporation to surrender its rights. The statute was held unconstitutional.

There were three separate dissents by Justices Holmes, Brandeis and Stone. Holmes said:

"I THINK that the judgment should be affirmed. The principle that I think should govern is the same that I stated in *Louisville Gas & Electric Co.* v. *Coleman.* Although this principle was not applied in that case I do not suppose it to have been denied that taxing acts, like other rules of law, may be determined by differences of degree and that to some extent States may have a domestic policy that they constitutionally may enforce. . . .

"If usually there is an important difference of degree between business done by corporations and that done by individuals, I see no reason why the larger businesses may not be taxed and the small ones disregarded, and I think it would be

[141]

immaterial if here and there exceptions were found to the general rule. . . . Furthermore, if the State desired to discourage this form of activity in corporate form and expressed its desire by a special tax I think that there is nothing in the Fourteenth Amendment to prevent it."

Quaker City Cab. Co. v. *Commonwealth of Pennsylvania*
277 U. S. 389, 403

Chain Drug Stores

(*Louis K. Liggett Co.* v. *Baldridge*, 1928)

PENNSYLVANIA TRIED TO CHECK THE GROWTH OF CHAIN DRUG stores by requiring that no new drug stores be set up or acquired unless every stockholder or partner were a licensed pharmacist. Two shops added by Liggett to its chain in that State were refused permits. The company lost its case in the District Court, which held that the ownership of a store compounding prescriptions bore a substantial relation to the public interest.

In the Supreme Court the Liggett business was held to be a property right and the statute an arbitrary invasion of it; a foreign corporation permitted to do business in a State could not be subjected to State laws conflicting with the Federal Constitution, nor could the State interfere under the guise of protecting health, said Mr. Justice Sutherland.

And the Court took judicial notice of the fact that the stock of chain drug store corporations was bought and sold on the exchanges and necessarily was owned largely by laymen; the operation of such chains throughout the country for many years was "a matter of public notoriety."

Holmes dissented (Brandeis concurring):

"A STANDING criticism of the use of corporations in business is that it causes such business to be owned by people who do not know anything about it. Argument has not been supposed to be necessary in order to show that the divorce between the power of control and knowledge is an evil. The selling of drugs and poisons calls for knowledge in a high degree, and Penn-

[143]

sylvania after enacting a series of other safeguards has provided that in that matter the divorce shall not be allowed.

"Of course, notwithstanding the requirement that in corporations hereafter formed all the stockholders shall be licensed pharmacists, it still would be possible for a stockholder to content himself with drawing dividends and to take no hand in the company's affairs. But obviously he would be more likely to observe the business with an intelligent eye than a casual investor who looked only to the standing of the stock in the market. The Constitution does not make it a condition of preventive legislation that it should work a perfect cure. It is enough if the questioned act has a manifest tendency to cure or at least make the evil less. It has been recognized by the professions, by statutes and by decisions, that a corporation offering professional services is not placed beyond legislative control by the fact that all the services in question are rendered by qualified members of the profession. . . .

"But for decisions to which I bow I should not think any conciliatory phrase necessary to justify what seems to me one of the incidents of legislative power. I think, however, that the police power, as that term has been defined and explained, clearly extends to a law like this, whatever I may think of its wisdom, and that the decree should be affirmed.

"Of course the appellant cannot complain of the exception in its favor that allows it to continue to own and conduct the drug stores that it now owns. The Fourteenth Amendment does not forbid statutes and statutory changes to have a beginning and thus to discriminate between the rights of an earlier and those of a later time. . . ."

Louis K. Liggett Co. v. *Baldridge, Attorney General of Pennsylvania, et al.*
278 U. S. 105, 114

Labor Contract Frauds

(*Bailey* v. *Alabama*, 1910)

THE SUBJECT OF ALLEGED NEGRO PEONAGE AROSE IN ALABAMA. A farmhand named Lonzo Bailey was sentenced to hard labor after taking $15 as an advance on a contract to work at $12 a month for a year and quitting soon after the first month. By an Alabama statute unjustified refusal or failure to perform the work or refund the money was *prima facie* evidence of intent to defraud.

Bailey's counsel argued that the law enforced involuntary servitude by compelling personal service in liquidation of a debt. The State replied that the law aimed to punish a certain class of frauds not then punished by any other statute.

"The point is that the statute *authorizes* the jury to convict," said the majority opinion of Mr. Justice Hughes. Bailey was charged with getting money with intent to injure or defraud; Alabama courts used a rule of evidence preventing an accused from testifying "as to his uncommunicated motives." According to Justice Hughes, this was a mere breach of contract for personal service, and the statute, making this a crime, provided means of compelling performance of the service— "a convenient instrument for coercion*** particularly effective against the poor and the ignorant, its most likely victims." An Act of Congress in 1867 had nullified State laws attempting to enforce service in liquidation of debts.

"As the case was given to the jury under instructions which authorized a verdict in accordance with the statutory presumption, and the opposing instructions requested by the accused were refused, the judgment must be reversed," said Justice Hughes. The statute was in conflict with the Thirteenth Amendment; it was, therefore, invalid.

Holmes (Lurton concurring) dissented:

"WE ALL agree that this case is to be considered and decided in the same way as if it arose in Idaho or New York. Neither public document nor evidence discloses a law which, by its administration, is made something different from what it appears on its face, and therefore the fact that in Alabama it mainly concerns the blacks does not matter. . . .

"I shall begin, then, by assuming for the moment what I think is not true and shall try to show not to be true, that this statute punishes the mere refusal to labor according to contract as a crime, and shall inquire whether there would be anything contrary to the Thirteenth Amendment or the statute if it did, supposing it to have been enacted in the State of New York.

"I cannot believe it. The Thirteenth Amendment does not outlaw contracts for labor. That would be at least as great a misfortune for the laborer as for the man that employed him. For it certainly would affect the terms of the bargain unfavorably for the laboring man if it were understood that the employer could do nothing in case the laborer saw fit to break his word. But any legal liability for breach of contract is a disagreeable consequence which tends to make the contractor do as he said he would. Liability to an action for damages has that tendency as well as a fine. If the mere imposition of such consequences as tend to make a man keep to his promise is the creation of peonage when the contract happens to be for labor, I do not see why the allowance of a civil action is not, as well as an indictment ending in fine.

"Peonage is service to a private master at which a man is kept by bodily compulsion against his will. But the creation of the ordinary legal motives for right conduct does not produce it. Breach of a legal contract without excuse is wrong conduct, even if the contract is for labor, and if a State adds to civil liability a criminal liability to fine, it simply intensifies the legal motive for doing right, it does not make the laborer a slave.

"But if a fine may be imposed, imprisonment may be imposed in case of a failure to pay it. Nor does it matter if labor is added to the imprisonment. Imprisonment with hard labor is not stricken from the statute books. On the contrary, involuntary servitude as a punishment for crime is excepted from the prohibition of the Thirteenth Amendment in so many words. Also the power of the States to make breach of contract a crime is not done away with by the abolition of slavery. But if breach of contract may be made a crime at all it may be made a crime with all the consequences usually attached to crime.

"There is produced a sort of illusion if a contract to labor ends in compulsory labor in a prison. But compulsory work for no private master in a jail is not peonage. If work in a jail is not condemned in itself, without regard to what the conduct is it punishes, it may be made a consequence of any conduct that the State has power to punish at all.

"I do not blink the fact that the liability to imprisonment may work as a motive when a fine without it would not, and that it may induce the laborer to keep on when he would like to leave. But it does not strike me as an objection to a law that it is effective. If the contract is one that ought not to be made, prohibit it. But if it is a perfectly fair and proper contract, I can see no reason why the State should not throw its weight on the side of performance. There is no relation between its doing so in the manner supposed and allowing a private master to use private force upon a laborer who wishes to leave.

"But all that I have said so far goes beyond the needs of the case as I understand it. I think it is a mistake to say that this statute attaches its punishment to the mere breach of a contract to labor. It does not purport to do so; what it purports to punish is fraudulently obtaining money by a false pretense of an intent to keep the written contract in consideration of which the money is advanced. (It is not necessary to cite cases to show that such an intent may be the subject of material false representation.)

"But the import of the statute is supposed to be changed

by the provision that a refusal to perform, coupled with a failure to return the money advanced, shall be *prima facie* evidence of fraudulent intent. I agree that if the statute created a conclusive presumption it might be held to make a disguised change in the substantive law. . . . But it only makes the conduct *prima facie* evidence,—a very different matter. Is it not evidence that a man had a fraudulent intent if he receives an advance upon a contract over night and leaves in the morning? I should have thought that it very plainly was.

"Of course the statute is in general terms and applies to a departure at any time without excuse or repayment, but that does no harm except on a tacit assumption that this law is not administered as it would be in New York, and that juries will act with prejudice against the laboring man. For *prima facie* evidence is only evidence, and as such may be held by the jury insufficient to make out guilt. . . . This was decided by the Supreme Court of Alabama and we should be bound by their construction of the statute, even if we thought it wrong. But I venture to add that I think it entirely right. . . .

"This being so, I take it that a fair jury would acquit if the only evidence were a departure after eleven months' work and if it received no color from some special well-known course of events. But the matter well may be left to a jury, because their experience as men of the world may teach them that in certain conditions it is so common for laborers to remain during a part of the season, receiving advances, and then to depart at the period of need in the hope of greater wages at a neighboring plantation, that when a laborer follows that course there is a fair inference of fact that he intended it from the beginning.

"The Alabama statute, as construed by the State court and as we must take it, merely says, as a court might say, that the prosecution may go to the jury. This means and means only that the court cannot say, from its knowledge of the ordinary course of events, that the jury could not be justified by its knowledge in drawing the inference from the facts proved. In my opinion the statute embodies little if anything more than what I should have told the jury was the law without it. The right of a State to regulate laws of evidence is admitted and the statute does not go much beyond the common law. . . .

"I do not see how the result that I have reached thus far is affected by the rule laid down by the Court, but not contained in the statute, that the prisoner cannot testify his uncommunicated intentions and therefore, it is assumed, would not be permitted to offer a naked denial of an intent to defraud. If there is an excuse for breaking the contract it will be found in external circumstances, and can be proved. So the sum of the wrong supposed to be inflicted is that the intent to go off without repaying may be put further back than it would be otherwise. But if there is a wrong it lies in leaving the evidence to the jury, a wrong that is not affected by the letting in or keeping out an item of evidence on the other side. I have stated why I think it was not a wrong.

"To sum up, I think that obtaining money by fraud may be made a crime as well as murder or theft; that a false representation, expressed or implied at the time of making a contract of labor, that one intends to perform it and thereby obtaining an advance, may be declared a case of fraudulently obtaining money as well as any other; that if made a crime it may be punished like any other crime, and that an unjustified departure from the promised service without repayment may be declared a sufficient case to go to the jury for their judgment; all without in any way infringing the Thirteenth Amendment or the statutes of the United States."

Bailey v. *State of Alabama*
219 U. S. 219, 245

Too Many Grade Crossings?

(Southern Ry. v. *King,* 1909)*

IN GEORGIA A MAN WAS KILLED AT A RAILROAD CROSSING WHILE riding in his buggy, and his widow sued the Southern Railway, alleging negligence under the Georgia Blow Post Law of 1852. This statute required every engineer to blow his whistle at each post (400 yards from a crossing) and to keep blowing until he arrived at the public road, checking his speed meantime so as to be able to stop should any person or thing be crossing the tracks.

The law was passed before the days of interstate railroads and was intended for State carriers, the defendant argued; the evolution of the business world had rendered the law obsolete; now it was a burden on interstate commerce rather than an exercise of State police power.

But Mr. Justice Day, for the majority, held that when such laws did not directly interfere with interestate commerce they were upheld by the Court. Their constitutionality depended on their effect, he said, and in the absence of congressional action on the present subject-matter the State rightly regulated how interstate trains should approach dangerous crossings.

Although the railroad contended that there were too many crossings in Georgia—to slow up and stop would "hinder and practically prevent interstate business"—Justice Day pointed out that this was averred but no facts were set forth. Two judgments (one for the widow and one for the dead man's injured companion) were affirmed.

Justice White agreed with Holmes' dissent:

"THE PETITIONER set up as a defense to these actions that the statute under which it was sued was such a burden on commerce among the States as to violate Article I, Section 8, of the Constitution of the United States—a pure issue of law. If in order to try this case intelligently it was necessary to take evidence of facts, I think the Court was bound to hear such evidence, even without any specific allegation of the facts that would maintain it, as it is the Court's duty to know and to declare the law.

"But I leave that question on one side because the petitioners did not stop with the naked proposition, but alleged further that 'it is impossible to observe said statute and carry the mails as the defendant is required to carry them under the contract it has with the Government; and it is likewise impossible to do an interstate business and at the same time comply with the terms of said statute.' These are pure allegations of fact. They mean on their face that the requirement that the engineer at every grade crossing should have his train under such control as to be able to stop if necessary to avoid running down a man or wagon crossing the track requires such delays as to prevent or seriously to interfere with commerce among the States. They refer to physical conditions and to physical facts; they can refer to nothing else. I think it obvious that they mean that the crossings are so numerous as to make the requirement impracticable, since I can think of nothing but the number of them that would have that effect.

"The statement may be called a conclusion, but it is a conclusion of fact, just as the statement that a certain liquid was beer is a conclusion of fact from certain impressions of taste, smell and sight. If the objection to the pleading had been that more particulars were wanted, although for my part I think it would have been unnecessarily detailed and prolix pleading to set forth what and where the crossings were, the pleading should not have been rejected but the details should have been required. The petitioner showed that it was ready to give them by its offer of proof.

"But evidently the answer was not held bad on that ground. Presumably at least, as stated by the counsel for the petitioner, it was held bad on the ground taken by the Supreme Court of that State, that although the requirement was impracticable it was the law. . . . For it is to be observed further that the facts involved were public facts, and that although the Court might not take notice of the precise situation of particular crossings it well might take notice, as the Supreme Court of Georgia seems to have taken notice in the case just mentioned, that they were numerous. . . . Again, if any merely technical objection had been thought fatal to the defense, the petitioner undoubtedly would have met it by a further amendment to its plea.

"It seems to me a miscarriage of justice to sustain liability under a statute which possibly, and I think probably, is unconstitutional, until the facts have been heard which the petitioner alleged and offered to prove. I think that the judgment should be reversed.

"I am authorized to say that Mr. Justice White concurs in this dissent."

Southern Railway Co. v. *Josephine King;*
Same v. *Inez King*
217 U. S. 524, 537

Liability in Panama

(*Panama Railroad* v. *Rock*, 1924)

THIS CASE RAISED A QUESTION OF A RIGHT OF ACTION UNDER THE law of the Canal Zone. A woman passenger was killed in an accident on the Panama Railroad in 1918 and her husband sought damages under the Civil Code of Panama which required a guilty person to repair his offense.

The rule of law, traced back to the Code Napoleon, was: "He who shall have been guilty of an offense or fault, which caused another damage, is obliged to repair it without prejudice to the principal penalty which the law imposes for the fault or offense committed." In Mr. Justice Sutherland's opinion a civil action for death was excluded; common-law principles must be applied to the population in the Zone, and the requirement that a civil liability for death must be definitely fixed was more familiar to the Americans in the Zone than the Napoleonic rule.

The District Court's verdict for the widower was reversed.

Chief Justice Taft and Justices McKenna and Brandeis concurred in Holmes' dissent:

"THERE IS no dispute that the language of the Civil Code of Panama, Article 2341, which has been quoted, is broad enough on its face to give an action for negligently causing the death of the plaintiff's wife. Taken literally it gives such an action in terms. The article of the Code Napoleon from which it is said to have been copied is construed by the French courts in accord with its literal meaning. . . . It would seem natural and

[153]

proper to accept the interpretation given to the article at its source, and by the more authoritative jurists who have had occasion to deal with it, irrespective of whether local interpretation was before or after its adoption by the Spanish States, so long as nothing seriously to the contrary is shown.

"The only thing that I know of to the contrary is the tradition of the later common law. The common-law view of the responsibility of a master for his servant was allowed to help in the interpretation of an ambiguous statute in *Panama R. R. Co.* v. *Bosse*, 249 U. S. 41, 45, for reasons there stated. But those reasons have far less application here, even if we refer to the common law apart from the statute, and in any case are not enough to override the plain meaning of the statutory words.

"The common law as to master and servant, whatever may be thought of it, embodied a policy that has not disappeared from life. But it seems to me that courts in dealing with statutes sometimes have been too slow to recognize that statutes, even when in terms covering only particular cases, may imply a policy different from that of the common law, and therefore may exclude a reference to the common law for the purpose of limiting their scope. . . .

"Without going into the reasons for the notion that an action (other than an appeal) does not lie for causing the death of a human being, it is enough to say that they have disappeared. The policy that forbade such an action, if it was more profound than the absence of a remedy when a man's body was hanged and his goods confiscated for the felony, has been shown not to be the policy of present law by statutes of the United States and of most if not all of the States. In such circumstances it seems to me that we should not be astute to deprive the words of the Panama Code of their natural effect.

"The decision in the *Hubgh Case*, 6 La. Ann. 495 [cited by majority], stands on nothing better than the classic tradition that the life of a free human being (it was otherwise with regard to slaves) did not admit of valuation, which no longer is true sentimentally, as is shown by the statutes, and which is economically false. I think that the judgment should be affirmed."

Panama Railroad Co. v. Rock
266 U. S. 209, 215

A Philippine Question

(Springer v. *Philippine Islands,* 1927)

THE PHILIPPINE LEGISLATURE CREATED A NATIONAL BANK IN 1916 and a national coal company in 1917, the Government holding most of the shares and private individuals the remainder. The voting-power of the Government's stock was vested in a Board of Control in both cases.

The Governor-General protested that the voting-power of Government-owned stock was in effect a public office; to provide for others besides himself on either board was an invasion of his power. (The President of the Philippine Senate and the Speaker of the Philippine House were included.) The majority of both Houses was thus taking over his control and was proceeding along the same lines in forming national petroleum, iron, cement and development companies.

Mr. Justice Sutherland held that to engraft executive duties on a legislative office was to usurp the power of appointment by indirection. He said that this attempt violated the Organic Act of 1916 (passed by the Congress of the United States and bestowed on the Philippines) which separated these departments of government. The appointment of directors was an executive act performed by the Legislature without the capacity to do so.

Justices Holmes, Brandeis and McReynolds dissented, but only Brandeis concurred in this opinion of Holmes':

"THE GREAT ordinances of the Constitution do not establish and divide fields of black and white. Even the more specific of them are found to terminate in a penumbra shading gradually from one extreme to the other. Property must not be taken without compensation, but with the help of a phrase (the police power) some property may be taken or destroyed for public use without paying for it, if you do not take too much. When we come to the fundamental distinctions it is still more obvious that they must be received with a certain latitude or our Government could not go on.

"To make a rule of conduct applicable to an individual who but for such action would be free from it is to legislate —yet it is what the judges do whenever they determine which of two competing principles of policy shall prevail. At an early date it was held that Congress could delegate to the courts the power to regulate process, which certainly is law-making so far as it goes. . . . With regard to the executive, Congress has delegated to it or to some branch of it the power to impose penalties . . . to make conclusive determination of dutiable values . . . to establish standards for imports . . . to make regulations as to forest reserves . . . and other powers not needing to be stated in further detail. . . .

"Congress has authorized the President to suspend the operation of a statute, even one suspending commercial intercourse with another country . . . and very recently it has been decided that the President might be given power to change the tariff. . . . It is said that the powers of Congress cannot be delegated, yet Congress has established the Interstate Commerce Commission, which does legislative, judicial and executive acts, only softened by a *quasi;* makes regulations . . . issues reparation orders, and performs executive functions in connection with Safety Appliance Acts, Boiler Inspection Acts, &c.

"Congress also has made effective excursions in the other direction. It has withdrawn jurisdiction of a case after it has been argued. . . . It has granted amnesty, notwithstanding the grant to the President of the power to pardon. . . . A terri-

torial legislature has granted a divorce. . . . Congress has declared lawful an obstruction to navigation that this Court has
declared unlawful. . . . Parallel to the case before us, Congress long ago established the Smithsonian Institution, to question which would be to lay hands on the Ark of the Covenant;
not to speak of later similar exercises of power hitherto unquestioned, so far as I know.

"It does not seem to need argument to show that however
we may disguise it by veiling words we do not and cannot carry
out the distinction between legislative and executive action with
mathematical precision and divide the branches into watertight
compartments, were it ever so desirable to do so, which I am
far from believing that it is, or that the Constitution requires.

"The only qualification of such latitude as otherwise would
be consistent with the three-fold division of power is the proviso in § 22 of the Organic Act 'that all executive functions of
the Government must be directly under the Governor-General
or within one of the executive departments,' &c. . . . That
does not appear to me to govern the case. The corporations concerned were private corporations which the Legislature had
power to incorporate. Whoever owned the stock, the corporation did not perform functions of the Government. This would
be plain if the stock were in private hands, and if the Government bought the stock from private owners the functions of the
corporations would not be changed.

"If I am right in what I have said I think that ownership
would not make voting upon the stock an executive function of the Government when the acts of the corporation were
not. I cannot believe that the Legislature might not have provided for the holding of the stock by a board of private persons with no duty to the Government other than to keep it in-
formed and to pay over such dividends as might accrue.

"It is said that the functions of the Board of Control are not
legislative or judicial and therefore they must be executive. I

should say rather that they plainly are no part of the executive functions of the Government but rather fall into the indiscriminate residue of matters within legislative control. I think it would be lamentable even to hint a doubt as to the legitimacy of the action of Congress in establishing the Smithsonian as it did, and I see no sufficient reason for denying the Philippine Legislature a similar power."

Springer et al. v. *Government of the Philippine Islands;*
Agoncillo v. *Same*
277 U. S. 189, 209

IV. On Usurping Power

Full Sway for Competition

(Northern Securities Co. v. United States, 1903)

THE SUPREME COURT HELD THAT J. PIERPONT MORGAN, JAMES J. Hill and associates had formed a trust in turning over the majority stock of the Northern Pacific and the Great Northern railroads to a holding company, the Northern Securities, incorporated in New Jersey in 1901.

The Fourteenth Amendment protects property rights, the defendants pointed out, and the right to sell was included in this guaranty; the Northern Securities was enlarging commerce, not restraining it, and was organized to buy stock from those who wished to sell. The Tenth Amendment reserves to the States those powers not delegated to the Federal Government, the corporation further argued, and its New Jersey charter authorized its action.

Mr. Justice Harlan, for the majority, emphasized the power of Congress to regulate interstate commerce; no State, by creating a corporation, could project its authority across the continent so as to prevent Congress from exerting this power, nor could a State exempt a corporation from obeying a rule lawfully established by Congress for such commerce: the Sherman Anti-Trust Law. This device of Messrs. Morgan and Hill, if permitted, would lead the way to absolute mastery of passenger and freight rates throughout the country and it would be impossible for Congress to protect the public against their exactions, Justice Harlan said.

"The advantages that would naturally come to the public under the operation of the general laws of competition" would be lost, he added; no scheme could more certainly come within the words of the Act: "combination in the form of a trust or otherwise*** in re-

straint of commerce among the several States or with foreign nations";
nor could any plan more effectively suppress free competition between
the Great Northern and the Northern Pacific.

To the majority of the Court the Act was a recognition of the rule
of free competition. To Justice Holmes a loose interpretation seemed
a blow at coöperation. Justice White, who also dissented, asserted that
stock ownership was not embraced in the term "interstate commerce,"
and he was joined by Chief Justice Fuller and Justices Peckham and
Holmes.

This was Holmes' first dissent, and the others in the minority concurred in it:

"**I** AM unable to agree with the judgment of the majority
of the Court, and although I think it useless and undesirable,
as a rule, to express dissent, I feel bound to do so in this case
and to give my reasons for it.

"Great cases like hard cases make bad law. For great cases
are called great not by reason of their real importance in shaping
the law of the future but because of some accident of immediate
overwhelming interest which appeals to the feelings and dis-
torts the judgment. These immediate interests exercise a kind
of hydraulic pressure which makes what previously was clear
seem doubtful, and before which even well-settled principles
of law will bend.

"What we have to do in this case is to find the meaning of
some not very difficult words. We must try, I have tried, to do
it with the same freedom of natural and spontaneous interpretation that one would be sure of if the same question arose upon
an indictment for a similar act which excited no public attention and was of importance only to a prisoner before the court.
Furthermore, while at times judges need for their work the
training of economists or statesmen, and must act in view of
their foresight of consequences, yet when their task is to interpret and apply the words of a statute, their function is merely

academic to begin with—to read English intelligently—and a consideration of consequences comes into play, if at all, only when the meaning of the words used is open to reasonable doubt.

"The question to be decided is whether under the Act of July 2, 1890 . . . it is unlawful, at any stage of the process, if several men unite to form a corporation for the purpose of buying more than half the stock of each of two competing inter-state railroad companies, if they form the corporation, and the corporation buys the stock. I will suppose further that every step is taken from the beginning with the single intent of ending competition between the companies. I make this addition not because it may not be and is not disputed but because, as I shall try to show, it is totally unimportant under any part of the statute with which we have to deal.

"The statute of which we have to find the meaning is a criminal statute. The two sections on which the Government relies both make certain acts crimes. That is their immediate purpose and that is what they say. It is vain to insist that this is not a criminal proceeding. The words cannot be read one way in a suit which is to end in fine and imprisonment and another way in one which seeks an injunction. The construction which is adopted in this case must be adopted in one of the other sort. I am no friend of artificial interpretations because a statute is of one kind rather than another, but all agree that before a statute is to be taken to punish that which always has been lawful it must express its intent in clear words. So I say we must read the words before us as if the question were whether two small exporting grocers shall go to jail.

"Again, the statute is of a very sweeping and general character. It hits 'every' contract or combination of the prohibited sort, great or small, and 'every' person who shall monopolize or attempt to monopolize, in the sense of the Act, 'any part' of the trade or commerce among the several States. There is a natural inclination to assume that it was directed against certain great combinations and to read it in that light. It does not say so. On the contrary, it says 'every' and 'any part.' Still less was it directed specially against railroads. There even was a reasonable doubt whether it included railroads until the point was decided by this Court.

"Finally, the statute must be construed in such a way as not merely to save its constitutionality but, so far as is consistent with a fair interpretation, not to raise grave doubts on that score. I assume for purposes of discussion, although it would be a great and serious step to take, that in some case that seemed to it to need heroic measures Congress might regulate not only commerce but instruments of commerce or contracts the bearing of which upon commerce would be only indirect. But it is clear that the mere fact of an indirect effect upon commerce not shown to be certain and very great would not justify such a law.

"The point decided in *United States* v. *E. C. Knight Co.,* 156 U. S. 1, 17, [the first Anti-Trust Act case] was that 'the fact that trade or commerce might be indirectly affected was not enough to entitle complainants to a decree.' Commerce depends upon population, but Congress could not, on that ground, undertake to regulate marriage and divorce. If the Act before us is to be carried out according to what seems to me the logic of the argument for the Government, which I do not believe that it will be, I can see no part of the conduct of life with which on similar principles Congress might not interfere.

"This Act is construed by the Government to affect the purchasers of shares in two railroad companies because of the effect it may have or, if you like, is certain to have upon the competition of these roads. If such a remote result of the exercise of an ordinary incident of property and personal freedom is enough to make that exercise unlawful, there is hardly any transaction concerning commerce between the States that may not be made a crime by the finding of a jury or a court.

The personal ascendancy of one man may be such that it would give to his advice the effect of a command if he owned but a single share in each road. The tendency of his presence in the stockholders' meetings might be certain to prevent competition, and thus his advice, if not his mere existence, become a crime.

"I state these general considerations as matters which I should have to take into account before I could agree to affirm the decree appealed from, but I do not need them for my own opinion, because when I read the Act I cannot feel sufficient doubt as to the meaning of the words to need to fortify my conclusion by any generalities. Their meaning seems to me plain on their face.

"The first section makes 'every contract, combination in the form of trust or otherwise, or conspiracy in restraint of trade or commerce among the several States, or with foreign nations,' a misdemeanor punishable by fine, imprisonment or both. Much trouble is made by substituting other phrases assumed to be equivalent, which then are reasoned from as if they were in the Act. The court below argued as if maintaining competition were the expressed object of the Act. The Act says nothing about competition.

"I stick to the exact words used. The words hit two classes of cases, and only two—Contracts in restraint of trade and combinations or conspiracies in restraint of trade, and we have to consider what these respectively are. Contracts in restraint of trade are dealt with and defined by the common law. They are contracts with a stranger to the contractor's business (although in some cases carrying on a similar one) which wholly or partially restrict the freedom of the contractor in carrying on that business as otherwise he would. The objection of the common law to them was primarily on the contractor's own account. The notion of monopoly did not come in unless the contract covered the whole of England. . . . Of course this objection did not apply to partnerships or other forms, if there were any, of substituting a community of interest where there had been competition. There was no objection to such combinations merely as in restraint of trade or otherwise unless they amounted to a monopoly. Contracts in restraint of trade, I repeat, were contracts with strangers to the contractor's business, and the trade restrained was the contractor's own.

"Combinations or conspiracies in restraint of trade, on the other hand, were combinations to keep strangers to the agreement out of the business. The objection to them was not an objection to their effect upon the parties making the contract, the members of the combination or firm, but an objection to their intended effect upon strangers to the firm and their supposed consequent effect upon the public at large. In other words, they were regarded as contrary to public policy because they monopolized or attempted to monopolize some portion of the trade or commerce of the realm. . . .

"All that is added to the first section by § 2 is that like penalties are imposed upon every single person who, without combination, monopolizes, or attempts to monopolize, commerce among the States; and that the liability is extended to attempting to monopolize any part of such trade or commerce. It is more important as an aid to the construction of § 1 than it is on its own account. It shows that whatever is criminal when done by way of combination is equally criminal if done by a single man. That I am right in my interpretation of the words of § 1 is shown by the words 'in the form of a trust or otherwise.' The prohibition was suggested by the trusts, the objection to which, as everyone knows, was not the union of former competitors but the sinister power exercised or supposed to be exercised by the combination in keeping rivals out of the business and ruining those who already were in. It was the ferocious extreme of competition with others, not the cessation of competition among the partners, that was the evil feared.

"Further proof is to be found in § 7, giving an action to

any person injured in his business or property by the forbidden conduct. This cannot refer to the parties of the agreement and plainly means that outsiders who are injured in their attempt to compete with a trust or other similar combination may recover for it. . . . How effective the section may be or how far it goes is not material to my point. My general summary of the two classes of cases which the Act affects is confirmed by the title, 'An Act to protect Trade and Commerce against unlawful Restraints and Monopolies.'

"What I now ask is under which of the foregoing classes this case is supposed to come; and that question must be answered as definitely and precisely as if we were dealing with the indictments which logically ought to follow this decision. The provision of the statute against contracts in restraint of trade has been held to apply to contracts between railroads, otherwise remaining independent, by which they restricted their respective freedom as to rates. This restriction by contract with a stranger to the contractor's business is the ground of the decision in *United States* v. *Joint Traffic Association*, 171 U. S. 505, following and affirming *United States* v. *Trans-Missouri Freight Association*, 166 U. S. 290. I accept those decisions absolutely, not only as binding upon me but as decisions which I have no desire to criticize or abridge.

"But the provision has not been decided and, it seems to me, could not be decided without a perversion of plain language to apply to an arrangement by which competition is ended through community of interest—an arrangement which leaves the parties without external restriction. That provision, taken alone, does not require that all existing competitions shall be maintained. It does not look primarily, if at all, to competition. It simply requires that a party's freedom in trade between the States shall not be cut down by contract with a stranger.

"So far as that phrase goes, it is lawful to abolish competition by any form of union. It would seem to me impossible

[169]

to say that the words 'every contract in restraint of trade is a crime punishable with imprisonment' would send the members of a partnership between, or a consolidation of, two trading corporations to prison—still more impossible to say that it forbade one man or corporation to purchase as much stock as he liked in both. Yet those words would have that effect if this clause of § 1 applies to the defendants here. For it cannot be too carefully remembered that that clause applies to 'every' contract of the forbidden kind—a consideration which was the turning point of the *Trans-Missouri Freight Association's* case.

"If the statute applies to this case it must be because the parties or some of them, have formed, or because the Northern Securities Company is, a combination in restraint of trade among the States, or, what comes to the same thing in my opinion, because the defendants or some one of them are monopolizing or attempting to monopolize some part of the commerce between the States. But the mere reading of those words shows that they are used in a limited and accurate sense.

"According to popular speech, every concern monopolizes whatever business it does, and if that business is trade between two States it monopolizes a part of the trade among the States. Of course the statute does not forbid that. It does not mean that all business must cease. A single railroad down a narrow valley or through a mountain gorge monopolizes all the railroad transportation through that valley or gorge. Indeed, every railroad monopolizes, in a popular sense, the trade of some area. Yet I suppose no one would say that the statute forbids a combination of men into a corporation to build and run such a railroad between the States.

"I assume that the Minnesota charter of the Great Northern and the Wisconsin charter of the Northern Pacific both are valid. Suppose that, before either road was built, Minnesota, as part of the system of transportation between the States, had created a railroad company authorized singly to build all the lines in the States now actually built, owned and controlled by either of the two existing companies. I take it that that charter would have been just as good as the present one, even if the statutes which we are considering had been in force. In whatever sense it would have created a monopoly the present charter does. It would have been a large one, but the Act of Congress makes no discrimination according to size. Size has nothing to do with the matter. A monopoly of 'any part' of commerce among the States is unlawful. The supposed company would have owned lines that might have been competing—probably the present one does. But the Act of Congress will not be construed to mean the universal disintegration of society into single men, each at war with all the rest, or even the prevention of all further combinations for a common end.

"There is a natural feeling that somehow or other the statute meant to strike at combinations great enough to cause just anxiety on the part of those who love their country more than money, while it viewed such little ones as I have supposed with just indifference. This notion, it may be said, somehow breathes from the pores of the Act, although it seems to be contradicted in every way by the words in detail. And it has occurred to me that it might be that when a combination reached a certain size it might have attributed to it more of the character of a monopoly merely by virtue of its size than would be attributed to a smaller one.

"I am quite clear that it is only in connection with monopolies that size could play any part. But my answer has been indicated already. In the first place, size in the case of railroads is an inevitable incident and if it were an objection under the Act, the Great Northern and the Northern Pacific already were too great and encountered the law. In the next place in the case of railroads it is evident that the size of the combination is reached for other ends than those which would make them monopolies. The combinations are not formed for the purpose

[171]

of excluding others from the field. Finally, even a small rail-road will have the same tendency to exclude others from its narrow area that great ones have to exclude others from the greater one, and the statute attacks the small monopolies as well as the great. The very words of the Act make such a distinction impossible in this case and it has not been attempted in express terms.

"If the charter which I have imagined above would have been good notwithstanding the monopoly, in a popular sense, which it created, one next is led to ask whether and why a combination or consolidation of existing roads, although in actual competition, into one company of exactly the same powers and extent, would be any more obnoxious to the law. Although it was decided . . . that since the statute, as before, the States have the power to regulate the matter, it was said in the argument that such a consolidation would be unlawful, and it seems to me that the Attorney General was compelled to say so in order to maintain his case. But I think that logic would not let him stop there or short of denying the power of a State at the present time to authorize one company to construct and own two parallel lines that might compete. The monopoly would be the same as if the roads were consolidated after they had begun to compete—and it is on the footing of monopoly that I now am supposing the objection made.

"But to meet the objection to the prevention of competition at the same time, I will suppose that three parties apply to a State for charters; one for each of two new and possibly competing lines respectively, and one for both of these lines, and that the charter is granted to the last. I think that charter would be good and I think the whole argument to the contrary rests on a popular instead of an accurate and legal conception of what the word 'monopolize' in the statute means.

"I repeat, that in my opinion there is no attempt to monopolize, and what, I have said, in my judgment amounts to the same thing, that there is no combination in restraint of trade, until something is done with the intent to exclude strangers to the combination from competing with it in some part of the business which it carries on.

"Unless I am entirely wrong in my understanding of what a 'combination in restraint of trade' means, then the same monopoly may be attempted and effected by an individual and is made equally illegal in that case by § 2. But I do not expect to hear it maintained that Mr. Morgan could be sent to prison for buying as many shares as he liked of the Great Northern and the Northern Pacific, even if he bought them both at the same time and got more than half the stock of each road.

"There is much that was mentioned in argument which I pass by. But in view of the great importance attached by both sides to the supposed attempt to suppress competition, I must say a word more about that. I said at the outset that I should assume, and I do assume, that one purpose of the purchase was to suppress competition between the two roads. I appreciate the force of the argument that there are independent stockholders in each; that it cannot be presumed that the respective boards of directors will propose any illegal act; that if they should they could be restrained, and that all that has been done as yet is too remote from the illegal result to be classed even as an attempt. Not every act done in furtherance of an unlawful end is an attempt or contrary to the law. There must be a certain nearness to the result. It is a question of proximity and degree. . . .

"So, as I have said, is the amenability of acts in furtherance of interference with commerce among the States to legislation by Congress. So, according to the intimation of this Court, is the question of liability under the present statute. . . . But I assume further, for the purposes of discussion, that what has been done is near enough to the result to fall under the law, if the law prohibits that result, although that assumption very nearly if not quite contradicts the decision in *United States* v. *E. C. Knight Co.*, 156 U. S. 1. But I said that the law does not prohibit the result. If it does it must be because there is some further meaning than I have yet discovered in the words 'combinations in restraint of trade.' I think that I have exhausted the meaning of those words in what I already have said. But they certainly do not require all existing competitions to be kept on foot, and, on the principle of the *Trans-Missouri Freight Association's* case, invalidate the continuance of old contracts by which former competitors united in the past.

"A partnership is not a contract or combination in restraint of trade between the partners unless the well-known words are to be given a new meaning invented for the purposes of this Act. It is true that the suppression of competition was referred to in *United States* v. *Trans-Missouri Freight Association*, 166 U. S. 290, but, as I have said, that was in connection with a contract with a stranger to the defendant's business—a true contract in restraint of trade. To suppress competition in that way is one thing, to suppress it by fusion is another.

"The law, I repeat, says nothing about competition and only prevents its suppression by contracts or combinations in restraint of trade, and such contracts or combinations derive their character as restraining trade from other features than the suppression of competition alone.

"To see whether I am wrong, the illustrations put in the argument are of use. If I am, then a partnership between two stage drivers who had been competitors in driving across a state line, or two merchants once engaged in rival commerce among the States, whether made after or before the Act, if now continued, is a crime. For, again I repeat, if the restraint on the freedom of the members of a combination caused by their entering into partnership is a restraint of trade, every such combination, as well the small as the great, is within the Act.

"In view of my interpretation of the statute I do not go

further into the question of the power of Congress. That has been dealt with by my brother White and I concur in the main with his views. I am happy to know that only a minority of my brethren adopt an interpretation of the law which in my opinion would make eternal the *bellum omnium contra omnes* and disintegrate society so far as it could into individual atoms.* If that were its intent I should regard calling such a law a regulation of commerce as a mere pretense. It would be an attempt to reconstruct society. I am not concerned with the wisdom of such an attempt but I believe that Congress was not entrusted by the Constitution with the power to make it and I am deeply persuaded that it has not tried.

"I am authorized to say that the Chief Justice [Fuller], Mr. Justice White and Mr. Justice Peckham concur in this dissent."

Northern Securities Co. v. *United States*
193 U. S. 197, 400

* Of the majority of five Mr. Justice Brewer alone held that the Anti-Trust Act included only *unreasonable* restraints in its scope.

Communal Benefits Denied

(American Column v. United States, 1921)

THE AMERICAN HARDWOOD MANUFACTURERS' ASSOCIATION, WHICH exchanged information on sales, prices and production among its 365 members, was held to be a conspiracy in restraint of trade. Government counsel contended that such open-price associations were so numerous and so extensively organized as to threaten an economic revolution; that their chief design was to destroy competition and substitute coöperation.

The association insisted that its reports did not carry any tinge of price-fixing, although containing estimates of future production and tabulations of supply on hand, and that its sales records showed variations in prices received by members.

"Plainly it would not be very difficult to devise a more minute disclosure of everything connected with one's business," wrote Mr. Justice Clarke in the majority opinion, and he quoted from letters sent out to the manufacturers as well as from the minutes of their meetings. One member wrote in to headquarters, "We had just taken a small order at what we thought a satisfactory price, but discovered immediately that others were getting more money, and since that time we have booked orders for a number of these special items at an increase of six dollars per thousand." Justice Clarke also recited the price rises that took place in 1919.

He considered the "open competition plan" a misnomer, not a new form of competition but an old form of combination in restraint of trade, skilfully devised to evade the law.

Holmes dissented:

"WHEN THERE are competing sellers of a class of goods, knowledge of the total stock on hand, of the probable total demand and of the prices paid of course will tend to equalize the prices asked. But I should have supposed that the Sherman Act did not set itself against knowledge—did not aim at a transitory cheapness unprofitable to the community as a whole because not corresponding to the actual conditions of the country.

"I should have thought that the ideal of commerce was an intelligent interchange made with full knowledge of the facts as a basis for a forecast of the future on both sides. A combination to get and distribute such knowledge notwithstanding its tendency to equalize, not necessarily to raise, prices, is very far from a combination in unreasonable restraint of trade.

"It is true that it is a combination of sellers only, but the knowledge acquired is not secret, it is public, and the buyers, I think I may assume, are not less active in their efforts to know the facts.

"A combination in unreasonable restraint of trade imports an attempt to override normal market conditions. An attempt to conform to them seems to me the most reasonable thing in the world. I see nothing in the conduct of the appellants that binds the members even by merely social sanctions to anything that would not be practiced, if we can imagine it, by an all-wise socialistic government acting for the benefit of the community as a whole. The parties to the combination are free to do as they will.

"I must add that the decree as it stands seems to me surprising in a country of free speech that affects to regard education and knowledge as desirable. It prohibits the distribution of stock, production or sales reports, the discussion of prices at association meetings, and the exchange of predictions of high prices. It is true that these acts are the main evidence of the supposed conspiracy, but that to my mind only shows the weakness of the Government's case.

"I cannot believe that the fact, if it be assumed, that the acts have been done with a sinister purpose, justifies excluding mills in the backwoods from information in order to enable centralized purchasers to take advantage of their ignorance of the facts.

"I agree with the more elaborate discussion of the case by my brother Brandeis." *

American Column & Lumber Co. et al. v. *United States*
257 U. S. 377, 412

* With whose separate dissent Mr. Justice McKenna agreed.

Presidential Authority

(*Myers* v. *United States*, 1926)

IN 1920 PRESIDENT WILSON REMOVED, WITHOUT CONSENT OF THE
Senate, the postmaster of Portland, Oregon, whom he had appointed
and who now claimed back pay. Congress had empowered the President in 1876 to name first-class postmasters with "advice and consent"
and provided for removals by the same method, but the Government
cited Article II of the Constitution as a defense, saying that the right
of appointment implied the right of removal.

Chief Justice Taft held the consent requirement invalid; the
framers of the Constitution and the early Congresses made no move
to curb the President's power in this direction, and the absence of an
express limit was "convincing indication that none was intended."

Mr. Justice McReynolds, dissenting, said that "a certain repug-
nance must attend the suggestion that the President may ignore any
provision of an Act of Congress under which he has proceeded. He
should promote and not subvert orderly government."

Mr. Justice Brandeis, himself an appointee of President Wilson's,
also dissented. "Nothing in support of the claim of uncontrollable
power can be inferred from the silence of the Convention of 1787 on
the subject of removal," he said; the protection of individuals, including
officials, from "the arbitrary or capricious exercise of power" was believed in 1787 to be an essential of free government.

And Holmes added:

"MY BROTHERS McReynolds and Brandeis have discussed
the question before us with exhaustive research and I say a few

words merely to emphasize my agreement with their conclusion.

"The arguments drawn from the executive power of the President, and from his duty to appoint officers of the United States (when Congress does not vest the appointment elsewhere), to take care that the laws be faithfully executed, and to commission all officers of the United States, seem to me spiders' webs inadequate to control the dominant facts.

"We have to deal with an office that owes its existence to Congress and that Congress may abolish tomorrow. Its duration and the pay attached to it while it lasts depend on Congress alone.

"Congress alone confers on the President the power to appoint to it and at any time may transfer the power to other hands. With such power over its own creation, I have no more trouble in believing that Congress has power to prescribe a term of life for it free from any interference than I have in accepting the undoubted power of Congress to decree its end. I have equally little trouble in accepting its power to prolong the tenure of an incumbent until Congress or the Senate shall have assented to his removal.

"The duty of the President to see that the laws be executed is a duty that does not go beyond the laws or require him to achieve more than Congress sees fit to leave within his power."

Myers v. *United States*
272 U. S. 52, 177

Concerning Immorality

(Keller v. United States, 1908)

IMPORTING A WOMAN FOR IMMORAL PURPOSES WAS FORBIDDEN BY Act of Congress in 1907. If she were found out within three years after her arrival she was to be deported, and anyone who harbored her in that time was guilty of a felony.

Did the concerns of morality belong within the province of Congress or were they part of the powers reserved to the States? Here was a landlord accused of harboring an Hungarian prostitute. She came to this country in 1905, and went to Chicago in 1907. The landlord said she was already an occupant when he bought the house. Tried in 1908, he was sentenced to sixteen months in the penitentiary.

The entire Court acknowledged the right of Congress to exclude aliens or provide terms of stay. But the charge was not against a prostitute, it was against a person who enabled her to ply her trade. On that score the Justices disagreed.

"It does not follow that Congress has the right to punish those whose acts furnish evidence from which the Government may determine the question of her expulsion," said Mr. Justice Brewer in the majority opinion; the Constitution gives no grant of police power to Congress. An enormous field of legislation would otherwise be taken away from the States: "Then we should be brought face to face with such a change in the internal conditions of this country as never was dreamed of by the framers of the Constitution." The indictment was ordered quashed.

Holmes (joined by Harlan and Moody) dissented:

"For the purpose of excluding those who unlawfully enter this country Congress has power to retain control over aliens long enough to make sure of the facts. . . . To this end it may make their admission conditional for three years. . . . If the ground of exclusion is their calling, practice of it within a short time after arrival is or may be made evidence of what it was when they came in.

"Such retrospective presumptions are not always contrary to experience or unknown to the law. . . . If a woman were found living in a house of prostitution within a week of her arrival, no one, I suppose, would doubt that it tended to show that she was in the business when she arrived. But how far back such an inference shall reach is a question of degree like most of the questions of life. And while a period of three years seems to be long I am not prepared to say, against the judgment of Congress, that it is too long.

"The statute does not state the legal theory upon which it was enacted. If the ground is that which I have suggested, it is fair to observe that the presumption that it creates is not open to rebuttal. I should be prepared to accept even that, however, in view of the difficulty of proof in such cases. Statutes of which the justification must be the same are familiar in the States. For instance, one creating the offense of being present when gaming implements are found . . . or punishing the sale of intoxicating liquors without regard to knowledge of their intoxicating quality . . . or throwing upon a seducer the risk of the woman turning out to be married or under a certain age. . . .

"It is true that in such instances the legislature has power to change the substantive law of crimes, and it has been thought that when it is said to create a conclusive presumption as to a really disputable fact, the proper mode of stating what it does, at least as a general rule, is to say that it has changed the substantive law. . . . This may be admitted without denying that considerations of evidence are what lead to the change. And if it should be thought more philosophical to express this law in substantive terms, I think that Congress may require, as a condition of the right to remain, good behavior for a certain time in matters deemed by it important to the public welfare and of a kind that indicates a pre-existing habit that would have excluded the party if it had been known. Therefore I am of opinion that it is within the power of Congress to order the deportation of a woman found practicing prostitution within three years.

"If Congress can forbid the entry and order the subsequent deportation of professional prostitutes, it can punish those who coöperate in their fraudulent entry. 'If Congress has power to exclude such laborers*** it has the power to punish any who assist in their introduction.' That was a point decided *Lees* v. *United States,* 150 U. S. 476, 480. The same power must exist as to coöperation in an equally unlawful stay. The indictment sets forth the facts that constitute such coöperation and need not allege the conclusion of law.

"On the principle of the cases last cited, in order to make its prohibition effective, the law can throw the burden of finding out the fact and date of a prostitute's arrival from another country upon those who harbor her for a purpose that presumably they know, in any event, to be contrary to law. Therefore, while I have admitted that the time fixed seems to me to be long, I can see no other constitutional objection to the Act, and, as I have said, I think that that one ought not to prevail."

Keller v. *United States*
213 U. S. 138, 149

Evidence by Wire-Tapping

(*Olmstead* v. *United States*, 1927)

A RUM-RUNNING RING IN SEATTLE WAS CONVICTED, ON EVIDENCE obtained by the tapping of its telephones, of conspiring to violate the Prohibition Act. Prohibition officers had inserted small wires along the phone lines leading to the homes and central office of four partners and, listening in for months, had overheard orders and acceptances. Their stenographic notes revealed conversations among the conspirators.

"It is no crime to exchange messages relating to the possession and sale of liquor. The crime is to possess and sell liquor," the petitioners argued; wire-tapping was comparable to breaking through a window and seizing letters. The Fourth Amendment secures persons, houses, papers, against trespass and seizure. The Fifth forbids compelling one to be a witness against oneself.

The Government answered that its evidence was not extorted confessions; the conversations were part of the crime. The officers in relating what they had heard testified as witnesses; no self-incrimination was involved. And the Supreme Court agreed: there was no searching, no seizure, no entry; the only thing employed was the sense of hearing, said Chief Justice Taft.

"The language of the Amendment cannot be extended and expanded to include telephone wires reaching to the whole world from the defendant's house or office," he held. "The intervening wires are not part of his house or office any more than are the highways along which they are stretched." He pointed out that the wire-tapping was done in the basement of the office-building and in the streets near the conspirators' homes; hence there had been no trespass.

To Mr. Justice Brandeis it was a plain case of invasion, as much as if a telephone message were a sealed letter. Why be so literal about the Fourth Amendment? he asked; decency, security and liberty demanded that Government officials be subjected to the same rules of conduct that other citizens must obey; otherwise we would be upholding the pernicious doctrine of committing crime to punish criminals.

Mr. Justice Butler suggested a new trial. Mr. Justice Stone concurred with Brandeis, and also with Holmes, who wrote:

"MY BROTHER Brandeis has given this case so exhaustive an examination that I desire to add but a few words. While I do not deny it, I am not prepared to say that the penumbra of the Fourth and Fifth Amendments covers the defendant, although I fully agree that courts are apt to err by sticking too closely to the words of a law where those words import a policy that goes beyond them. . . . But I think, as Mr. Justice Brandeis says, that apart from the Constitution the Government ought not to use evidence obtained and only obtainable by a criminal act.

"There is no body of precedents by which we are bound, and which confines us to logical deduction from established rules. Therefore we must consider the two objects of desire, both of which we cannot have, and make up our minds which to choose. It is desirable that criminals should be detected, and to that end that all available evidence should be used. It also is desirable that the Government should not itself foster and pay for other crimes, when they are the means by which the evidence is to be obtained.

"If it pays its officers for having got evidence by crime I do not see why it may not as well pay them for getting it in the same way, and I can attach no importance to protestations of disapproval if it knowingly accepts and pays and announces that in future it will pay for the fruits. We have to choose, and for my part I think it a less evil that some criminals should escape than that the Government should play an ignoble part.

"For those who agree with me, no distinction can be taken between the Government as prosecutor and the Government as judge. If the existing code does not permit district attorneys to have a hand in such dirty business it does not permit the judge to allow such iniquities to succeed. . . . And if all that I have said so far be accepted, it makes no difference that in this case wire-tapping is made a crime by the law of the State, not by the law of the United States.

"It is true that a State cannot make rules of evidence for courts of the United States, but the State has authority over the conduct in question, and I hardly think that the United States would appear to greater advantage when paying for an odious crime against State law than when inciting to the disregard of its own.

"I am aware of the often repeated statement that in a criminal proceeding the Court will not take notice of the manner in which papers offered in evidence have been obtained. But that somewhat rudimentary mode of disposing of the question has been overthrown. . . . I have said that we are free to choose between two principles of policy. But if we are to confine ourselves to precedent and logic the reason for excluding evidence obtained by violating the Constitution seems to me logically to lead to excluding evidence obtained by a crime of the officers of the law."

Olmstead et al. v. *United States*
Green et al. v. *Same*
McInnis et al. v. *Same*
277 U. S. 438, 469

Uncle Sam as Tenant

(Goodyear v. United States, 1927)

THE UNITED STATES VETERANS' BUREAU LEASED PREMISES IN CIN-
cinnati from the Goodyear Tire and Rubber Co. in 1921 for five
years, subject to an appropriation from Congress each year, which was
tantamount to a one-year lease with option to renew. At the end of
the fiscal year in 1923 the Bureau was undecided as to how long it
would remain, but it stayed into the next fiscal year and received an
appropriation covering 1924.

Then the Bureau notified the Goodyear Company that it would
not pay rent for a longer time than actual tenancy, but when it moved
in December, 1923, Goodyear claimed rent up to the end of the
fiscal year 1924 under the Ohio laws.

Affirmative renewal of the lease was lacking, said Mr. Justice Sanford; notice had been given before holding over and it was immaterial
that under the common law in Ohio a lessee holding over after expiration was bound for another year. The right to sue must rest on the
existence of a contract express or implied in fact.

Justices Sutherland and Stone concurred in Holmes' dissent:

"THERE WAS no adverse holding in this case. The United
States admitted that it occupied the premises under a contract
as lessee until June 30, 1923. One consequence of this contract
by the law that governed it and by the stipulation of the lessor
was that if the lessee held over he held over for a year. I do not
see how the United States could accept the contract and repudiate the consequence, or accept the permission of the lessor to

continue in possession upon the express condition that it be bound for a year and repudiate the condition, except in the event of there being no appropriation, in which case the paramount law of the United States would prevail.

"There was an appropriation here and therefore there was nothing to hinder the United States being bound until June 30, 1924, except the statement of the agents that it did not mean to be, which seems to me merely the statement that it did not mean to accept the legal consequence of its act."

Goodyear Tire & Rubber Co. v. *United States*
276 U. S. 287, 293

Where to Try Conspiracies

(*Hyde* v. *United States*, 1911)

DEFENDANTS IN A LAND-GRAB CONSPIRACY IN OREGON AND CALI-
fornia protested against trial in the District of Columbia. The Sixth
Amendment of the Constitution requires criminal prosecutions to be
held in the place "wherein the crime shall have been committed."
Here the alleged crime was the conspiracy and not the overt acts,
which were performed in the District. By Federal statute an overt
act was essential to prosecuting a conspiracy, and the trial court in the
District ruled that "the defendants thereby conspired here."

Yet another statute provided that when any offense began in one
judicial district and ended in another it should be deemed as committed in either and punishable in either.

Mr. Justice McKenna pointed out that there may be a constructive presence in a State, as distinct from a personal presence, by which
a crime may be consummated. He reasoned: "It is not an oppression
in the law to accept the place where an unlawful purpose is attempted
to be executed as the place of its punishment, and rather conspirators
be taken from their homes than the victims and witnesses of the conspiracy be taken from theirs."

Mr. Justice Holmes was spokesman for a minority of four, including Justices Lurton, Hughes and Lamar, in this and in another conspiracy case decided on the same day:

"THIS IS an indictment under Revised Statutes § 5440,
amended, Act of May 17, 1879, c. 8, 21 Stat. 4, for conspiracy
to defraud the United States. The petitioners were tried and

convicted in the District of Columbia, the conviction was affirmed by the Court of Appeals, 35 App. D. C. 451, and thereupon a writ of certiorari was granted by this Court. The scheme was to obtain by fraudulent devices from the States of California and Oregon school lands lying within forest reserves, to exchange them for public lands of the United States open to selection, and then to sell the lands so obtained.

"Hyde and Schneider were in California and never were actually in the District in aid of the conspiracy, but overt acts are alleged to have been done there to effect the objects in view. Most of these acts are innocent, taken by themselves, consisting mainly of the entry of appearance by Hyde's lawyer in the matter of different selections, the filing of papers concerning them, and letters urging speed. Hyde is alleged to have caused some documents affecting the same to be transmitted from California to the Commissioner at Washington, and in the last six counts payments to employees in the Land Office are alleged to have been made with corrupt purpose and in aid of the plan by a person who was included in the indictment as a conspirator, but whom the jury did not convict.

"The court instructed the jury that if the defendants agreed to accomplish their purpose by having any of the alleged overt acts done in the District of Columbia and any of those acts were done there, the conspiracy was in the District, whether the defendants were there or not. The defendants excepted to this instruction, as well as to many others.

"I have said enough to show that there was more than one question in the case, but as the first and also the most important one is whether the court had jurisdiction of the alleged offense, I shall confine myself to that.

"The conspiracy was continuous in its nature and is averred to have been so. . . . Therefore, wherever it was formed, it might have been continued in the District of Columbia as, for instance, if the conspirators had met there for the purposes of their scheme. Moreover, in order to narrow the question, I will assume that, so far as the statute of limitations is concerned, an overt act done anywhere with the express or implied consent of conspirators would show the conspiracy to be continuing between the parties so consenting, and leave them open to prosecution for three years from that date. But it does not follow that an overt act draws the conspiracy to wherever such overt act may be done, and whether it does so or not is the question before us now.

"In order to answer this question it is not enough to say that as the overt act was one that was contemplated by the conspirators it is treated as the act of them all, and that this is equivalent to saying that they were constructively present. That would be passing a *dicto secundum quid ad dictum simpliciter*. They are chargeable there for the act, but it does not follow that they were there to other intents. They are shown not to have been by the fact that they could not be treated as fugitives from justice even in respect of that very act, when and although that act was itself a crime. . . .

"To speak of constructive presence is to use the language of fiction, and so to hinder precise analysis. When a man is said to be constructively present where the consequences of an act done elsewhere are felt, it is meant that for some special purpose he will be treated as he would have been treated if he had been present, although he was not. For instance, if a man acting in one State sets forces in motion that kill a man in another, or produces or induces some consequence in that other that it regards as very hurtful and wishes to prevent, the latter State is very likely to say that if it can catch him it will punish him, although he was not subject to its laws when he did the act. . . . But as States usually confine their threats to those within the jurisdiction at the time of the act . . . the symmetry of general theory is preserved by saying that the offender was constructively present in the case supposed. . . . We must not forget facts, however. He was not present in fact, and in theory of law he was present only so far as to be charged with the act.

"Obviously the use of this fiction or form of words must not be pushed to such a point in the administration of the national law as to transgress the requirement of the Constitution that the trial of crimes shall be held in the State and district where the crimes shall have been committed (Article III, Section 2, Clause 3; Amendments, Article VI). With the country extending from ocean to ocean this requirement is even more important now than it was a hundred years ago and must be enforced in letter and spirit if we are to make impossible hardships amounting to grievous wrongs.

"In the case of conspiracy the danger is conspicuously brought out. Every overt act done in aid of it of course is attributed to the conspirators, and if that means that the conspiracy is present as such wherever every overt act is done, it might be at the choice of the Government to prosecute in any one of the twenty States in none of which the conspirators had been. And as wherever two or more have united for the commission of a crime there is a conspiracy, the opening to opression thus made is very wide indeed. It is even wider if success should be held not to merge the conspiracy in the crime intended and achieved. I think it unnecessary to dwell on oppressions that I believe have been practiced or on the constitutional history impressively adduced by Mr. A. S. Worthington [counsel for the petitioners] to show that this is one of the wrongs that our forefathers meant to prevent.

"No distinction can be taken based on the gravity of the overt act, or the fact that it was contemplated, or that it is important for the accomplishment of the substantive evil that the conspiracy aims to bring about and the law seeks to prevent. That would be carrying over the law of attempts to where it does not belong. Although both are adjective crimes, a conspiracy is not an attempt, even under Revised Statutes § 5440, which requires an overt act. When I first read that section I thought that it was an indefinite enlargement of the law of attempts. But reflection and the decisions both convinced me that I was wrong. The statute simply did away with a doubt as to the requirements of the common law. . . . An attempt, in the strictest sense, is an act expected to bring about a substantive wrong by the forces of nature. With it is classed the kindred offense where the act and the natural conditions present or supposed to be present are not enough to do the harm without a further act, but where it is so near to the result that if coupled with an intent to produce that result, the danger is very great. . . .

"But combination, intention, and overt act may all be present without amounting to a criminal attempt—as if all that were done should be an agreement to murder a man fifty miles away and the purchase of a pistol for the purpose. There must be dangerous proximity to success. But when that exists the overt act is the essence of the offense. On the other hand, the essence of the conspiracy is being combined for an unlawful purpose—and if an overt act is required, it does not matter how remote the act may be from accomplishing the purpose if done to effect it; that is, I suppose, in furtherance of it in any degree. In this case the statute treats the conspiracy as the crime and the indictment follows the statute.

"The cases in this Court have agreed that the statute has not made the overt act a part of the crime, which still remains the conspiracy alone. By the same reasoning the overt act gives no ground for the application of Revised Statutes § 731, creating a double jurisdiction when an offense against the United States is begun in one district and completed in another. The act is no part of the conspiracy even if it is an element in some other crime, as is stated in so many words in *Hyde* v. *Shine*, 199 U. S. 62, 76, quoting the well-known statement in *United States* v. *Britton*, 108 U. S. 199, 204, that the statutory requirement merely affords a *locus penitentiae.* . . . The overt act is simply evidence that the conspiracy has passed beyond words and is on foot when the act is done. As a test of actuality it is made a condition to punishment, but it is no more a part of the crime than it was at common law, where it was customary to allege such an act; or than is the fact that the statute of limitations has not run.

"I can think of no other case in which it would be argued that an act constituting no part of the crime charged draws jurisdiction to the place where it is done. Even when the act is the substance of a felony the history of law shows that the courts only slowly and with hesitation came to the admission that a man, although within the jurisdiction, could be a principal when he was not present at the accomplishment of the crime. . . . The distinction between principal and accessory before the fact is a late surviving expression of the doubt. . . . When the accessory is in a different jurisdiction it has been held that he could not be convicted as such in the place of the crime, even in modern cases. . . . It would be an amazing extension of even the broadest form of fiction if it should be held that an otherwise innocent overt act done in one State drew to itself a conspiracy in another State to defraud people in the latter, even though the first State would punish a conspiracy to commit a fraud beyond its own boundaries.

"Of course in the present case the conspiracy as well as the overt act was within the United States, but the case that I have supposed of different jurisdictions is a perfect test of where the crime was committed. If a conspiracy exists wherever an overt act is done in aid of it, the act ought to give jurisdiction over conspirators in a foreign State, if later they should be caught in the place where the act was done.

"The defendants were in California and never left the State, so far as this case is concerned. The fraud, assuming as I do for the purpose of the decision that there was one, was to get land from the United States there and elsewhere on the Pacific Coast. If successful it would be punished there. The crime with which the defendants are charged is having been engaged in or members of a conspiracy, nothing else; no act, other than what is implied as necessary to signify their understanding to each other. It is punished only to create a further obstacle to the ultimate crime in California. The defendants never were members of a conspiracy within a thousand miles of the District in fact. Yet if a lawyer entered his appearance there in a case before the Land Department, and the defendants directed it and expected to profit by it in carrying out their plans, it is said that we should feign that they were here in order to warrant their being taken across the continent and tried in this place.

"The Constitution is not to be satisfied with a fiction. When a man causes an unlawful act, as in the case of a prohibited use of the mails, it needs no fiction to say that the crime is committed at the place of the act wherever the man may be. . . . But when the offense consists solely in relation to other men with a certain intent, it is pure fiction to say that the relation is maintained and present in the case supposed. If the Government, instead of prosecuting for the substantive offense, charges only conspiracy to commit it, trial ought to be where the conspiracy exists in fact.

"The effect of an overt act upon the statute of limitations is consistent with what I have said. If an overt act is done with the consent of the conspirators, and to effect their end, the reason why the statute begins to run afresh is not that a new conspiracy is made or the old one renewed by the act, but that the facts supposed show conclusively that the conspiracy is continuing in life. So long as it does so it cannot be barred, although the earlier years of it may be.

"To avoid misapprehension the distinction should be noted between acts done in aid of a conspiracy and acts that constitute and call it into being. If a conspiracy should be formed by letters between men living in California, Louisiana and Massachusetts, who never left their several States, nothing that I have said would disparage the right of the Government to indict them where in contemplation of the law the agreement was made.

"It is said that the conspiracy may be a secret one; but that cannot affect the tests of jurisdiction. The overt act may amount to evidence not only of its existence but of its place. But to treat overt acts as evidence is one thing; it is quite another to treat any overt act as sufficient in itself to give jurisdiction, although the conspiracy exists only in another place.

"The intimations that are to be found, opposed to the view that I take, appear to have been induced by the confusion that I have tried to dispel, and to assume that an overt act creates jurisdiction over a conspiracy on the same ground that causing a death may give jurisdiction in murder; or perhaps, in *The King* v. *Brisac*, 4 East 164, 171, to proceed on the dangerous analogy of treasonable conspiracies to levy war or compass the death of the sovereign. The dictum in that case gains no new force from the repetition by text writers. It is one of the misfortunes of the law that ideas become encysted in phrases and thereafter for a long time cease to provoke further analysis.

"On the other hand, if overt acts had been regarded as founding jurisdiction, the petitioners could not have been discharged in *Tinsley* v. *Treat*, 205 U. S. 20, where overt acts of other conspirators within the jurisdiction were alleged and not denied. Although the point was not mentioned in the opinion, it was argued and was not overlooked. At least in the absence of clear statutory words I am of opinion that logic and the policy and general intent of the Constitution agree in refusing to extend the fiction of constructive presence to a case like this. I think that the true view still is that of *Reg.* v. *Best*, 1 Salk. 174, 'The *venue* must be where the conspiracy was, not where the result of the conspiracy is put in execution,' quoted as correct in principle in Markby's edition of *Roscoe's Criminal Evidence*, 6th ed., 391; and that to decide otherwise is to overrule not only the often expressed and settled understanding but the express decisions of this Court."

Hyde and Schneider v. *United States*
225 U. S. 347, 384

(*Brown* v. *Elliott*, 1911)

"THESE ARE appeals from orders denying writs of habeas corpus on the same state of facts, which can be set out in a few words. The petitioners were taken into custody in California for removal to Omaha, in the District of Nebraska, for trial before the District Court there, and severally petitioned for habeus corpus on the ground that the indictment showed that the Omaha court had no jurisdiction of the alleged offense. The indictment is under Revised Statutes § 5440 . . . for conspiring to commit an offense against the United States, namely, to send and receive letters through the Post Office in pursuance of a complex scheme to defraud various people, contrary to Revised Statutes § 5480. . . .

"The scheme contemplated the hiring of Post Office boxes in Omaha and other places, in six different States; and the hiring of a box there and the posting and receiving of letters in that place by conspirators other than the petitioners, are alleged as overt acts done in pursuance of the scheme. But it is alleged that the place where the conspiracy was formed is unknown, no place is laid for its continuance, and the petitioners are not shown to have been engaged in it in Omaha or ever to have been in the place. Therefore no jurisdiction is shown unless the averment of the above-mentioned overt acts makes up for all that is left out.

"To deny the jurisdiction, however, I must go farther than was necessary in *Hyde* v. *United States*. For in this case the offense against the United States named as the proximate object of the conspiracy, viz., the sending of letters through the Post Office in aid of the ultimately intended fraud, is alleged to have been accomplished, and indeed is laid as the overt act. But all the parties to the conspiracy could have been indicted in Omaha for the use of the Post Office there in pursuance of their plan by some of their number, and it naturally may be asked how it can be possible that the petitioners should be collectively guilty of unlawfully using the mails in Omaha but not guilty of being combined there for that purpose.

"The answer has been suggested at least by what I have said in the case of *Hyde*. The parties are liable to punishment where the prohibited act was done, not on the ground of a fiction that they were present, but in spite of the fact that they were not present. And they well may be dealt with there if they can be reached for bringing about what is deemed a harm in that place. But when they are punished for being and not for doing, when the offense consists in no act beyond the osmose of mutual understanding, they should be punished only where they are,—only where the wrongful relation exists.

"The United States can reach them equally, it is true, in either case, but as it can try them only where the crime has been committed, the test to be applied is the same that would be applied if the crime arose under the law of one of the States. It does not follow from the defendants' liability in Omaha for certain results of their conspiracy that they can be tried there for the conspiracy itself. I assume for purposes of decision, whatever misgivings may be felt as to the justice of indicting for a conspiracy to do what actually has been done, that an indictment will lie. . . . But I am of opinion that Omaha is not the proper jurisdiction in which to bring it.

"If the case were decided on the narrow ground that for the purposes of removal an allegation of conspiracy 'then and there' in the middle of the indictment was to be taken to refer to the caption and the place where the indictment was found, I should say nothing. But as general principles are thought to be involved I think it proper to state my opinion about them."

Brown v. *Elliott*
225 U. S. 392, 402

V. On Escaping Taxes

Wisconsin's Loss

(*Schlesinger* v. *Wisconsin*, 1925)

A WISCONSIN LAW PROVIDED THAT EVERY TRANSFER MADE WITHIN six years of the death of the grantor, vendor or donor of a material part of his estate shall be construed to have been made in contemplation of death. The statute affected the widow and three children of one Schlesinger who had made gifts to them totaling five million dollars before he died in 1921. Ordered to pay an inheritance tax, the executors said that they were being deprived of property without due process of law and attacked the statute as denying equal protection of the laws.

On both grounds Mr. Justice McReynolds held the law in conflict with the Fourteenth Amendment. It was arbitrary to tax gifts made six years before death and not to tax earlier ones, he said; a State is forbidden to deny due process whether to prevent evasion or for any other purpose.

Justices Brandeis and Stone joined in Holmes' dissent:

"IF THE Fourteenth Amendment were now before us for the first time I should think it ought to be construed more narrowly than it has been construed in the past. But even now it seems to me not too late to urge that in dealing with State legislation upon matters of substantive law we should avoid with great caution attempts to substitute our judgment for that of the body whose business it is in the first place with regard to questions of domestic policy that are fairly open to debate.

[203]

"The present seems to me one of those questions. I leave aside the broader issues that might be considered and take the statute as it is written, putting the tax on the ground of an absolute presumption that gifts of a material part of the donor's estate made within six years of his death were made in contemplation of death.

"If the time were six months instead of six years I hardly think that the power of the State to pass the law would be denied, as the difficulty of proof would warrant making the presumption absolute; and while I should not dream of asking where the line can be drawn, since the great body of the law consists in drawing such lines, yet when you realize that you are dealing with a matter of degree you must realize that reasonable men may differ widely as to the place where the line should fall.

"I think that our discussion should end if we admit, what I certainly believe, that reasonable men might regard six years as not too remote. Of course many gifts will be hit by the tax that were made with no contemplation of death. But the law allows a penumbra to be embraced that goes beyond the outline of its object in order that the object may be secured.

"A typical instance is the prohibition of the sale of unintoxicating malt liquors in order to make effective a prohibition of the sale of beer. The power 'is not to be denied simply because some innocent articles or transactions may be found within the proscribed class.' . . . In such cases (and they are familiar) the Fourteenth Amendment is invoked in vain. Later cases follow the principle. . . .

"I am not prepared to say that the Legislature of Wisconsin, which is better able to judge than I am, might not believe, as the Supreme Court of the State confidently affirms, that by far the larger proportion of gifts coming under the statute actually were made in contemplation of death. I am not prepared to say that if the Legislature held that belief, it might not extend the tax to gifts made within six years of death in order to make sure that its policy of taxation should not be escaped. I think that with the States as with Congress, when the means are not prohibited and are calculated to effect the object, we ought not to inquire into the degree of the necessity for resorting to them. . . .

"It may be worth noticing that the gifts of millions taxed in this case were made from about four years before death to a little over one year. The statute is not called upon in its full force in order to justify this tax. If I thought it necessary I should ask myself whether it should not be construed as intending to get as near to six years as it constitutionally could, and whether it would be bad for a year and a month."

Schlesinger et al., Executors, etc., v. Wisconsin et al.
270 U. S. 230, 241

A Judge's Immunity

(*Evans* v. *Gore*, 1919)

A DISTRICT COURT JUDGE IN KENTUCKY, WALTER EVANS, PAID HIS income tax under protest. An Act of 1919, under the authority of the Sixteenth Amendment, levied a direct income tax on all residents of this country without excluding federal office-holders. It was void, Evans contended, because the Constitution stipulates that their compensation "shall not be diminished"—and the Act in effect reduced his salary.

In the majority opinion Mr. Justice Van Devanter recalled the discussion that had taken place in Congress when the statute was being passed and the expectation there that the Supreme Court would settle the point. He declared that the Amendment did not authorize that tax; that Article III of the Constitution was meant to safeguard the judges' independence and was not a private grant to them but a limitation in the public interest.

"We conclude that the tax was imposed contrary to the constitutional prohibition and so must be adjudged invalid," said the majority.

Holmes dissented (Brandeis concurring):

"THIS IS an action brought by the plaintiff in error against an acting Collector of Internal Revenue to recover a portion of income tax paid by the former. The ground of the suit is that the plaintiff is entitled to deduct from the total of his net income six thousand dollars, being the amount of his salary as a judge of the District Court of the United States. The Act of February 24, 1919 . . . taxes the net income of every individual and requires the compensation received by the judges of the United States to be included in the gross income from which the net income is to be computed. This was done by the plaintiff in error and the tax was paid under protest. He contends that the requirement mentioned and the tax, to the extent that it was enhanced by consideration of the plaintiff's salary, are contrary to Article III, § 1, of the Constitution, which provides that the compensation of judges shall not be diminished during their continuance in office. Upon demurrer judgment was entered for the defendant, and the case comes here upon the single question of the validity of the above-mentioned provisions of the Act.

"The decision below seems to me to have been right for two distinct reasons: that this tax would have been valid under the original Constitution, and that if not so, it was made lawful by the Sixteenth Amendment. In the first place, I think that the clause protecting the compensation of judges has no reference to a case like this. The exemption of salaries from diminution is intended to secure the independence of the judges on the ground, as it was put by Hamilton in the *Federalist* (No. 79) that 'a power over a man's subsistence amounts to a power over his will.' That is a very good reason for preventing attempts to deal with a judge's salary as such, but it seems to me no reason for exonerating him from the ordinary duties of a citizen, which he shares with all others. To require a man to pay the taxes that all other men have to pay cannot possibly be made an instrument to attack his independence as a judge. I see nothing in the purpose of this clause of the Constitution to indicate that the judges were to be a privileged class free from bearing their share of the cost of the institutions upon which their well-being if not their life depends.

"I see equally little in the letter of the clause to indicate the intent supposed. The tax on net incomes is a tax on the balance of a mutual account in which there always are some and may be many items on both sides. It seems to me that it cannot be affected by an inquiry into the source from which the items more or less remotely are derived. Obviously there is some point at which the immunity of a judge's salary stops, or to put it in the language of the clause, a point at which it could not be said that his compensation was diminished by a charge. If he bought a house the fact that a part or the whole of the price had been paid from his compensation as judge would not exempt the house. So if he bought bonds. Yet in such cases the advantages of his salary would be diminished. Even if the house or bonds were bought with other money the same would be true, since the money would not have been free for such an application if he had not used his salary to satisfy other more peremptory needs.

"At some point, I repeat, money received as salary loses its specific character as such. Money held in trust loses its identity by being mingled with the general funds of the owner. I see no reason why the same should not be true of a salary. But I do not think that the result could be avoided by keeping the salary distinct. I think that the moment the salary is received, whether kept distinct or not, it becomes part of the general income of the owner and is mingled with the rest, in theory of law, as an item in the mutual account with the United States. I see no greater reason for exempting the recipients while they still have the income as income than when they have invested it in a house or bond.

"The decisions heretofore reached by this Court seem to me to justify my conclusion. In *Peck & Co.* v. *Lowe*, 247 U. S. 165, a tax was levied by Congress upon the income of the plaintiff corporation. More than two-thirds of the income were derived from exports and the Constitution in terms prohibits any tax on articles exported from any State. By construction it had been held to create 'a freedom from any tax which directly burdens the exportation.' . . . The prohibition was unequivocal and express, not merely an inference as in the present case. Yet it was held unanimously that the tax was valid. 'It is not laid on income from exportation because of its source, in a discriminative way, but just as it is laid on other income.*** There is no discrimination. At most, exportation is affected only indirectly and remotely. The tax is levied*** after the recipient of the income is free to use it as he chooses. Thus what is taxed —the net income—is as far removed from exportation as are articles intended for export before the exportation begins.' . . . And all this applies with even greater force when, as I have observed, the Constitution has no words that forbid a tax. In *United States Glue Co.* v. *Oak Creek*, 247 U. S. 321, 329, the same principle was affirmed as to interstate commerce and it was said that if there was no discrimination against such commerce the tax constituted one of the ordinary burdens of government from which parties were not exempted because they happened to be engaged in commerce among the States.

"A second and independent reason why this tax appears to me valid is that, even if I am wrong as to the scope of the original document, the Sixteenth Amendment justifies the tax, whatever would have been the law before it was applied. By that Amendment, Congress is given power to 'collect taxes on incomes, from whatever source derived.' It is true that it goes on 'without apportionment among the several States, and without regard to any census or enumeration,' and this shows the particular difficulty that led to it. But the only cause of that difficulty was an attempt to trace income to its source, and it seems to me that the Amendment was intended to put an end to the cause and not merely to obviate a single result. I do not see how judges can claim an abatement of their income tax on the ground that an item in their gross income is salary, when the power is given expressly to tax incomes from whatever source derived."

Evans v. *Gore, Deputy and Acting Collector of Internal Revenue for the Western District of Kentucky*
253 U. S. 245, 264

[209]

Deeds Instead of Wills

(Chanler v. Kelsey, 1906)

WILLIAM B. ASTOR EXECUTED A NUMBER OF DEEDS FROM 1844 TO 1865, giving his daughter, Mrs. Delano, the power to appoint heirs to his property so that there would be no succession in the legal sense (and no succession tax) as the property did not belong to her. But the State of New York taxed the inheritances which fell to her heirs. The tax was imposed by virtue of an Act of 1897 which provided that when a power of appointment was made the appointment should be deemed a transfer, whether the power came from a disposition of the property made before the passage of the law or after.

The beneficiaries of Mrs. Delano invoked the Fourteenth Amendment: the tax took property without due process. They called Article I to their aid: the tax impaired a contract.

Mr. Justice Day, for the majority, found no violation of the Constitution on either score; the statute was valid. Estates created by the execution of a power took effect in common law as if created by the original deeds, and there was no error in the surrogate's judgment.

Mr. Justice Holmes dissented (Justice Moody concurring):

"I HAVE the misfortune to differ from the majority of my brethren in this case, and although the argument which seemed and still seems to me unanswerable was presented and has not prevailed, I think that the principles involved are of sufficient importance to justify a statement of the reasons of my dissent. A State succession tax stands on different grounds from a similar tax by the United States or a general tax upon transfers.

It is more unlimited in its possible extent, if not altogether unlimited, and therefore it is necessary that the boundaries of the
power to levy such taxes should be accurately understood and
defined.

"I always have believed that a state inheritance tax was an
exercise of the power of regulating the devolution of property
by inheritance or will upon the death of the owner,—a power
which belongs to the States; and I have been fortified in my
belief by the utterances of this Court from the time of Chief
Justice Taney to the present day. . . . For that reason the
power is more unlimited than the power of a State to tax transfers generally or the power of the United States to levy an inheritance tax. The distinction between State and United States
inheritance taxes was recognized in *Knowlton* v. *Moore,* 178
U. S. 41, 58, and whatever may be thought of the decision in
Snyder v. *Bettman,* 190 U. S. 249, I do not understand it to
import a denial of the distinction, reaffirmed by the dissenting
members of the Court. . . .

"If then a given State tax must be held to be a succession
tax in order to maintain its validity, or if in fact it is held to be
a succession tax by the State court of which it is the province to
decide the matter, it follows that such a tax cannot be levied
except where there is a succession, and when some element or
step necessary to complete it still is wanting when the tax law
goes into effect.

"If some element is wanting at that time, the succession depends for taking effect on the continuance of the permission to
succeed or grant of the right on the part of the State; and as
the grant may be withdrawn, it may be qualified by a tax. But
if there is no succession, or if the succession has fully vested
or has passed beyond dependence upon the continuing of the
State's permission or grant, an attempt to levy a tax under the
power to regulate succession would be an attempt to appropriate
property in a way which the Fourteenth Amendment has been

construed to forbid. No matter what other taxes might be levied, a succession tax could not be, and so it has been decided in New York. . . .

"It is not denied that the tax under consideration is a succession tax. The Court of Appeals treated it as such in the present case. It said: 'If the power had been exercised by deed a different question would have arisen, but it was exercised by will and, owing to the full and complete control by the Legislature of the making, the form, and the substance of wills, it can impose a charge or tax for doing anything by will.' . . . That it was such a tax and valid for that reason was decided in *Matter of Dows*, 167 N. Y. 227, affirmed by this Court. . . . And these decisions and some of the other decisions of this Court cited above were relied upon by the Court of Appeals. . . . Probably the tax would be invalid for other local reasons besides those mentioned in *Matter of Dows*, but for the construction which it has received. . . .

"This being then a succession tax, I should have thought it plain that there was no succession for it to operate upon. More precisely, even if otherwise any element of succession could have been found, a matter that I think would need explanation, the execution of the power did not depend in any way upon the continued coöperation of the laws of New York by way of permission or grant.

"I am not concerned to criticize the statement of the Court of Appeals that in substance it is the execution of the power that gives to the grantee the property passing under it. It is enough if it is remembered that the instrument executing the power derives none of its efficiency in that respect from the present laws of New York. It is true that the instrument happens to be a will, and that it could not have operated as a will except by the grant of the privilege from the State at the time when Mrs. Delano died. But what would execute the power depended, in the first place, upon the deed creating it, and if that deed did not require a will but only an instrument otherwise sufficiently characterized, it did not matter whether the instrument was also good as a will or not. . . .

"What the deeds which I am considering required was 'an instrument in its nature testamentary to be acknowledged by her (Mrs. Delano) as a deed in the presence of two witnesses or published by her as a will.' The language was chosen carefully, I presume, in view of the incapacities of married women at that time. By the terms used a will was unnecessary. It was enough if Mrs. Delano sealed and acknowledged an instrument in its nature testamentary in the presence of two witnesses, whether it was good as a will or not. . . . This she did. In *Orr* v. *Gilman*, 183 U. S. 278, the power was created by will, and, what is more obviously material, it required a will for its execution, and so might be held to invoke and submit itself to the law in force when the execution should take place. Therefore that case has no bearing upon this.

"The ground upon which this tax is imposed is, I repeat, the right of the State to regulate or, if it sees fit, to destroy inheritances. If it might not have appropriated the whole it cannot appropriate any part by the law before us. And I also repeat that it has no bearing upon the matter that by a different law the State might have derived an equal revenue from those donees in the form of a tax. I do not understand it to be suggested that the State without compensation could have appropriated the remainder after Mrs. Delano's life, which Mr. Astor parted with in 1844 and shortly following years. If it could not have done so I am unable to see on what ground this tax is not void. The English decisions throw no light upon the question before us because they are concerned only with the construction of statutes which, however construed, are law."

Chanler v. *Kelsey, Comptroller of the State of New York*
205 U. S. 466, 479

[213]

Stock Dividends

(*Eisner* v. *Macomber*, 1919)

INSTEAD OF GIVING CASH, THE STANDARD OIL CO. OF CALIFORNIA declared a stock dividend of about $25,000,000 in 1916. Under the Revenue Act of that year stock dividends were to be regarded as income. One of the holders paid her tax on the new stock but protested and sued to recover, contending that it was a direct tax on property violating Article I of the Constitution and not within the meaning of the Sixteenth Amendment.

Holmes had delivered the majority opinion in *Towne* v. *Eisner*, finding stock dividends not taxable under the Revenue Act of 1913, and on this authority a District Court ordered the tax returned. But the Government maintained the right of Congress to tax gains (cash dividends) "when wearing a new dress"; the same earnings were passed to stockholders in an equally concrete form. On the other side it was said that a stock dividend was a capital gain, a mere increase in valuation, a certified expression of undivided surplus and capitalization, and was not income until realized.

Mr. Justice Pitney agreed that there was a distinction between gain derived from capital (income) and gain accruing to capital (growth of investment). The Sixteenth Amendment speaks of "incomes from whatever source derived." Such a tax as the Act of 1916 laid was a tax on capital increase, he said, forbidden by Article I; a tax on property must be apportioned according to population. Although Pitney held that *Towne* v. *Eisner* controlled, Holmes differed (as did Brandeis and Day):

"I THINK that *Towne* v. *Eisner* was right in its reasoning and result, and that on sound principles the stock dividend was not income. But it was clearly intimated in that case that the construction of the statute then before the Court might be different from that of the Constitution. . . . I think that the word 'incomes' in the Sixteenth Amendment should be read in 'a sense most obvious to the common understanding at the time of its adoption.' . . . For it was for public adoption that it was proposed. . . .

"The known purpose of this Amendment was to get rid of nice questions as to what might be direct taxes, and I cannot doubt that most people not lawyers would suppose when they voted for it that they put a question like the present to rest. I am of opinion that the Amendment justifies the tax. . . ."

Eisner, as Collector of U. S. Internal Revenue for the Third District of the State of New York, v. *Macomber*
252 U. S. 189, 219

Foreign Insurance Policies

(*Compania General* v. *Collector*, 1927)

THE PHILIPPINE INSURANCE ACT PROVIDED FOR A TAX OF ONE percent payable by insurance companies on all premiums paid in the Islands. Where policies were obtained from foreign companies having no agents there the same amount was levied, but as a direct tax on the policyholder. Was this a denial of equal protection? Was the tax really a penalty? These were the questions.

The Court considered the policies separately. Where fire risks involved the right of a London insurance company (which had an agent in the Philippines) to do business in the Islands, the tax had to be paid, although the policy was issued from London to the Barcelona headquarters of the insured. But where a marine policy was issued to Barcelona by a Paris firm having no agent in the Islands, the tax was outside the Government's jurisdiction.

Chief Justice Taft said that the latter tax was manifestly a fine to discourage insurance companies not paying tribute to the State; it was not laid on insured property but on a contract or its proceeds, which were not in the Philippines nor expected to be there.

Holmes wrote:

"THIS IS a suit to recover the amount of a tax alleged to have been illegally imposed. The plaintiff is a Spanish corporation licensed to do business in the Philippine Islands and having an office in Manila. In 1922 from time to time it bought goods and put them in its Philippine warehouses. It notified its head office in Barcelona, Spain, of the value of the goods and that office thereupon insured them under open policies issued by a company of London.

"From time to time also the Philippine branch shipped goods abroad for sale and secured insurance upon the shipments in the same manner, the premiums being charged to it in both cases.

"By the Philippine Insurance Act . . . where owners of property obtain insurance directly with foreign companies, the owners are required to report each case to the Collector of Internal Revenue and to 'pay the tax of one per centum on premium paid, in the manner required by law of insurance companies.'

"The defendant Collector collected this tax on the above-mentioned premiums from the plaintiff against its protest. The plaintiff bases its suit upon the contentions that the statute is contrary to the Act of Congress of August 29, 1916, c. 416, § 3 (the Jones Act), 39 Stat. 545, 546, 547, as depriving it of its property without due process of law, and also as departing from the requirement in the same section that the rules of taxation shall be uniform. The Supreme Court of the Philippines upheld the tax. A writ of certiorari was granted by this Court. . . .

"The plaintiff's reliance is upon *Allgeyer* v. *Louisiana,* 165 U. S. 578, in which it was held that a fine could not be imposed by the State for sending a notice similar to the present to an insurance company out of the State. But it seems to me that the tax was justified and that this case is distinguished from that of *Allgeyer* and from *St. Louis Cotton Compress Co.* v. *Arkansas,* 260 U. S. 346, by a difference between a penalty and a tax.

"It is true, as indicated in the last cited case, that every exaction of money for an act is a discouragement to the extent of the payment required, but that which in its immediacy is a discouragement may be part of an encouragement when seen in its organic connection with the whole. Taxes are what we pay for civilized society, including the chance to insure. A penalty on the other hand is intended altogether to prevent the thing punished. It readily may be seen that a State may tax things that under the Constitution as interpreted it cannot prevent. The constitutional right asserted in *Allgeyer* v. *Louisiana* to earn one's livelihood by any lawful calling certainly is consistent, as we all know, with the calling being taxed.

"Sometimes there may be a difficulty in deciding whether an imposition is a tax or a penalty, but generally the intent to prohibit, when it exists, is plainly expressed. Sometimes even when it is called a tax the requirement is shown to be a penalty by its excess in amount over the tax in similar cases, as in *St. Louis Cotton Compress Co.* v. *Arkansas.* But in the present instance there is no room for doubt. The charge not only is called a tax but is the same in amount as that imposed where the right to impose it is not denied.

"The Government has the insured within its jurisdiction. I can see no ground for denying its right to use its power to tax unless it can be shown that it has conferred no benefit of a kind that would justify the tax, as is held with regard to property outside of a State belonging to one within it. . . . But here an act was done in the Islands that was intended by the plaintiff to be and was an essential step towards the insurance, and, if that is not enough, the Government of the Islands was protecting the property at the very moment in respect of which it levied the tax. Precisely this question was met and disposed of in *Equitable Life Assur. Soc.* v. *Pennsylvania,* 238 U. S. 143, 147.

"The result of upholding the Government's action is just. When it taxes domestic insurance it reasonably may endeavor not to let the foreign insurance escape. If it does not discriminate against the latter, it naturally does not want to discriminate against its own.

"The suggestion that the rule of taxation is not uniform

may be disposed of in a few words. The uniformity required is uniformity in substance, not in form. The insurance is taxed uniformly, and although in the case of domestic insurance the tax is laid upon the company whereas here it is laid upon the insured, it must be presumed that in the former case the company passes the tax on to the insured as an element in the premium charged.

"For these reasons Mr. Justice Brandeis and I are of opinion that the judgment of the Supreme Court of the Islands should be affirmed."

Compania General de Tabacos de Filipinas
v. Collector of Internal Revenue
275 U. S. 87, 99

Authority of Congress

(*Untermyer* v. *Anderson*, 1927)

A RESIDENT OF NEW YORK GAVE AWAY PROPERTY WHILE A BILL TO make gifts taxable was under discussion in Congress. Two days later it was passed as the Revenue Act of 1924.

The Court held that the Act applied to the full calendar year; therefore, by affecting bona fide gifts made before the law was proclaimed, the gift-tax provisions were arbitrary and invalid. (Due process clause, Fifth Amendment.)

Taxpayers ought not be required to guess the outcome of pending measures, said Mr. Justice McReynolds.

Mr. Justice Holmes had dwelt in *Adkins* v. *Children's Hospital* on "the vague contours of the Fifth Amendment," Brandeis recalled in his dissent in which Justices Stone and Holmes concurred.

Holmes himself wrote:

"**A**s I think the construction of the Act . . . adopted by four of us in *Blodgett* v. *Holden*, 275 U. S. 142, the proper one, I shall not go into the question of constitutionality beyond saying that I find it hard to state to myself articulately the ground for denying the power of Congress to lay the tax. We all know that we shall get a tax bill every year. I suppose that the taxing act may be passed in the middle as lawfully as at the beginning of the year. A tax may be levied for past privileges and protection as well as for those to come. . . . I do not imagine that the authority of Congress to tax the exercise of the legal power to make a gift will be doubted any more than its authority to tax a sale. Apart from its bearing upon construction and constitutionality I am not at liberty to consider the justice of the Act."

Untermyer, Executrix, et al.
v. Anderson, Collector
276 U. S. 440, 446

Royalties on Patents

(*Long* v. *Rockwood*, 1927)

WHERE A QUESTION OF STATE INCOME TAX ON PATENT ROYALTIES was raised the Court said that it was "almost absurd" to contend that a power given by the United States may be subject to state taxation; this would be equivalent to a tax on the patent right itself.

The Massachusetts tax commissioner contended that neither the purpose of the Government in promoting science nor the exclusive right granted to patentees was thus hampered. The Federal purpose was accomplished when a limited monopoly was granted in return for disclosing the process, he said.

But the Court considered patents in the light of instrumentalities of the Government's policy, as provided in Article I and in the patent laws; there was a benefit to the public in addition to the monopoly of the patentee. The courts of last resort in Pennsylvania and New York, as well as Massachusetts, had held so. "No opinion to the contrary has been cited," Mr. Justice McReynolds pointed out. Judgments recovering taxes were sustained.

Justices Brandeis, Sutherland and Stone agreed with Holmes' dissent:

"THESE ARE complaints brought by the respondent against the Commissioner of Corporations and Taxation of Massachusetts for the abatement of income taxes for the years 1921 and 1922. The question raised as stated by the Supreme Judicial Court of the State is whether the Commonwealth has the right to tax the income received from royalties for the use of patents issued by the United States. That court held that the Commonwealth had no such right under the Constitution of the

[222]

United States and the Commissioner obtained a writ of certiorari from this Court.

"The reasoning of the court is simple. If the State 'cannot tax the patent, it cannot tax the royalties received from its use.' The postulate is founded on the casual intimation of Chief Justice Marshall in *McCulloch* v. *Maryland*, 4 Wheat. 316, 432, and is said to have been conceded below by the Commissioner. It hardly is conceded here, and whether it is or not, if this Court should be of opinion that the conclusion urged by the Commissioner can be supported upon broader grounds than he felt at liberty to take, the Court is not estopped by his doubts. Why then cannot a State tax a patent by a tax that in no way discriminates against it?

"Obviously it is not true that patents are instrumentalities of the Government. They are used by the patentees for their private advantage alone. If the Government uses them it must pay like other people. . . . The use made by the patentee may be not to make and sell the patented article but simply to keep other people from doing so in aid of some collateral interest of his own. . . . National banks really are instrumentalities of the Government and directly concern the national credit. Indians are wards of the nation. Interstate commerce is left expressly to regulation by Congress, and the States can intermeddle only by its consent. In this case the advantages expected by the Government are mainly the benefits to the public when the patent has expired and secondarily the encouragement of invention. . . .

"The most that can be said is that a tax is a discouragement so far as it goes and to that extent in its immediate operation runs counter to the Government intent. But patents would be valueless to their owner without the organized societies constituted by the States, and the question is why patents should not contribute as other property does to maintaining that without which they would be of little use.

[223]

"Most powers conceivably may be exercised beyond the limits allowed by the law. Rights that even seem absolute have these qualifications. . . . But we do not on that account resort to the blunt expedient of taking away the power or the right. . . . The power to tax is said to be the power to destroy. But, to repeat what I have just now had occasion to say in another case, this Court, which so often has defeated the attempt to tax in certain ways, can defeat an attempt to discriminate or otherwise to go too far without wholly abolishing the power to tax.

"The power to fix rates is the power to destroy, but this Court while it endeavors to prevent confiscation does not prevent the fixing of rates. Even with regard to patents some laws of a kind that might destroy the use of them within the State have been upheld. . . . They must be reasonable or they will be held void, but if this Court deems them reasonable they stand. . . . The fact that the franchise came from a grant by the United States is no more reason for exemption, standing by itself, than is the derivation of the title to a lot of land from the same source. . . .

"In *Baltimore Shipbuilding & Dry Dock Co.* v. *Baltimore,* 195 U. S. 375, the land was conveyed subject to a condition that a dry-dock should be built upon it which the United States was to have the right to use free from charge for docking and which was to revert to the United States on a diversion of the land to any other use or on the dry-dock being unfit for use for six months. Certainly a case in which the United States was much more clearly interested than in an ordinary patent. Yet there it was held that neither the company nor the land was an instrumentality of the United States and that there was nothing to hinder the right of the State to tax. . . ."

Long, Commissioner, v. *Rockwood*
277 U. S. 142, 149

Sales to the Government

(*Panhandle* v. *United States*, 1927)

A MISSISSIPPI GASOLINE DEALER REFUSED TO PAY A STATE EXCISE TAX on certain sales because they had been made to the Federal Government. Mississippi countered that she was not demanding a tax from the United States but from gasoline dealers for the right to do business. Mr. Justice Butler held that the State did not give the dealer the right to sell to the United States, nor did that right depend upon state law but on the authority of the Government to choose its sources of supply.

The Constitution empowered the Government to operate the hospital to which the gasoline was sold, he said; authorization laws are supreme over conflicting state enactments; Mississippi could not tax transactions by which the United States obtained the supplies required for governmental purposes.

Four Justices dissented. McReynolds, in his opinion, dwelt on the doctrine of immunity while Brandeis and Stone joined with Holmes:

"THE STATE of Mississippi in 1924 and 1926 imposed upon distributors and retail dealers of gasoline, for the privilege of engaging in the business, an excise tax of three cents and four cents respectively per gallon sold in the State. The Supreme Court of the State declared it to be a privilege tax but points out that whether this tax is on the privilege or on the property it is imposed before the gasoline has left the dealer's hands.

"The plaintiff in error, a dealer, was sued by the State for certain sums that were due under the statutes. It pleaded that the sales in respect of which the tax was demanded were sales to the United States for the use of its Coast Guard and Veterans' Hospital, that these being instrumentalities of the Government it did not include the amount of the tax in the price charged, and that the statute did not and could not tax the dealer for them consistently with the Constitution of the United States. The Supreme Court of the State upheld the tax and pointed out the extreme consequence to which a different decision might lead.

"It seems to me that the state court was right. I should say plainly right but for the effect of certain dicta of Chief Justice Marshall which culminated in or rather were founded upon his often quoted proposition that the power to tax is the power to destroy. In those days it was not recognized as it is today that most of the distinctions of law are distinctions of degree. If the States had any power it was assumed that they had all power and that the necessary alternative was to deny it altogether.

"But this Court, which so often has defeated the attempt to tax in certain ways, can defeat an attempt to discriminate or otherwise go too far without wholly abolishing the power to tax. The power to tax is not the power to destroy while this Court sits. The power to fix rates is the power to destroy if unlimited, but this Court while it endeavors to prevent confiscation does not prevent the fixing of rates. A tax is not an unconstitutional regulation in every case where an absolute prohibition of sales would be one. . . .

"To come down more closely to the question before us, when the Government comes into a State to purchase I do not perceive why it should be entitled to stand differently from any other purchaser. It avails itself of the machinery furnished by the State and I do not see why it should not contribute in the same proportion that every other purchaser contributes for the privileges that it uses. It has no better or other right to use them than anyone else.

"The cost of maintaining the State that makes the business possible is just as necessary an element in the cost of production as labor or coal. If the plaintiff in error had paid the tax and had added it to the price, the Government would have had nothing to say. It could take the gasoline or leave it but it could not require the seller to abate his charge even if it had been arbitrarily increased in the hope of getting more from the Government than could be got from the public at large.

"But in fact the Government has not attempted to say anything in this case, which is simply that of a dealer trying to cut down a legitimate tax on his business because certain purchasers proposed to use the goods in a certain way, although so far as the sale was concerned they were free to turn the gasoline into the ocean, use it for private purposes, or sell it again. It does not appear that the Government would have refused to pay a price that included the tax if demanded, but if the Government had refused, it would not have exonerated the seller. . . .

"An imperfect analogy with taxation that affects interstate commerce is relied upon. Even the law on that subject has been liberalized since the decision of most of the cases cited. . . . But obviously it does not follow from the invalidity of a tax directly burdening interstate commerce that a tax upon a domestic seller is bad because he may be able to shift the burden to a purchaser, even though an agency of the Government, who is willing to pay the price with the tax and who had no rational ground for demanding favor.

"I am not aware that the President, the Members of Congress, the Judiciary or, to come nearer to the case in hand, the Coast Guard or the officials of the Veterans' Hospital, because they are instrumentalities of the Government and cannot function naked and unfed, hitherto have been held entitled to have their bills for food and clothing cut down so far as their butchers and tailors have been taxed on their sales; and I had not supposed that the butchers and tailors could omit from their tax returns all receipts from the large class of customers to which I have referred. The question of interference with Government, I repeat, is one of reasonableness and degree, and it seems to me that the interference in this case is too remote. . . ."

Panhandle Oil Co. v. *Mississippi,*
ex. rel. Knox, Attorney General
277 U. S. 218, 222

THE ESPIONAGE ACT: MAJORITY OPINIONS

Free Speech Not Free

(Schenck v. United States, 1918)

MR. JUSTICE HOLMES WAS SELECTED TO DELIVER THE OPINION OF the unanimous Court in the three Espionage Act cases which follow:

"THIS IS an indictment in three counts. The first charges a conspiracy to violate the Espionage Act of June 15, 1917 . . . by causing and attempting to cause insubordination, &c., in the military and naval forces of the United States, and to obstruct the recruiting and enlistment service of the United States, when the United States was at war with the German Empire, to-wit, that the defendants wilfully conspired to have printed and circulated to men who had been called and accepted for military service under the Act of May 18, 1917, a document set forth and alleged to be calculated to cause such insubordination and obstruction. The count alleges overt acts in pursuance of the conspiracy, ending in the distribution of the document set forth.

"The second count alleges a conspiracy to commit an offense against the United States, to-wit, to use the mails for transmission of matter declared to be non-mailable by Title XII, § 2, of the Act of June 15, 1917, to-wit, the above-mentioned document, with an averment of the same overt acts. The third count charges an unlawful use of the mails for the transmission of the same matter and otherwise as above. The defendants were found guilty on all the counts. They set up the First Amendment to the Constitution forbidding Congress to

[231]

make any law abridging the freedom of speech, or of the press, and bringing the case here on that ground have argued some other points also of which we must dispose.

"It is argued that the evidence, if admissible, was not sufficient to prove that the defendant Schenck was concerned in sending the documents. According to the testimony Schenck said he was general secretary of the Socialist Party and had charge of the Socialist headquarters from which the documents were sent. He identified a book found there as the minutes of the Executive Committee of the party. The book showed a resolution of August 13, 1917, that fifteen thousand leaflets should be printed on the other side of one of them in use, to be mailed to men who had passed exemption boards, and for distribution.

"Schenck personally attended to the printing. On August 20 the general secretary's report said, 'Obtained new leaflets from printer and started work addressing envelopes,' &c.; and there was a resolve that Comrade Schenck be allowed $125 for sending leaflets through the mail. He said that he had about fifteen or sixteen thousand printed. There were files of the circular in question in the inner office which he said were printed on the other side of the one-sided circular and were there for distribution. Other copies were proved to have been sent through the mails to drafted men. Without going into confirmatory details that were proved, no reasonable man could doubt that the defendant Schenck was largely instrumental in sending the circulars about. As to the defendant Baer, there was evidence that she was a member of the Executive Board and that the minutes of its transactions were hers. The argument as to the sufficiency of the evidence that the defendants conspired to send the documents only impairs the seriousness of the real defense.

"It is objected that the documentary evidence was not admissible because obtained upon a search warrant, valid so far as appears. The contrary is established. . . . The search warrant did not issue against the defendant but against the Socialist headquarters at 1326 Arch Street [Philadelphia] and it would seem that the documents technically were not even in the defendant's possession. . . . Notwithstanding some protest in argument the notion that evidence even directly proceeding from the defendant in a criminal proceeding is excluded in all cases by the Fifth Amendment is plainly unsound. . . .

"The document in question upon its first printed side recited the first section of the Thirteenth Amendment, said that the idea embodied in it was violated by the Conscription Act and that a conscript is little better than a convict. In impassioned language it intimated that conscription was despotism in its worst form and a monstrous wrong against humanity in the interest of Wall Street's chosen few. It said, 'Do not submit to intimidation,' but in form at least confined itself to peaceful measures such as a petition for the repeal of the Act.

"The other and later printed side of the sheet was headed, 'Assert Your Rights.' It stated reasons for alleging that anyone violated the Constitution when he refused to recognize 'your right to assert your opposition to the draft,' and went on, 'If you do not assert and support your rights, you are helping to deny or disparage rights which it is the solemn duty of all citizens and residents of the United States to retain.' It described the arguments on the other side as coming from cunning politicians and a mercenary capitalist press, and even silent assent to the conscription law as helping to support an infamous conspiracy. It denied the power to send our citizens away to foreign shores to shoot up the people of other lands, and added that words could not express the condemnation such cold-blooded ruthlessness deserves, &c., winding up, 'You must do your share to maintain, support and uphold the rights of the people of this country.' Of course the document would not have been sent unless it had been intended to have some effect, and

[233]

we do not see what effect it could be expected to have upon persons subject to the draft except to influence them to obstruct the carrying of it out. The defendants do not deny that the jury might find against them on this point.

"But it is said, suppose that that was the tendency of this circular, it is protected by the First Amendment to the Constitution. Two of the strongest expressions are said to be quoted respectively from well-known public men. It well may be that the prohibition of laws abridging the freedom of speech is not confined to previous restraints, although to prevent them may have been the main purpose, as intimated in *Patterson* v. *Colorado*. [See page 251.]

"We admit that in many places and in ordinary times the defendants in saying all that was said in the circular would have been within their constitutional rights. But the character of every act depends upon the circumstances in which it is done. . . . The most stringent protection of free speech would not protect a man in falsely shouting fire in a theater and causing a panic. It does not even protect a man from an injunction against uttering words that may have all the effect of force. . . . The question in every case is whether the words used are used in such circumstances and are of such a nature as to create a clear and present danger that they will bring about the substantive evils that Congress has a right to prevent. It is a question of proximity and degree.

"When a nation is at war many things that might be said in time of peace are such a hindrance to its effort that their utterance will not be endured so long as men fight and that no court could regard them as protected by any constitutional right. It seems to be admitted that if an actual obstruction of the recruiting service were proved, liability for words that produced that effect might be enforced. The statute of 1917 in § 4 punishes conspiracies to obstruct as well as actual obstruction. If the act (speaking, or circulating a paper), its tendency and the intent with which it is done are the same, we perceive no ground for saying that success alone warrants making the act a crime. (*Goldman* v. *United States*, 245 U. S. 474). Indeed that case might be said to dispose of the present contention if the precedent covers all *media concludendi*. But as the right to free speech was not referred to specially, we have thought fit to add a few words.

"It was not argued that a conspiracy to obstruct the draft was not within the words of the Act of 1917. The words are 'obstruct the recruiting or enlistment service,' and it might be suggested that they refer only to making it hard to get volunteers. Recruiting heretofore usually having been accomplished by getting volunteers, the word is apt to call up that method only in our minds. But recruiting is gaining fresh supplies for the forces, as well by draft as otherwise. It is put as an alternative to enlistment or voluntary enrollment in this Act. The fact that the Act of 1917 was enlarged by the amending Act of May 16, 1918 . . . of course does not affect the present indictment and would not, even if the former Act had been repealed. . . ."

Schenck v. *United States*
Baer v. *Same*
249 U. S. 47

When Congress Makes War

(*Frohwerk* v. *United States*, 1918)

"THIS IS an indictment in thirteen counts. The first alleges a conspiracy between the plaintiff in error and one Carl Gleeser, they then being engaged in the preparation and publication of a newspaper, the *Missouri Staats Zeitung,* to violate the Espionage Act of June 15, 1917. . . . It alleges as overt acts the preparation and circulation of twelve articles, &c., in the said newspaper at different dates from July 6, 1917, to December 7 of the same year. The other counts allege attempts to cause disloyalty, mutiny and refusal of duty in the military and naval forces of the United States, by the same publications, each count being confined to the publication of a single date.

"Motion to dismiss and a demurrer on constitutional and other grounds, especially that of the First Amendment as to free speech, were overruled, subject to exception, and the defendant refusing to plead, the court ordered a plea of not guilty to be filed. There was a trial and Frohwerk was found guilty on all the counts except the seventh, which needs no further mention. He was sentenced to a fine and to ten years' imprisonment on each count, the imprisonment on the latter counts to run concurrently with that on the first.

"Owing to unfortunate differences no bill of exceptions is before us. Frohwerk applied to this Court for leave to file a petition for a writ of mandamus requiring the judge to sign a proper bill of exceptions, but a case was not stated that would

warrant the issuing of the writ and leave was denied. . . .
The absence of a bill of exceptions and the suggestions in the
application for mandamus have caused us to consider the case
with more anxiety than if it presented only the constitutional
question which was the theme of the principal argument here.

"With regard to that argument we think it necessary to
add to what has been said in *Schenck* v. *United States*, only that
the First Amendment, while prohibiting legislation against free
speech as such, cannot have been, and obviously was not, intended to give immunity for every possible use of language.
. . . We venture to believe that neither Hamilton nor Madi-
son, nor any other competent person then or later, ever supposed that to make criminal the counselling of a murder within
the jurisdiction of Congress would be an unconstitutional interference with free speech.

"Whatever might be thought of the other counts on the
evidence, if it were before us, we have decided in *Schenck* v.
United States that a person may be convicted of a conspiracy
to obstruct recruiting by words of persuasion. The Government
argues that on the record the question is narrowed simply to the
power of Congress to punish such a conspiracy to obstruct, but
we shall take it in favor of the defendant that the publications
set forth as overt acts were the only means and, when coupled
with the joint activity in producing them, the only evidence of
the conspiracy alleged. Taking it that way, however, so far as
the language of the articles goes there is not much to choose
between expressions to be found in them and those before us in
Schenck v. *United States*.

"The first begins by declaring it a monumental and inex-
cusable mistake to send our soldiers to France, says that it
comes no doubt from the great trusts, and later that it appears
to be outright murder without serving anything practical;
speaks of the unconquerable spirit and undiminished strength of
the German nation, and characterizes its own discourse as words

[237]

of warning to the American people. Then comes a letter from one of the counsel who argued here, stating that the present force is a part of the regular army raised illegally; a matter discussed at length in his voluminous brief, on the ground that before its decision to the contrary the Solicitor General misled this Court as to the law. Later, on August 3, came discussion of the causes of the war, laying it to the Administration and saying 'that a few men and corporations might amass unprecedented fortunes, we sold our honor, our very soul,' with the usual repetition that we went to war to protect the loans of Wall Street. Later, after more similar discourse, comes, 'We say therefore, cease firing.'

"Next, on August 10, after deploring 'the draft riots in Oklahoma and elsewhere' in language that might be taken to convey an innuendo of a different sort, it is said that the previous talk about legal remedies is all very well for those who are past the draft age and have no boys to be drafted, and the paper goes on to give a picture, made as moving as the writer was able to make it, of the sufferings of a drafted man, of his then recognizing that his country is not in danger and that he is being sent to a foreign land to fight in a cause that neither he nor anyone else knows anything of, and reaching the conviction that this is but a war to protect some rich men's money. Who then, it is asked, will pronounce a verdict of guilty upon him if he stops reasoning and follows the first impulse of nature: self-preservation; and further, whether, while technically he is wrong in his resistance, he is not more sinned against than sinning; and yet again whether the guilt of those who voted the unnatural sacrifice is not greater than the wrong of those who now seek to escape by ill-advised resistance.

"On August 17, there is quoted and applied to our own situation a remark to the effect that when rulers scheme to use it for their own aggrandizement loyalty serves to perpetuate wrong. On August 31, with more of the usual discourse, it is said that the sooner the public wakes up to the fact that we are led and ruled by England, the better; that our sons, our taxes and our sacrifices are only in the interest of England. On September 28, there is a sneering contrast between Lord Northcliffe and other Englishmen spending many hundreds of thousands of dollars here to drag us into the war and Count Bernstorff spending a few thousand to maintain peace between his own country and us. Later followed some compliments to Germany and a statement that the Central Powers are carrying on a defensive war.

"There is much more to the general effect that we are in the wrong and are giving false and hypocritical reasons for our course, but the foregoing is enough to indicate the kind of matter with which we have to deal.

"It may be that all this might be said or written even in time of war in circumstances that would not make it a crime. We do not lose our right to condemn either measures or men because the country is at war. It does not appear that there was any special effort to reach men who were subject to the draft; and if the evidence should show that the defendant was a poor man, turning out copy for Gleeser, his employer, at less than a day laborer's pay, for Gleeser to use or reject as he saw fit, in a newspaper of small circulation, there would be a natural inclination to test every question of law to be found in the record very thoroughly before upholding the very severe penalty imposed. But we must take the case on the record as it is, and on that record it is impossible to say that it might not have been found that the circulation of the paper was in quarters where a little breath would be enough to kindle a flame and that the fact was known and relied upon by those who sent the paper out. Small compensation would not exonerate the defendant if it were found that he expected the result, even if pay were his chief desire. When we consider that we do not know how strong the Government's evidence may have been we find ourselves unable to say that the articles could not furnish a basis for a conviction upon the first count at least. We pass therefore to the other points that are raised.

"It is said that the first count is bad because it does not allege the means by which the conspiracy was to be carried out. But a conspiracy to obstruct recruiting would be criminal even if no means were agreed upon specifically by which to accomplish the intent. It is enough if the parties agreed to set to work for that common purpose. That purpose could be accomplished or aided by persuasion as well as by false statements, and there was no need to allege that false reports were intended to be made or made.

"It is argued that there is no sufficient allegation of intent, but intent to accomplish an object cannot be alleged more clearly than by stating that parties conspired to accomplish it. The overt acts are alleged to have been done to effect the object of a conspiracy and that is sufficient under § 4 of the Act of 1917. Countenance, we believe, has been given by some courts to the notion that a single count in an indictment for conspiring to commit two offenses is bad for duplicity. This Court has given it none. . . . The conspiracy is the crime, and that is one, however diverse its objects.

"Some reference was made in the proceedings and in argument to the provision in the Constitution concerning treason, and it was suggested on the one hand that some of the matters dealt with in the Act of 1917 were treasonable and punishable as treason or not at all, and on the other hand that the acts complained of not being treason could not be punished. These suggestions seem to us to need no more than to be stated. The amendment of the Act of 1917 in 1918 did not affect the present indictment. (*Schenck* v. *United States*.) Without pursuing the matter further we are of opinion that the indictment must stand.

"Before the demurrer was disposed of the court had ordered jurymen to be summoned to serve for the April term of the court and to report for service on June 25, 1918, as of course it might. The demurrer was overruled on June 24, and on the following day the plea of not guilty was ordered to be entered, a continuance was refused, a jury was impanelled and the trial set to begin the next morning. There is nothing before us that makes it possible to say that the judge's discretion was wrongly exercised. Upon the whole case we are driven to the conclusion that the record shows no ground upon which the judgment can be reversed."

Frohwerk v. *United States*
249 U. S. 204

The Case of Eugene V. Debs

(*Debs* v. *United States*, 1918)

"THIS IS an indictment under the Espionage Act of June 15, 1917 . . . as amended by the Act of May 16, 1918. . . . It has been cut down to two counts, originally the third and fourth. The former of these alleges that on or about June 16, 1918, at Canton, Ohio, the defendant caused and incited and attempted to cause and incite insubordination, disloyalty, mutiny and refusal of duty in the military and naval forces of the United States and with intent so to do delivered, to an assembly of people, a public speech, set forth. The fourth count alleges that he obstructed and attempted to obstruct the recruiting and enlistment service of the United States and to that end and with that intent delivered the same speech, again set forth.

"There was a demurrer to the indictment on the ground that the statute is unconstitutional as interfering with free speech, contrary to the First Amendment, and to the several counts as insufficiently stating the supposed offense. This was overruled, subject to exception. There were other exceptions to the admission of evidence with which we shall deal. The defendant was found guilty and was sentenced to ten years' imprisonment on each of the two counts, the punishment to run concurrently on both.

"The main theme of the speech was socialism, its growth, and a prophecy of its ultimate success. With that we have nothing to do, but if a part or the manifest intent of the more general utterances was to encourage those present to obstruct the recruiting service and if in passages such encouragement was directly given, the immunity of the general theme may not be enough to protect the speech.

"The speaker began by saying that he had just returned from a visit to the workhouse in the neighborhood where three of their most loyal comrades were paying the penalty for their devotion to the working class—these being Wagenknecht, Baker and Ruthenberg, who had been convicted of aiding and abetting another in failing to register for the draft. . . . He said that he had to be prudent or might not be able to say all that he thought, thus intimating to his hearers that they might infer that he meant more, but he did say that those persons were paying the penalty for standing erect and for seeking to pave the way to better conditions for all mankind. Later he added further eulogies and said that he was proud of them. He then expressed opposition to Prussian militarism in a way that naturally might have been thought to be intended to include the mode of proceeding in the United States.

"After considerable discourse that it is unnecessary to follow, he took up the case of Kate Richards O'Hare, convicted of obstructing the enlistment service, praised her for her loyalty to socialism and otherwise, and said that she was convicted on false testimony, under a ruling that would seem incredible to him if he had not had some experience with a Federal court. We mention this passage simply for its connection with evidence put in the trial.

"The defendant spoke of other cases, and then, after dealing with Russia, said that the master class has always declared the wars and the subject class has always fought the battles— that the subject class has had nothing to gain and all to lose, including their lives; that the working class who furnish the corpses have never yet had a voice in declaring war and have never yet had a voice in declaring peace. 'You have your lives to lose; you certainly ought to have the right to declare war if you consider a war necessary.'

"The defendant next mentioned Rose Pastor Stokes, convicted of attempting to cause insubordination and refusal of duty in the military forces of the United States and obstructing the recruiting service. He said that she went out to render her service to the cause in this day of crises, and they sent her to the penitentiary for ten years; that she had said no more than the speaker had said that afternoon; that if she was guilty so was he, and that he would not be cowardly enough to plead his innocence; but that her message that opened the eyes of the people must be suppressed, and so, after a mock trial before a packed jury and a corporation tool on the bench, she was sent to the penitentiary for ten years.

"There followed personal experiences and illustrations of the growth of socialism, a glorification of minorities, and a prophecy of the success of the international socialist crusade, with the interjection that 'you need to know that you are fit for something better than slavery and cannon fodder.' The rest of the discourse had only the indirect though not necessarily ineffective bearing on the offenses alleged that is to be found in the usual contrasts between capitalists and laboring men, sneers at the advice to cultivate war gardens, attribution to plutocrats of the high price of coal, &c., with the implication running through it all that the working men are not concerned in the war, and a final exhortation, 'Don't worry about the charge of treason to your masters; but be concerned about the treason that involves yourselves.'

"The defendant addressed the jury himself, and while contending that his speech did not warrant the charges, said, 'I have been accused of obstructing the war. I admit it. Gentlemen, I abhor war. I would oppose war if I stood alone.' The statement was not necessary to warrant the jury in finding that one purpose of the speech, whether incidental or not does not matter, was to oppose not only war in general but this war, and that the opposition was so expressed that its natural and intended effect would be to obstruct recruiting. If that was intended and if, in all the circumstances, that would be its probable effect, it would not be protected by reason of its being part of a general program and expressions of a general and conscientious belief.

"The chief defenses upon which the defendant seemed willing to rely were the denial that we have dealt with and that based upon the First Amendment to the Constitution, disposed of in *Schenck* v. *United States*. His counsel questioned the sufficiency of the indictment. It is sufficient in form. (*Frohwerk* v. *United States*.) The most important question that remains is raised by the admission in evidence of the record of the conviction of Ruthenberg, Wagenknecht and Baker, Rose Pastor Stokes, and Kate Richards O'Hare. The defendant purported to understand the grounds on which these persons were imprisoned and it was proper to show what those grounds were in order to show what he was talking about, to explain the true import of his expression of sympathy and to throw light on the intent of the address, so far as the present matter is concerned.

"There was introduced also an 'Anti-War Proclamation and Program' adopted at St. Louis in April, 1917, coupled with testimony that about an hour before his speech the defendant had stated that he approved of that platform in spirit and in substance. The defendant referred to it in his address to the jury, seemingly with satisfaction and willingness that it should be considered in evidence. But his counsel objected and has argued against its admissibility, at some length.

"This document contained the usual suggestion that capitalism was the cause of the war and that our entrance into it 'was instigated by the predatory capitalists in the United

States.' It alleged that the war of the United States against Germany could not 'be justified even on the plea that it is a war of defense of American rights or American "honor." ' It said, 'We brand the declaration of war by our Government as a crime against the people of the United States and against the nations of the world. In all modern history there has been no war more unjustifiable than the war in which we are about to engage.' Its first recommendation was 'continuous, active and public opposition to the war, through demonstrations, mass petitions, and all other means within our power.' Evidence that the defendant accepted this view and this declaration of his duties at the time that he made his speech is evidence that if in that speech he used words tending to obstruct the recruiting service he meant that they should have that effect. The principle is too well established and too manifestly good sense to need citation of the books. We should add that the jury were most carefully instructed that they could not find the defendant guilty for advocacy of any of his opinions unless the words used had as their natural tendency and reasonable, probable effect to obstruct the recruiting service, &c., and unless the defendant had the specific intent to do so in his mind.

"Without going into further particulars, we are of opinion that the verdict on the fourth count, for obstructing and attempting to obstruct the recruiting service of the United States, must be sustained. Therefore it is less important to consider whether that upon the third count, for causing and attempting to cause insubordination, &c., in the military and naval forces, is equally impregnable. The jury were instructed that for the purposes of the statute the persons designated by the Act of May 18, 1917, registered and enrolled under it, and thus subject to be called into the active service, were a part of the military forces of the United States. The Government presents a strong argument from the history of the statutes that the in-

struction was correct and in accordance with established legislative usage. We see no sufficient reason for differing from the
conclusion but think it unnecessary to discuss the question in
detail."

Debs v. *United States*
249 U. S. 211

EXCERPTS FROM OTHER MAJORITY OPINIONS

Punishing a Free Press

(*Patterson* v. *Colorado*, 1906)

CITED FOR CONTEMPT BY THE COLORADO SUPREME COURT FOR RE-flecting on the motives of its judges, ex-Senator Thomas M. Patterson was fined $1,000. He had published a charge in his Denver paper that two of the judges obtained seats on the bench in a scheme to put Republican candidates into office, and he made this charge while election fraud cases were pending before the court. Holmes saw fit to uphold the judgment, while Mr. Justice Harlan dissented.

Harlan's point was that the Fourteenth Amendment prevents a State from abridging the privileges and immunities of citizens of the United States; that freedom of speech and of the press was an attribute of national citizenship before the Amendment was added to the Constitution. These rights are an essential part of every man's liberty, he said, and cannot be reduced even if a legislature thinks the public welfare requires this to be done. It is impossible to conceive of liberty which does not embrace the right to enjoy free speech and a free press, he said.

Justice Holmes said in part:—

"THE DEFENSE upon which the plaintiff in error most relies is raised by the allegation that the articles complained of are true and the claim of the right to prove the truth. He claimed this right under the Constitutions both of the State and of the United States, but the latter ground alone comes into consideration here, for reasons already stated. . . . We do not pause to consider whether the claim was sufficient in point

[251]

of form, although it is easier to refer to the Constitution gen erally for the supposed right than to point to the clause from which it springs. We leave undecided the question whether there is to be found in the Fourteenth Amendment a prohibition similar to that in the First. But even if we were to assume that freedom of speech and freedom of the press were protected from abridgment on the part of not only the United States but also the States, still we should be far from the conclusion that the plaintiff in error would have us reach.

"In the first place, the main purpose of such constitutional provisions is 'to prevent all such *previous restraints* upon publications as had been practiced by other governments,' and they do not prevent the subsequent punishment of such as may be deemed contrary to the public welfare. . . . The preliminary freedom extends as well to the false as to the true; the subsequent punishment may extend as well to the true as to the false. This was the law of criminal libel apart from statute in most cases, if not in all. . . .

"In the next place, the rule applied to criminal libel applies yet more clearly to contempts. A publication likely to reach the eyes of a jury, declaring a witness in a pending cause a perjurer, would be none the less a contempt that it was true. It would tend to obstruct the administration of justice, because even a correct conclusion is not to be reached or helped in that way, if our system of trials is to be maintained. The theory of our system is that the conclusions to be reached in a case will be induced only by evidence and argument in open court, and not by any outside influence, whether of private talk or public print.

"What is true with reference to a jury is true also with reference to a court. Cases like the present are more likely to arise, no doubt, when there is a jury and the publication may affect their judgment. Judges generally, perhaps, are less apprehensive that publications impugning their own reasoning or motives will interfere with their administration of the law. But if a court regards, as it may, a publication concerning a matter of law pending before it, as tending toward such an interference, it may punish it as in the instance put.

"When a case is finished, courts are subject to the same criticism as other people, but the propriety and necessity of preventing interference with the course of justice by premature statement, argument or intimidation hardly can be denied. . . . It is objected that the judges were sitting in their own case. But the grounds upon which contempts are punished are impersonal. . . . No doubt judges naturally would be slower to punish when the contempt carried with it a personally dishonoring charge, but a man cannot expect to secure immunity from punishment by the proper tribunal by adding to illegal conduct a personal attack.

"It only remains to add that the plaintiff in error had his day in court and opportunity to be heard. We have scrutinized the case, but cannot say that it shows an infraction of rights under the Constitution of the United States, or discloses more than the formal appeal to that instrument in the answer to found the jurisdiction of this Court."

Patterson v. *Colorado*
205 U. S. 454

Disrespect for the Law

(Fox v. *State of Washington,* 1914)

IN AN EFFORT TO ESCAPE FROM SOCIETY A GROUP FOUNDED A colony of its own, only to learn that laws could reach through the woods. The bitterness of the Utopians expressed itself in print—and once more the colony ran afoul of the law. This time the colony came into conflict with a Washington statute which made it a misdemeanor to distribute matter "which shall tend to encourage or advocate disrespect for the law." After describing the situation Holmes continued:

"THE PRINTED matter in question is an article entitled 'The Nude and the Prudes,' reciting in its early part that 'Home is a community of free spirits, who came out into the woods to escape the polluted atmosphere of priest-ridden conventional society'; that 'one of the liberties enjoyed by Homeites was the privilege to bathe in the evening dress or merely with the clothes nature gave them, just as they chose'; but that 'eventually a few prudes got into the community and proceeded in the brutal, unneighborly way of the outside world to suppress the people's freedom' and that they had four persons arrested on the charge of indecent exposure, followed in two cases, it seems, by sentences to imprisonment.

" 'And the perpetrators of this vile action wonder why they are being boycotted,'—it goes on.—'The well-merited indignation of the people has been aroused. Their liberty has been attacked. The first step in the way of subjecting the community to all the persecution of the outside has been taken. If this was let go without resistance the progress of the prudes would be easy.' It then predicts and encourages the boycott of those who thus interfere with the freedom of Home, concluding: 'The boycott will be pushed until these invaders come to see the brutal mistake of their action and so inform the people.' Thus by indirection but unmistakably the article encourages and incites a persistence in what we must assume would be a breach of the state laws against indecent exposure; and the jury so found.

"So far as statutes fairly may be construed in such a way as to avoid doubtful constitutional questions they should be so construed . . . and it is to be presumed that state laws will be construed in that way by the state courts. We understand the state court by implication at least to have read the statute as confined to encouraging an actual breach of law. Therefore the argument that this Act is both an unjustifiable restriction of liberty and too vague for criminal law must fail. It does not appear and it is not likely that the statute will be construed to prevent publications merely because they tend to produce unfavorable opinions of a particular statute or of law in general. In this present case the disrespect for law that was encouraged was disregard of it—an overt breach and technically criminal act. It would be in accord with the usages of English to interpret disrespect as manifested disrespect, as active disregard going beyond the line drawn by the law. That is all that has happened as yet, and we see no reason to believe that the statute will be stretched beyond that point.

"If the statute should be construed as going no farther than it is necessary to go in order to bring the defendant within it, there is no trouble with it for want of definiteness. . . . It lays hold of encouragements that, apart from statute, if directed to a particular person's conduct, generally would make him who uttered them guilty of a misdemeanor if not an accomplice or a principal in the crime encouraged, and deals with the publi-

[255]

cation of them to a wider and less selected audience. Laws of this description are not unfamiliar. Of course we have nothing to do with the wisdom of the defendant, the prosecution, or the Act. All that concerns us is that it cannot be said to infringe the Constitution of the United States."

Fox v. *State of Washington*
236 U. S. 273

An Arrest Under Martial Law

(*Moyer* v. *Peabody*, 1908)

GOVERNOR PEABODY OF COLORADO CALLED OUT THE MILITIA WHEN the town of Telluride got out of control during a miners' outbreak. He ordered the arrest of Charles H. Moyer, president of the Western Federation of Miners, who had returned to town after being deported as the ringleader. Although the courts were open Moyer was prevented from having access to them. Moyer sued Peabody for redress but did not obtain it. Holmes said in part:

"OF COURSE the plaintiff's position is that he has been deprived of his liberty without due process of law. But it is familiar that what is due process of law depends on circumstances. It varies with the subject-matter and the necessities of the situation.*** The facts that we are to assume are that a state of insurrection existed and that the Governor, without sufficient reason but in good faith, in the course of putting the insurrection down held the plaintiff until he thought that he safely could release him.

"It would seem to be admitted by the plaintiff that he was president of the Western Federation of Miners and that, whoever was to blame, trouble was apprehended with the members of that organization. We mention these facts not as material but simply to put in more definite form the nature of the occasion on which the Governor felt called upon to act. In such a situation we must assume that he had a right under the state constitu-

[257]

tion and laws to call out troops, as was held by the Supreme Court of the State. The constitution is supplemented by an act providing that 'when an invasion of or insurrection in the State is made or threatened the Governor shall order the National Guard to repel or suppress the same.'*** That means that he shall make the ordinary use of the soldiers to that end; that he may kill persons who resist and, of course, that he may use the milder measure of seizing the bodies of those whom he considers to stand in the way of restoring peace.

"Such arrests are not necessarily for punishment, but are by way of precaution to prevent the exercise of hostile power. So long as such arrests are made in good faith and in the honest belief that they are needed in order to head the insurrection off, the Governor is the final judge and cannot be subjected to an action after he is out of office on the ground that he had not reasonable ground for his belief. If we suppose a Governor with a very long term of office, it may be that a case could be imagined in which the length of the imprisonment would raise a different question. But there is nothing in the duration of the plaintiff's detention or in the allegations of the complaint that would warrant submitting the judgment of the Governor to revision by a jury. It is not alleged that his judgment was not honest, if that be material, or that the plaintiff was detained after fears of the insurrection were at an end.

"No doubt there are cases where the expert on the spot may be called upon to justify his conduct later in court, notwithstanding the fact that he had sole command at the time and acted to the best of his knowledge. That is the position of the captain of a ship. But even in that case great weight is given to his determination and the matter is to be judged on the facts as they appeared then and not merely in the light of the event. . . . When it comes to a decision by the head of the State upon a matter involving its life, the ordinary rights of individuals must yield to what he deems the necessities of the moment.

Public danger warrants the substitution of the executive process for the judicial process. . . . This was admitted with regard to killing men in the actual clash of arms, and we think it obvious, although it was disputed, that the same is true of temporary detention to prevent apprehended harm.

"As no one would deny that there was immunity for ordering a company to fire upon a mob in insurrection, and that a state law authorizing the Governor to deprive citizens of life under such circumstances was consistent with the Fourteenth Amendment, we are of opinion that the same is true of a law authorizing by implication what was done in this case. As we have said already, it is unnecessary to consider whether there are other reasons why the Circuit Court was right in its conclusion. It is enough that in our opinion the declaration does not disclose a 'suit authorized by law to be brought to redress the deprivation of any right secured by the Constitution of the United States.' " . . .

Moyer v. *Peabody*
212 U. S. 78

Pitfalls for Labor

(*Lawlor* v. *Loewe*, 1914)

WHEN THE UNITED HATTERS OF NORTH AMERICA CAMPAIGNED TO unionize workers in their trade, the hat manufacturers uncovered a combination and conspiracy in restraint of interstate commerce. Part of the scheme was to have the American Federation of Labor declare a boycott against hats made by non-union labor and against dealers who sold them. Suit was brought against certain members of the union under the Sherman Act.

Holmes cited a recent case holding illegal the circulation of a list of "unfair dealers" and added:

"WE AGREE with the Circuit Court of Appeals that a combination and conspiracy forbidden by the statute were proved, and that the question is narrowed to the responsibility of the defendants for what was done by the sanction and procurement of the societies above-named.*** It is a tax on credulity to ask anyone to believe that members of labor unions at that time did not know that the primary and secondary boycott and the use of the 'We don't patronize' and 'Unfair' list were means expected to be employed in the effort to unionize shops. Very possibly they were thought to be lawful. . . . By the constitution of the United Hatters the directors are to use 'all the means in their power' to bring shops 'not under our jurisdiction' 'into the trade.' The by-laws provide a separate fund to be kept for strikes, lockouts, and agitation for the union label. Members are forbidden to sell non-union hats.

"The Federation of Labor with which the Hatters were affiliated had organization of labor for one of its objects, helped affiliated unions in trade disputes, and to that end, before the present trouble, had provided in its constitution for prosecuting and had prosecuted many what it called legal boycotts. Their conduct in this and former cases was made public especially among members in every possible way.

"If the words of the documents on their face and without explanation did not authorize what was done, the evidence of what was done publicly and habitually showed their meaning and how they were interpreted. The jury could not but find that by the usage of the unions the acts complained of were authorized, and authorized without regard to their interference with commerce among the States. We think it unnecessary to repeat the evidence of the publicity of this particular struggle, in the common newspaper and union prints, evidence that made it almost inconceivable that the defendants, all living in the neighborhood of the plaintiffs, did not know what was done in the specific case. If they did not know that, they were bound to know the constitution of their societies, and at least well might be found to have known how the words of those constitutions had been construed in the Act."

Lawlor v. *Loewe*
235 U. S. 522

Tried by White Men

I

(*United States* v. *Shipp*, 1906)

A NEGRO IN CHATTANOOGA WAS SENTENCED TO DEATH FOR CRIM-
inally assaulting a white woman. He appealed that Negroes had been illegally excluded from the jury that tried him and, though the Circuit
Court refused a writ of habeas corpus, Mr. Justice Harlan granted an
appeal. On the night when the local papers printed the news that the
proceedings had been ordered stopped, the sheriff withdrew his customary guard and left the prisoner under the watch of only the jailkeeper.

Sheriff Shipp was charged with conspiring to permit the lynching
that followed and he was cited for contempt. Holmes said in part:

"THE FIRST question, naturally, is that of the jurisdiction of
this Court. The jurisdiction to punish for a contempt is not
denied as a general abstract proposition as, of course, it could
not be with success. . . . But it is argued that the Circuit
Court had no jurisdiction in the habeas corpus case, unless Johnson was in custody in violation of the Constitution, and that the
appellate jurisdiction of this Court was dependent upon the Act
of March 3, 1891 . . . and by that Act did not exist unless the
case involved 'the construction and application of the Constitution of the United States.'

"If the case did not involve the application of the Constitution, otherwise than by way of pretense, it is said that this
Court was without jurisdiction, and that its order might be

[262]

contemned with impunity. And it is urged that an inspection of the evidence before the Circuit Court, if not the face of the petition, shows that the ground alleged for the writ was only a pretense.

"We regard this argument as unsound.*** But even if the Circuit Court had no jurisdiction to entertain Johnson's petition, and if this Court had no jurisdiction of the appeal, this Court and this Court alone could decide that such was the law. It and it alone necessarily had jurisdiction to decide whether the case was properly before it. On that question, at least, it was its duty to permit argument and to take the time required for such consideration as it might need.***

"We cannot regard the grounds upon which the petition for habeas corpus was presented as frivolous or a mere pretense. The murder of the petitioner has made it impossible to decide that case, and what we have said makes it unnecessary to pass upon it as a preliminary to deciding the question before us.***

"The defendants severally have denied under oath in their answer that they had anything to do with the murder. It is urged that the sworn answers are conclusive, that if they are false the parties may be prosecuted for perjury, but that in this proceeding they are to be tried, if they so elect, simply by their oaths. It has been suggested that the Court is a party and therefore leaves the fact to be decided by the defendant. But this is a mere afterthought to explain something not understood. The Court is not a party. There is nothing that affects the judges in their own persons. Their concern only is that the law should be obeyed and enforced, and their interest is no other than that they represent in every case.***

"The question was touched, in argument, whether the acts charged constitute a contempt. We are of opinion that they do, and that their character does not depend upon a nice inquiry whether, after the order made by this Court, the sheriff was to be regarded as bailee of the United States or still held the prisoner in the name of the State alone. Either way, the order suspended further proceedings of the State against the prisoner and required that he should be forthcoming to abide the further order of this Court. It may be found that what created the mob and led to the crime was the unwillingness of its members to submit to the delay required for the trial of the appeal. From that to the intent to prevent that delay and the hearing of the appeal is a short step. If that step is taken the contempt is proved.

"These preliminaries being settled, the trial of the case will proceed."

II

(*Brownfield* v. *South Carolina,* 1902)

CONVICTED OF MURDER, A NEGRO ALLEGED THAT THE GRAND JURY was composed wholly of white persons, that Negroes were excluded on account of their race and color although they constituted four-fifths of the registered voters of the county. He contended that his civil rights and the equal protection of the laws had been denied to him, but Holmes observed:

"THE TROUBLE with the case is that we are not warranted in assuming that the allegations are true. The record contains an agreed statement, called a brief, in which it appears that the defendant below made a motion to quash on the grounds stated, and in which it is said that the defendant offered to introduce testimony to support these grounds. But this agreed statement is 'signed with relation to case as settled by judge.' It appears that the parties agreed that the judge before whom the case was tried should 'make a statement as to his rulings upon the motion to quash an indictment, and also as to the motion to challenge the arrays of grand and petit jurors in the case, and also as to requests to charge, and such statement shall be the agreed statement for the purposes of this appeal.'

"The challenge of the array referred to was upon the same grounds as the motion to quash. In pursuance of this agreement the judge made a statement of the grounds on which he over-ruled the motion. 'Because the statement of facts set out in the grounds for quashing the same did not appear from the records or otherwise. . . . In the absence of any showing to the contrary I was bound to assume that the jury commissioners had done their duty.'

"The foregoing language is quite inconsistent with there having been an offer to prove the allegations of the motion, as is the further fact that the record discloses no exception to the supposed refusal to hear evidence offered to that end. If these considerations were not enough, we have, in addition, the absence of any suggestion of a refusal to admit evidence in the reasons for appeal to the Supreme Court, and the statement of the Supreme Court [of South Carolina] that it was not contended at the hearing of the appeal that there was any offer to introduce testimony on the point 'other than the offer therein made.' The last words refer, we assume, to the concluding words of the motion: 'All of which the defendant is ready to verify.' Upon the whole record we are compelled to infer that the statement that the defendant offered to introduce evidence was inserted in the so-called brief by his counsel, but was not agreed to except so far as it might be confirmed by the statement of the judge, and that he did not confirm it.

"We see no ground for the suggestion that this fact was outside the matters submitted to the judge, and therefore must be taken to have been admitted. Evidently that was not the understanding on the part of the State. It is suggested that the allegations of the motion to quash not having been controverted and having been supported by the affidavit of the defendant, must be taken to be true. But a motion, although reduced to writing, is not a pleading and does not require a written answer. It appears from the grounds on which the judge decided it, apart from anything else, that the allegations were controverted, and under such circumstances it was necessary for the defendant to make an attempt to introduce evidence. The formal words of the motion were not enough. . . .

"A provisional objection is made to the constitution of South Carolina, in case it should be held to exclude Negroes from the jury. But the ground of the motion was not that Negroes were excluded by an invalid constitutional provision, but that they were excluded in the administration of the law, although they were qualified under it to serve. The case involves questions of the gravest character, but we must deal with it according to record, and the record discloses no wrong."

United States v. *Shipp*
203 U. S. 563
Brownfield v. *South Carolina*
189 U. S. 426

Setting the 8-Hour Standard

(*Ellis* v. *United States*, 1906)

CONTRACTORS DOING WORK IN THE BOSTON NAVY YARD WERE FINED under an act of 1892 which limited the work-day of laborers and mechanics employed on public works of the United States to eight hours, except in a case of "extraordinary emergency." After stating the facts Holmes said:

"THE CONTENTION that the Act is unconstitutional is not frivolous, since it may be argued that there are relevant distinctions between the power of the United States and that of a State. But the arguments naturally urged against such a statute apply equally for the most part to the two jurisdictions, and are answered, so far as a State is concerned, by *Atkin* v. *Kansas*, 191 U. S. 207. In that case a contractor for work upon a municipal boulevard was sentenced to a fine under a similar law of Kansas, and the statute was upheld.

"We see no reason to deny the United States the power thus established for the States. Like the States, it may sanction the requirements made of contractors employed upon its public works by penalties in case those requirements are not fulfilled. It would be a strong thing to say that a legislature that had power to forbid or to authorize and enforce a contract had not also the power to make a breach of it criminal, but however that may be, Congress, as incident to its power to authorize and enforce contracts for public works, may require that they shall be carried out only in a way consistent with its views of public policy, and may punish a departure from that way. It is true that it has not the general power of legislation possessed by the legislatures of the States, and it may be true that the object of this law is of a kind not subject to its general control. But the power that it has over the mode in which contracts with the United States shall be performed cannot be limited by a speculation as to motives. If the motive be conceded, however, the fact that Congress has not general control over the conditions of labor does not make unconstitutional a law otherwise valid, because the purpose of the law is to secure to it certain advantages, so far as the law goes.

"One other argument is put forward, but it hardly needs an answer. A ruling was asked in Ellis's case, and is attempted to be sustained, to the effect that the Government waived its sovereignty by making a contract, and that even if the Act of 1892 were read into the contract, a breach of its requirements would be only a breach of contract and could not be made a crime. This is a mere confusion of ideas. The Government purely as contractor, in the absence of special laws, may stand like a private person, but by making a contract it does not give up its power to make law, and it may make a law like the present for the reasons that we have stated. We are of opinion that the Act is not contrary to the Constitution of the United States.***

"It needs no argument to show that the disappointment of a contractor with regard to obtaining some of his materials, a matter which he knew involved some difficulty of which he took the risk, does not create such an emergency as is contemplated in the exception to the law. Again, the construction of the pier was desirable for the more convenient repair of warships, but it was not essential. Vessels had been docked without it since 1835 or 1836, so that there was no hot haste on that account, if under any circumstances that kind of need would have been enough.

[268]

"There is only one other question raised in Ellis's case. It is admitted that he was a contractor within the meaning of the Act and that the workmen permitted to work more than eight hours a day were employed upon 'public works,' and it is not denied that these workmen were 'mechanics.' The jury were instructed, subject to exception, that if the defendant intended to permit the men to work over eight hours on the calendar day named he intended to violate the statute. The argument against the instruction is that the word 'intentionally' in the statute requires knowledge of the law; or at least that, to be convicted, Ellis must not have supposed, even mistakenly, that there was an emergency extraordinary enough to justify his conduct. The latter proposition is only the former a little disguised. Both are without foundation. If a man intentionally adopts certain conduct in certain circumstances known to him, and that conduct is forbidden by the law under those circumstances, he intentionally breaks the law in the only sense in which the law ever considers intent."

Ellis v. *United States*
206 U. S. 246

Combining on Rates

(Carroll v. Greenwich Ins. Co., 1905)

HOLMES HELD CONSTITUTIONAL AN IOWA STATUTE PROHIBITING fire insurance companies doing business in the State from agreeing on rates, etc. He made an analogy of the Sherman Anti-Trust Law and remarked that ordinarily if an Act of Congress is valid under the Fifth Amendment so is a similar State law under the Fourteenth. Continuing, he wrote:

"IT IS only on the ground that the right to combine at will is a fundamental personal right that it can be held to be protected by the Fourteenth Amendment from any abridgment by the States. . . . Many State laws which limit the freedom of contract have been sustained by this Court, and therefore an objection to this law on the general ground that it limits that freedom cannot be upheld.

"There is no greater sanctity in the right to combine than in the right to make other contracts. Indeed, Mr. Dicey in his recent work on *Law and Public Opinion in England during the Nineteenth Century* indicates that it is out of the very right to make what contract one chooses, so strenuously advocated by Bentham, that combinations have arisen which restrict the very freedom that Bentham sought to attain, and which even might menace the authority of the State. If then the statute before us is to be overthrown more special reasons must be assigned.

"At the argument before us more special reasons were assigned. It was pressed that there is no justification for the particular selection of fire insurance companies for the prohibitions discussed. With regard to this it should be observed, as is noticed by the appellees, that a general statute of Iowa prohibits all contracts or combinations to fix the price of any article of merchandise or commodity, or to limit the quantity of the same produced or sold in the State, Code of 1897, § 5060, and that this section covers fire insurance. . . . Therefore the Act in question does little if anything more than apply and work out the policy of the general law in a particular case.

"Again, if an evil is specially experienced in a particular branch of business, the Constitution embodies no prohibition of laws confined to the evil, or doctrinaire requirement that they should be couched in all-embracing terms. It does not forbid the cautious advance, step by step, and the distrust of generalities which sometimes have been the weakness, but often the strength, of English legislation. . . . And if this is true, then in view of the possible teachings to be drawn from a practical knowledge of the business concerned, it is proper that courts should be very cautious in condemning what legislatures have approved.

"If the Legislature of the State of Iowa deems it desirable artificially to prevent, so far as it can, the substitution of combination for competition, this Court cannot say that fire insurance may not present so conspicuous an example of what that Legislature thinks an evil as to justify special treatment."

Carroll v. *Greenwich Ins. Co.*
199 U. S. 401

Near-War of the States

(Missouri v. Illinois, 1905)*

MISSOURI COMPLAINED THAT HER DRINKING WATER WAS BEING POL-
luted by the new artificial channel through which the sewage of Chicago was disgorged—"fifteen hundred tons of poisonous filth daily"—
and finally emptied into a tributary of the Mississippi River. St. Louis
alone reported an increase of seventy-seven percent in her death rate
from typhoid.

Holmes said in part:

"THE NUISANCE set forth in the bill was one which would
be of international importance—a visible change of a great river
from a pure stream into a polluted and poisoned ditch. The
only question presented was whether as between the States of
the Union this Court was competent to deal with a situation
which, if it arose between independent sovereignties, might lead
to war.

"Whatever difference of opinion there might be upon matters of detail, the jurisdiction and authority of this Court to
deal with such a case as that is not open to doubt. But the evidence now is in, the actual facts have required for their establishment the most ingenious experiments, and for their interpretation the most subtle speculations, of modern science,
and therefore it becomes necessary at the present stage to con-

sider somewhat more nicely than heretofore how the evidence in it is to be approached.***

"If one State raises a controversy with another, this Court must determine whether there is any principle of law and, if any, what, on which the plaintiff can recover. But the fact that this Court must decide does not mean, of course, that it takes the place of a legislature. Some principles it must have power to declare. For instance, when a dispute arises about boundaries, this Court must determine the line and in doing so must be governed by rules explicitly or implicitly recognized. . . . It must follow and apply those rules even if legislation of one or both of the States seems to stand in the way. But the words of the Constitution would be a narrow ground upon which to construct and apply to the relations between States the same system of municipal law in all its details which would be applied between individuals. If we suppose a case which did not fall within the power of Congress to regulate, the result of a declaration of rights by this Court would be the establishment of a rule which would be irrevocable by any power except that of this Court to reverse its own decision, an amendment of the Constitution, or possibly an agreement between the States sanctioned by the legislature of the United States.

"The difficulties in the way of establishing such a system of law might not be insuperable but they would be great and new. Take the question of prescription in a case like the present. The reasons on which prescription for a public nuisance is denied or may be granted to an individual as against the sovereign power to which he is subject have no application to an independent State.***

"It may be imagined that a nuisance might be created by a State upon a navigable river like the Danube, which would amount to a *casus belli* for a State lower down, unless removed. If such a nuisance were created by a State upon the Mississippi

[273]

the controversy would be resolved by the more peaceful means of a suit in this Court. But it does not follow that every matter which would warrant a resort to equity by one citizen against another in the same jurisdiction equally would warrant an interference by this Court with the action of a State. It hardly can be that we should be justified in declaring statutes ordaining such action void in every instance where the Circuit Court might intervene in a private suit, upon no other ground than analogy to some selected system of municipal law, and the fact that we have jurisdiction over controversies between States.*** Before this Court ought to intervene the case should be of serious magnitude clearly and fully proved, and the principle to be applied should be one which the Court is prepared deliberately to maintain against all considerations on the other side. . . .

"As to the principle to be laid down the caution necessary is manifest. It is a question of the first magnitude whether the destiny of the great rivers is to be the sewers of the cities along their banks or to be protected against everything which threatens their purity. To decide the whole matter at one blow by an irrevocable fiat would be at least premature. If we are to judge by what the plaintiff itself permits, the discharge of sewage into the Mississippi by cities and towns is to be expected. We believe that the practice of discharging into the river is general along its banks except where the levees of Louisiana have led to a different course. The argument for the plaintiff asserts it to be proper within certain limits. These are facts to be considered.

"Even in cases between individuals some consideration is given to the practical course of events. In the back country of England parties would not be expected to stand upon extreme rights. . . . Where, as here, the plaintiff has sovereign powers and deliberately permits discharges similar to those of which it complains, it not only offers a standard to which the defendant has the right to appeal but, as some of those discharges are above the intake of St. Louis, it warrants the defendant in demanding the strictest proof that the plaintiff's own conduct does not produce the result, or at least so conduce to it that courts should not be curious to apportion the blame.***

"It is proved that the great volume of pure water from Lake Michigan which is mixed with the sewage at the start has improved the Illinois River in these respects to a noticeable extent. Formerly it was sluggish and ill-smelling. Now it is a comparatively clear stream to which edible fish have returned.*** The experiments of the defendant's experts lead them to the opinion that a typhoid bacillus could not survive the journey, while those on the other side maintain that it might live and keep its power for twenty-five days or more, and arrive at St. Louis. Upon the question at issue, whether the new discharge from Chicago hurts St. Louis, there is a categorical contradiction between the experts on the two sides.***

"The defendant's experts maintain that the water of the Missouri is worse than that of the Illinois, while it contributes a much larger proportion of the intake. The evidence is very strong that it is necessary for St. Louis to take preventive measures, by filtration and otherwise, against the dangers of the plaintiff's own creation or from other sources than the Illinois. What will protect against one will protect against another. The presence of causes of infection from the plaintiff's action makes the case weaker in principle as well as harder to prove than one in which all came from a single source.***

"The case stands no differently in point of law from a suit because of the discharge from Peoria into the Illinois, or from any other or all the other cities on the banks of that stream.

"We might go into detail, but we believe that we have said enough to explain our point of view and our opinion of the evidence as it stands. What the future may develop of course we cannot tell. But our conclusion upon the present evidence is that the case proved falls so far below the allegations of the bill that it is not brought within the principles heretofore established in the cause."

Bill dismissed without prejudice.

Missouri v. Illinois and Sanitary District of Chicago
200 U. S. 496

The Business of Being a Member of Society

"**I**N ORDER to enter into most of the relations of life people have to give up some of their constitutional rights. If a man makes a contract he gives up the constitutional right that previously he had to be free from the hamper that he puts upon himself."

(274 U. S. 490, 497 dissent)

"**M**OST RIGHTS are qualified. A man has at least as absolute a right to give his own money as he has to demand money from a party that has made no promise to him; yet if he gives it to induce another to steal or murder, the purpose of the act makes it a crime.*** A man has a right to give advice, but advice given for the sole purpose of injuring another's business and effective on a large scale might create a cause of action."

(256 U. S. 350)

"**E**VEN THE incidents of ownership may be cut down by the peculiar laws and usages of a State."

(201 U. S. 140)

"**W**HERE A RULE of conduct applies to more than a few people it is impracticable that everyone should have a direct

[277]

voice in its adoption. The Constitution does not require all public acts to be done in town meeting or an assembly of the whole. General statutes within the State power are passed that affect the person or property of individuals sometimes to the point of ruin, without giving them a chance to be heard. Their rights are protected in the only way that they can be in a complex society by their power, immediate or remote, over those who make the rule.

"If the result in this case [*Bi-Metallic Investment Co.* v. *State Board of Equalization of Colorado*] had been reached as it might have been reached by the State's doubling the rate of taxation, no one would suggest that the Fourteenth Amendment was violated unless every person affected had been allowed an opportunity to raise his voice against it before the body entrusted by the State Constitution with the power.*** There must be a limit to individual argument in such matters if government is to go on."

(239 U. S. 441)

"GOVERNMENT hardly could go on if to some extent values incident to property could not be diminished without paying for every such change in the general law. As long recognized, some values are enjoyed under an implied limitation and must yield to the police power. But obviously the implied limitation must have its limits or the contract and due process clauses are gone.

"One fact for consideration in determining such limits is the extent of the diminution. When it reaches a certain magnitude, in most if not in all cases there must be an exercise of eminent domain and compensation to sustain the Act. So the question depends upon the particular facts. The greatest weight is given to the judgment of the legislature, but it always is open to interested parties to contend that the legislature has gone beyond its constitutional power."

(260 U. S. 393)

[278]

"MANY LAWS which it would be vain to ask the Court to overthrow could be shown, easily enough, to transgress a scholastic interpretation of one or another of the great guaranties in the Bill of Rights. They more or less limit the liberty of the individual or they diminish property to a certain extent. We have few scientifically certain criteria of legislation, and as it often is difficult to mark the line where what is called the police power of the States is limited by the Constitution of the United States, judges should be slow to read into the latter a *nolumus mutare* as against the law-making power.***

"With regard to the police power, as elsewhere in the law, lines are pricked out by the gradual approach and contact of decisions on the opposing sides.***

"There are many things that a man might do at common law that the States may forbid."

(219 U. S. 104)

"AND YET again, the extent to which legislation may modify and restrict the uses of property consistently with the Constitution is not a question for pure abstract theory alone. Tradition and the habits of the community count for more than logic.

"Since, as before, the making of constitutions, regulation of burial and prohibition of it in certain spots, especially in crowded cities, have been familiar to the Western World. The plaintiff must wait until there is a change of practice or at least an established consensus of civilized opinion before it can expect this Court to overthrow the rules that the lawmakers and the court of his own State uphold."

(216 U. S. 358)

[279]

(An inmate of a Virginia state asylum opposed the statute permitting the superintendent to have her sterilized. Her mother was feeble-minded, she herself was feeble-minded, and so was her illegitimate child.)

"WE HAVE SEEN more than once that the public welfare may call upon the best citizens for their lives. It would be strange if it could not call upon those who already sap the strength of the State for these lesser sacrifices, often not felt to be such by those concerned, in order to prevent our being swamped with incompetence. It is better for all the world if, instead of waiting to execute degenerate offspring for crime or to let them starve for their imbecility, society can prevent those who are manifestly unfit from continuing their kind. The principle that sustains compulsory vaccination is broad enough to cover cutting the Fallopian tubes. Three generations of imbeciles are enough.

"But it is said, however it might be if this reasoning were applied generally, it fails when it is confined to the small number who are in the institutions named and is not applied to the multitudes outside. It is the usual last resort of constitutional arguments to point out shortcomings of this sort. But the answer is that the law does all that is needed when it does all that it can, indicates a policy, applies it to all within the lines, and seeks to bring within the lines all similarly situated so far and so fast as its means allow. Of course, so far as the operations enable those who otherwise must be kept confined to be returned to the world, and thus open the asylum to others, the equality aimed at will be more nearly reached."

(274 U. S. 200)

"THE PROSTITUTE is to be deported.*** It is thoroughly established that Congress has power to order the deportation of aliens whose presence in the country it deems hurtful. The determination by facts that might constitute a crime under local law is not a conviction of crime, nor is the deportation a punishment; it is simply a refusal by the Government to harbor persons whom it does not want."

(228 U. S. 585)

"ALL RIGHTS tend to declare themselves absolute to their logical extreme. Yet all in fact are limited by the neighborhood of principles of policy which are other than those on which the particular right is founded, and which become strong enough to hold their own when a certain point is reached.***

"It sometimes is difficult to fix boundary stones between the private right of property and the police power when, as in the case at bar, we know of few decisions that are very much in point.***

"The legal conception of the necessary is apt to be confined to somewhat rudimentary wants; and there are benefits from a great river that might escape a lawyer's view.***

"A man cannot acquire a right to property by his desire to use it in commerce among the States. Neither can he enlarge his otherwise limited and qualified right to the same end.*** It constantly is necessary to reconcile and to adjust different constitutional principles, each of which would be entitled to possession of the disputed ground but for the presence of the others, as we already have said that it is necessary to reconcile and to adjust different principles of the common law."

(209 U. S. 350)

"THE EIGHTEENTH AMENDMENT meant a great revolution in the policy of this country, and presumably and obviously meant to upset a good many things on as well as off the statute

[281]

book. It did not confine itself in any meticulous way to the use of intoxicants in this country. It forbade export for beverage purposes elsewhere. True, this discouraged production here, but that was forbidden already, and the provision applied to liquors already lawfully made.

"It is obvious that those whose wishes and opinions were embodied in the Amendment meant to stop the whole business. They did not want intoxicating liquor in the United States and reasonably may have thought that if they let it in some of it was likely to stay. When, therefore, the Amendment forbids not only importation into and exportation from the United States but transportation within it, the natural meaning of the words expresses an altogether probable intent."

(259 U. S. 80)

"In modern societies every part is related so organically to every other that what affects any portion must be felt more or less by all the rest. Therefore, unless everything is to be forbidden and legislation is to come to a stop, it is not enough to show that in the working of a statute there is some tendency logically discernible to interfere with commerce or existing contracts. Practical lines have to be drawn and distinctions of degree must be made."

(187 U. S. 611)

(Meat dealers, including Swift & Co., combined to affect prices as well as costs, agreeing not to bid against each other in the livestock markets of various States.)

"It is suggested that the several acts charged are lawful and that intent can make no difference. But they are bound together as the parts of a single plan. The plan may make the parts unlawful. . . . The statute gives this proceeding against combinations in restraint of commerce among the States and against attempts to monopolize the same. Intent is almost essential to such a combination and is essential to such an attempt.

"Where acts are not sufficient in themselves to produce a result which the law seeks to prevent—for instance, the monopoly—but require further acts in addition to the mere forces of nature to bring that result to pass, an intent to bring it to pass is necessary in order to produce a dangerous probability that it will happen. . . . But when that intent and the consequent dangerous probability exist, this statute, like many others and like the common law in some cases, directs itself against that dangerous probability as well as against the completed result. What we have said disposes incidentally of the objection to the bill as multifarious. The unity of the plan embraces all the parts.

"One further observation should be made. Although the combination alleged embraces restraint and monopoly of trade within a single State, its effect upon commerce among the States is not accidental, secondary, remote, or merely probable. On the allegations of the bill the latter commerce no less, perhaps even more, than commerce within a single State, is an object of attack. . . . Moreover, it is a direct object; it is that for the sake of which the several specific acts and courses of conduct are done and adopted.***

"The charge is not of a single agreement but of a course of conduct intended to be continued. Under the Act it is the duty of the Court, when applied to, to stop the conduct. The thing done and intended to be done is perfectly definite: with the purpose mentioned, directing the defendants' agents and inducing each other to refrain from competition in bids. The defendants cannot be ordered to compete but they properly can be forbidden to give directions or to make agreements not to compete."

(196 U. S. 375)

(Holmes concurred in the majority opinion on the *Arizona Employers' Liability Cases,* 1918, saying that to hold an employer liable for accidents was a worthy and constitutional policy. As for the burden imposed, he had a few words to add.)

"IF A BUSINESS is unsuccessful it means that the public does not care enough for it to make it pay. If it is successful the public pays its expenses and something more. It is reasonable that the public should pay the whole cost of producing what it wants and a part of that cost is the pain and mutilation incident to production. By throwing that loss upon the employer in the first instance we throw it upon the public in the long run and that is just. If a legislature should reason in this way and act accordingly it seems to me that it is within constitutional bounds."

(250 U. S. 400, 431)

Authority and Power

"IT MAY BE doubted how far any court can be bound by legislation after this Court has declared such legislation beyond the power of the State, any more than it would be if the law had been held unconstitutional."

(197 U. S. 233)

"ALTHOUGH RESEARCH has shown and practice has established the futility of the charge that it was a usurpation when this Court undertook to declare an Act of Congress unconstitutional, I suppose that we all agree that to do so is the gravest and most delicate duty that this Court is called on to perform. Upon this among other considerations the rule is settled that as between two possible interpretations of a statute, by one of which it would be unconstitutional and by the other valid, our plain duty is to adopt that which will save the Act. Even to avoid a serious doubt the rule is the same."

(275 U. S. 142, 147)

"WE ARE BOUND to be very cautious in coming to the conclusion that the Fourteenth Amendment has upset what thus far has been established and accepted for a long time."

(201 U. S. 140)

[285]

"Now and then an extraordinary case may turn up, but constitutional law like other mortal contrivances has to take some chances, and in the great majority of instances no doubt justice will be done."

(222 U. S. 1)

———

"While the courts must exercise a judgment of their own, it by no means is true that every law is void which may seem to the judges who pass upon it excessive, unsuited to its ostensible end, or based upon conceptions of morality with which they disagree. Considerable latitude must be allowed for differences of view as well as for possible peculiar conditions which this Court can know but imperfectly, if at all. Otherwise a constitution, instead of embodying only relatively fundamental rules of right, as generally understood by all English-speaking communities, would become the partisan of a particular set of ethical or economic opinions, which by no means are held *semper ubique et ab omnibus*.***

"No court would declare a usury law unconstitutional, even if every member of it believed that Jeremy Bentham had said the last word on that subject, and had shown for all time that such laws did more harm than good.

"The Sunday laws, no doubt, would be sustained by a bench of judges, even if every one of them thought it superstitious to make any day holy."

(187 U. S. 606)

———

"On the other hand, while this Court cannot refuse to exercise its own judgment, it naturally will lean toward the interpretation of a local statute adopted by a local court."

(206 U. S. 474)

(Missouri assailed the Migratory Bird Act, passed after a treaty had been signed with Canada, which regulated the shooting of game birds. Holmes answered both the complaint that the statute invaded Missouri's sovereign right and the assertion that she had a pecuniary interest as owner of the birds within her borders.)

"To put the claim of the State upon title is to lean upon a slender reed. Wild birds are not in the possession of anyone; and possession is the beginning of ownership. The whole foundation of the State's rights is the presence within their jurisdiction of birds that yesterday had not arrived, tomorrow may be in another State and in a week a thousand miles away. If we are to be accurate we cannot put the case of the State upon higher ground than that the treaty deals with creatures that for the moment are within the State borders, that it must be carried out by officers of the United States within the same territory, and that, but for the treaty, the State would be free to regulate this subject itself.***

"No doubt, the great body of private relations usually falls within the control of the State, but a treaty may override its power. We do not have to invoke the later developments of constitutional law for this proposition; it was recognized as early as [1806]. . . .

"Here a national interest of very nearly the first magnitude is involved. It can be protected only by national action in concert with that of another power. The subject-matter is only transitorily within the State and has no permanent habitat therein. But for the treaty and the statute there soon might be no birds for any powers to deal with. We see nothing in the Constitution that compels the Government to sit by while a food supply is cut off and the protectors of our forest and our crops are destroyed. It is not sufficient to rely upon the States. The reliance is vain, and were it otherwise the question is whether the United States is forbidden to act. We are of opinion that the treaty and the statute must be upheld."

(252 U. S. 416)

(Pennsylvania forbade aliens to kill wild birds or animals and to possess shotguns for that end.)

"THE QUESTION therefore narrows itself down to whether this Court can say that the Legislature of Pennsylvania was not warranted in assuming as its premise for the law that resident unnaturalized aliens were the peculiar source of the evil that it desired to prevent. Obviously the question so stated is one of local experience on which this Court ought to be very slow to declare that the state legislature was wrong in its facts. If we might trust popular speech in some States it was right—but it is enough that this Court has no such knowledge of local conditions as to be able to say that it was manifestly wrong.***

"It is to be remembered that the subject of this whole discussion is wild game, which the State may preserve for its own citizens if it pleases."

(232 U. S. 138)

———————

(Montana exacted a ten-dollar license fee from all engaged in the hand laundry business, exempting steam laundries and women workers where not more than two women were employed. A Chinese charged unequal protection and sued to recover his ten dollars.)

"A STATE does not deny the equal protection of the laws merely by adjusting its revenue laws and taxing system in such a way as to favor certain industries or forms of industry. Like the United States, although with more restriction and in less degree, a State may carry out a policy, even a policy with which we might disagree.*** If a State sees fit to encourage steam laundries and discourage hand laundries, that is its own affair. And if again it finds a ground of distinction in sex, that is not without precedent.*** If Montana deems it advisable to put a lighter burden upon women than upon men with regard to employment that our people commonly regard as more appropriate for the former, the Fourteenth Amendment does not interfere by creating a fictitious equality where there is a real difference. The particular points at which that difference shall be emphasized by legislation are largely in the power of the State.

"Another difficulty suggested by the statute is that it is impossible not to ask whether it is not aimed at the Chinese; which would be a discrimination that the Constitution does not allow.*** But this ground of objection was not urged and rather was disclaimed when it was mentioned from the Bench at the argument. It may or may not be that if the facts were called to our attention in a proper way the objection would prove to be real.*** Laws frequently are enforced which the Court recognizes as possibly or probably invalid if attacked by a different interest or in a different way. Therefore without prejudice to the question that we have suggested when it shall be raised, we must conclude that so far as the present case is concerned, the judgment must be affirmed."

(223 U. S. 59)

(The eight-hour day for female hotel and restaurant workers was opposed by an Arizona hotel because the State law provided that the time must be spent within a twelve-hour period, except in the case of eating places on a railroad right of way.)

"THE FOURTEENTH AMENDMENT is not a pedagogical requirement of the impracticable. The equal protection of the laws does not mean that all occupations that are called by the same name must be treated in the same way.*** Presumably, or at least possibly, the main custom of restaurants upon railroad rights of way comes from the passengers upon trains that stop to allow them to eat. The work must be adjusted to the hours of the trains. This fact makes a practical and, it may be, an important distinction between such restaurants and others.

"If in its theory the distinction is justifiable as for all that we know it is, the fact that some cases, including the plaintiff's, are very near to the line makes it none the worse. That is the inevitable result of drawing a line where the distinctions are distinctions of degree; and the constant business of the law is to draw such lines."

(249 U. S. 265)

"THE MAIN GROUND is the authority of the United States to remove obstructions to interstate and foreign commerce. There is no question that this power is superior to that of the States to provide for the welfare or necessities of their inhabitants.

"In matters where the States may act the action of Congress overrides what they have done. But in matters where the national importance is imminent and direct even where Congress has been silent, the States may not act at all.

"Evidence is sufficient, if evidence is necessary, to show that a withdrawal of water on the scale directed by the statute of Illinois threatens and will affect the level of the Lakes, and that is a matter which cannot be done without the consent of the United States, even were there no international covenant in the case."

(266 U. S. 405)

(A carpenters' union was called a conspiracy under the Sherman Law and the New York penal law by employers who found it impossible to have work done in Manhattan and Brooklyn except by union labor.)

[290]

"As this court is not the final authority concerning the laws of New York we say but a word about them. We shall not believe that the ordinary action of a labor union can be made the ground of an injunction under those laws until we are so instructed by the New York Court of Appeals. Certainly the conduct complained of has no tendency to produce a monopoly of manufacture or building since the more successful it is the more competitors are introduced into the trade."

(244 U. S. 459)

"If a case is carried through the state courts upon arguments drawn from the State constitution alone, the defeated party cannot try his chances here merely by suggesting for the first time when he takes his writ of error that the decision is wrong under the Constitution of the United States."

(204 U. S. 565)

"An osteopath undertakes to be something more than a nurse or a masseur, and the difference rests precisely in a claim to greater science, which the State requires him to prove."

(223 U. S. 288)

(The Court held that a State's liability law extended to the high seas in a case where there had been a collision between ships both owned by companies incorporated in that State. Holmes gave the reasons and made a few observations.)

"In short, the bare fact of the parties being outside the territory in a place belonging to no other sovereign would not

[291]

limit the authority of the State, as accepted by civilized theory. No one doubts the power of England or France to govern their own ships upon the high seas.***

"The doubt in this case arises as to the power of the States where Congress has remained silent. That doubt, however, cannot be serious. The grant of admiralty jurisdiction, followed and construed by the Judiciary Act of 1789, 'saving to suitors in all cases the right of a common-law remedy where the common law is competent to give it,' leaves open the common-law jurisdiction of the state courts over torts committed at sea. This, we believe, has always been admitted. . . . And as the State courts in their decisions would follow their own notions about the law and might change them from time to time, it would be strange if the State might not make changes by its other mouthpiece, the legislature. The same argument that deduces the legislative power of Congress from the jurisdiction of the National courts tends to establish the legislative power of the State where Congress has not acted.***

"Nor would there be produced any lamentable lack of uniformity. Courts constantly enforce rights arising from and depending upon other laws than those governing the local transactions of the jurisdiction in which they sit. But we are not concerned with these considerations. In this case the statutes of the United States have enabled the owner to transfer its liability to a fund and to the exclusive jurisdiction of the admiralty, and it has done so. That fund is being distributed. In such circumstances all claims to which the admiralty does not deny existence must be recognized, whether admiralty liens or not. This is not only a general principle but is the result of the statute which provides for as well as limits the liability and allows it to be proved against the fund."

(207 U. S. 398)

"THE FOURTEENTH AMENDMENT, itself a historical product, did not destroy history for the States and substitute mechanical compartments of law all exactly alike. If a thing has been practiced for two hundred years by common consent, it will need a strong case for the Fourteenth Amendment to affect it."

(260 U. S. 22)

"SOME RATHER WEAK cases must fall within any law which is couched in general words."

(188 U. S. 720)

(Virginia forbade mining and manufacturing firms to issue scrip in payment of labor. Employees of a protesting coke company were given orders to pay bearer "in merchandise only from your store.")

"THE OBJECTIONS that are urged here are that the statute interferes with freedom of contract, and, more especially, that it is class legislation of a kind supposed to be inconsistent with the Fourteenth Amendment, a West Virginia decision upon a similar statute being cited to that effect. . . . The former of these objections, however, is disposed of by *Knoxville Iron Co.* v. *Harbison,* 183 U. S. 13.

"It is more pressed that the Act discriminates unconstitutionally against certain classes. But while there are differences of opinion as to the degree and kind of discrimination permitted by the Fourteenth Amendment, it is established by repeated decisions that a statute aimed at what is deemed an evil, and hitting it presumably where experience shows it to be most felt, is not to be upset by thinking up and enumerating other instances to which it might have been applied equally well, so far as this Court can see. That is for the legislature to judge

[293]

unless the case is very clear. The suggestion that others besides mining and manufacturing companies may keep shops and pay their workmen with orders on themselves for merchandise is not enough to overthrow a law that must be presumed to be deemed by the legislature coextensive with the practical need."

(234 U. S. 224)

(A Negro in El Paso was not allowed to vote in a Democratic primary election because a Texas law forbade it in so many words. His suit for damages was dismissed by the District Court on the ground that the subject-matter was political and not in its jurisdiction.)

"THE OBJECTION that the subject-matter of the suit is political is little more than a play upon words. Of course the petition concerns political action but it alleges and seeks to recover for private damage. That private damage may be caused by such political action and may be recovered for in a suit at law hardly has been doubted for over two hundred years. . . . If the defendants' conduct was a wrong to the plaintiff the same reasons that allow a recovery for denying the plaintiff a vote at a final election allow it for denying a vote at the primary election that may determine the final result.

"The important question is whether the statute can be sustained. But although we state it as a question the answer does not seem to us open to a doubt. We find it unnecessary to consider the Fifteenth Amendment, because it seems to us hard to imagine a more direct and obvious infringement of the Fourteenth. That Amendment, while it applies to all, was passed, as we know, with a special intent to protect the blacks from discrimination against them.***

"States may do a good deal of classifying that it is difficult to believe rational, but there are limits, and it is too clear for ex-

[294]

tended argument that color cannot be made the basis of statutory classification affecting the right set up in this case."

(273 U. S. 536)

(One of the clauses in the Act of Congress creating the Federal Trade Commission empowered that body to make investigations.)

"THE MERE FACTS of carrying on a commerce not confined within state lines and of being organized as a corporation do not make men's affairs public, as those of a railroad company now may be. Anyone who respects the spirit as well as the letter of the Fourth Amendment would be loath to believe that Congress intended to authorize one of its subordinate agencies to sweep all our traditions into the fire . . . and to direct fishing expeditions into private papers on the possibility that they may disclose evidence of crime.***

"The interruption of business, the possible revelation of trade secrets, and the expense that compliance with the Commission's wholesale demand would cause are the least considerations. It is contrary to the first principles of justice to allow a search through all the respondents' records, revelant or irrelevant, in the hope that something will turn up."

(264 U. S. 298)

(Real estate belonging to a railroad was assessed for grading and paving. The property received no improvement, said the owners; on the contrary, increased travel would hurt it.)

"THERE IS A LOOK of logic when it is said that special assessments are founded on special benefits and that a law which makes it possible to assess beyond the amount of the special benefit attempts to rise above its source. But that mode of argument assumes an exactness in the premises which does not exist.

"The foundation of this familiar form of taxation is a question of theory. The amount of benefit which an improvement will confer upon particular land, indeed whether it is a benefit at all, is a matter of forecast and estimate. In its general aspects at least it is peculiarly a thing to be decided by those who make the law. The result of the supposed constitutional principle is simply to shift the burden to a somewhat large taxing district, the municipality, and to disguise rather than to answer the theoretic doubt.

"It is dangerous to tie down legislatures too closely by judicial constructions not necessarily arising from the words of the Constitution. Particularly, as was intimated in *Spencer* v. *Merchant*, 125 U. S. 345, it is important for this Court to avoid extracting from the very general language of the Fourteenth Amendment a system of delusive exactness in order to destroy methods of taxation which were well known when that Amendment was adopted and which it is safe to say that no one then supposed would be disturbed. It is now established beyond permissible controversy that laws like the one before us are not contrary to the Constitution of the United States.***

"If an occupant could not escape by professing his desire for solitude and silence, the legislature may make a similar desire fortified by structures equally ineffective. It may say that it is enough that the land could be turned to the purposes for which the paving would increase its value. Indeed, it is apparent that the prophecy in the answer cannot be regarded as absolute even while the present use of the land continues—for no one can say that changes might not make a station desirable at this point; in which case the advantages of a paved street could not be denied."

(197 U. S. 430)

(This was a case involving assessing for street-widening.)

"BUT WHEN the chance of the cost exceeding the benefit grows large and the amount of the not improbable excess is great, it may not follow that the case last cited [immediately above] will be a precedent. Constitutional rights like others are matters of degree. To illustrate: Under the police power, in its strict sense, a certain limit might be set to the height of buildings without compensation; but to make that limit five feet would require compensation and a taking by eminent domain. So it well might be that a form of assessment that would be valid for paving would not be valid for the more serious expenses involved in the taking of land."

(205 U. S. 135)

———

"THE STATE has absolute power over the subject [Prohibition of intoxicating liquor, 1904]. It does not abridge that power by adopting the form of reference to a local vote. It may favor prohibition to just such degree as it chooses, and to that end may let in a local vote upon the subject as much or as little as it may please. There is no such overmastering consideration of expediency attaching everywhere and always to the form of voting, still less is there any such principle to be drawn from the Fourteenth Amendment, as requires the two sides of a vote on prohibition to be treated with equal favor by the State, the subject-matter of the vote being wholly within the State's control."

(193 U. S. 504)

———

"WITH THE development of its effects there has been some reaction against the Benthamite doctrine of absolute freedom of contract. But courts are not legislatures and are not at liberty to invent and apply specific regulations according to their notions of convenience. In the absence of a statute their only duty is to discover the meaning of the contract and to enforce it, without leaning in either direction, when, as in the present case, the parties stood on equal footing and were free to do what they chose."

(205 U. S. 340)

(Massachusetts required half-fare for public school children.)

"IN THE NEXT PLACE, if the only ground were that the charter of the Elevated Railway contained a contract against the imposition of such a requirement, it would be attributing to the Fourteenth Amendment an excessively nice operation to say that the immunity of a single corporation prevented the passage of an otherwise desirable and wholesome law. It is unnecessary to consider what would be the effect on the statute by construction in Massachusetts if the exception could not be upheld. For, if in order to avoid the Scylla of unjustifiable class legislation, the law were read as universal, it might be thought by this Court to fall into the Charybdis of impairing the obligation of a contract with the elevated road, although that objection might perhaps be held not to be open to the plaintiff in error here.***

"Moreover, while it may be true that in some cases rates or fares may be reduced to an unprofitable point in view of the business as a whole or upon special considerations, it is not enough to justify a general law like this, that the companies concerned still may be able to make a profit from other sources for all that appears. Notwithstanding the foregoing considerations I hesitatingly agree with the State court that the requirement may be justified under what is commonly called the police power. The obverse way of stating this power in the sense in which I am using the phrase would be that constitutional rights like others are matters of degree, that the great constitutional provisions for the protection of property are not to be pushed to a logical extreme, but must be taken to permit the infliction of some fractional and relatively small losses without compensation, for some at least of the purposes of wholesome legislation.

"If the Fourteenth Amendment is not to be a greater hamper upon the established practices of the States in common with other governments than I think was intended, they must be allowed a certain latitude in the minor adjustments of life, even though by their action the burdens of a part of the community are somewhat increased. The traditions and habits of centuries were not intended to be overthrown when that Amendment was passed.

"Education is one of the purposes for which what is called police power may be exercised. Massachusetts always has recognized it as one of the first objects of public care. It does not follow that it would be equally in accord with the conceptions at the base of our constitutional law to confer equal favors upon doctors, or workingmen, or people who could afford to buy one-thousand-mile tickets. Structural habits count for as much as logic in drawing the line. And, to return to the taking of property, the aspect in which I am considering the case, general taxation to maintain public schools is an appropriation of property to a use in which the taxpayer may have no private interest, and, it may be, against his will. It has been condemned by some theorists on that ground. Yet no one denies its constitutionality. People are accustomed to it and accept it without doubt. The present requirement is not different in fundamental principle, although the tax is said to be in kind and falls only on the class capable of paying that kind of tax—a class of *quasi* public corporations specially subject to legislative control.

"Thus the question narrows itself down to the magnitude of the burden imposed—to whether the tax is so great as to exceed the limits of the police power. Looking at the law without regard to its special operation I should hesitate to assume that its total effect, direct and indirect, upon the roads outside of Boston amounted to a more serious burden than a change in the law of nuisance, for example, might be. Turning to the specific effect, the offer of proof was cautious. It was simply that a 'considerable percentage' of the passengers carried by the company consisted of pupils of the public schools. This might be true without the burden becoming serious. I am not prepared to overrule the decision of the Legislature and of the highest court of Massachusetts that the requirement is reasonable under the conditions existing there, upon evidence that goes no higher than this. It is not enough that a statute goes to the verge of constitutional power. We must be able to see clearly that it goes beyond that power. In case of real doubt a law must be sustained."

(207 U. S. 79)

"THE FOUNDATION of jurisdiction is physical power."

(244 U. S. 456)

(The State gives the railroad the right to occupy land and in return may insist that crossings should not be dangerous to the public. This was Holmes' answer to the plea of the Erie Railroad that compliance with a grade-crossing law would bankrupt it.)

"THAT THE STATES might be so foolish as to kill a goose that lays golden eggs for them has no bearing on their constitutional rights. If it reasonably can be said that safety requires the change it is for them to say whether they will insist upon it, and neither prospective bankruptcy nor engagement in interstate commerce can take away this fundamental right of the sovereign of the soil.*** Intelligent self-interest should lead to a careful consideration of what the road is able to do without ruin, but this is not a constitutional duty."

(254 U. S. 394)

(A suit to determine what proportion of Virginia's debt West Virginia had incurred before their separation.)

"THE CASE is to be considered in the untechnical spirit proper for dealing with a quasi-international controversy, remembering that there is no municipal code governing the matter, and that this Court may be called on to adjust differences that cannot be dealt with by Congress or disposed of by the legislature of either State alone.***

"As this is no ordinary commercial suit but, as we have said, a quasi-international difference referred to this Court in reliance upon the honor and constitutional obligations of the States concerned rather than upon ordinary remedies, we think it best at this stage to go no farther, but to await the effect of a conference between the parties, which, whatever the outcome, must take place. If the cause should be pressed contentiously to the end, it could be referred to a master to go over the figures that we have given provisionally, and to make such calculations as might become necessary. But this case is one that calls for forebearance on both sides. Great States have a temper superior to that of private litigants, and it is to be hoped that enough has been decided for patriotism, the fraternity of the Union and mutual consideration to bring it to an end."

(220 U. S. 1)

[301]

"IT IS a sufficient answer to say that you cannot carry a constitution out with mathematical nicety to logical extremes. If you could, we never should have heard of the police power. And this is still more true of taxation, which in most communities is a long way off from a logical and coherent theory."

(211 U. S. 446)

"AND IN STATES bound together by a Constitution and subject to the Fourteenth Amendment, great caution should be used not to let fiction deny the fair play that can be secured only by a pretty close adhesion to fact."

(243 U. S. 90)

"CONSTITUTIONS ARE intended to preserve practical and substantial rights, not to maintain theories."

(194 U. S. 451)

Words, Music and Copyrights

"**W**ORDS EXPRESS whatever meaning convention has attached to them."

(231 U. S. 683)

"**B**UT THE provisions of the Constitution are not mathematical formulas having their essence in their form; they are organic living institutions transplanted from English soil. Their significance is vital not formal; it is to be gathered not simply by taking the words and a dictionary, but by considering their origin and the line of their growth."

(233 U. S. 604)

(Although sustaining an injunction against infringement in the case of *Coca-Cola Co.* v. *Koke Co.*, Holmes' opinion modified the order in various respects.)

"**T**HE DECREE of the District Court restrains the defendant from using the word 'dope.' The plaintiff illustrated in a very striking way the fact that the word is one of the most featureless known even to the language of those who are incapable of discriminating speech. In some places it would be used to call for Coca-Cola. It equally would have been used to call for anything else having about it a faint aureole of poison."

(254 U. S. 143)

[303]

(Two copyrighted compositions of Victor Herbert, a march, *From Maine to Oregon*, and a song, *Sweethearts*, were played in a New York restaurant, infringing the exclusive right of copyright owners to perform their work publicly for profit. "There was no charge for admission to hear the music," was the defense.)

"IF THE RIGHTS under the copyright are infringed only by a performance where money is taken at the door they are very imperfectly protected. Performances not different in kind from those of the defendants could be given that might compete with and even destroy the success of the monopoly that the law intends the plaintiffs to have. It is enough to say that there is no need to construe the statute so narrowly.

"The defendants' performances are not eleemosynary. They are part of a total for which the public pays, and the fact that the price of the whole is attributed to a particular item which those present are expected to order, is not important. It is true that the music is not the sole object, but neither is the food, which probably could be got cheaper elsewhere. The object is a repast in surroundings that to people having limited powers of conversation or disliking the rival noise give a luxurious pleasure not to be had from eating a silent meal. If music did not pay it would be given up. If it pays it pays out of the public's pocket. Whether it pays or not, the purpose of employing it is profit and that is enough."

(242 U. S. 591)

(A department store put on sale a brand of hosiery imitating another firm's label—red square with diagonal black band—which had lost protection as a trademark.)

"ORDINARILY IMITATION is enough to imply that the matter imitated is important at least to the sale of the goods. But when the similarity arises as the one before us did, it indicates nothing except perhaps the poverty of the designer's invention. Furthermore the defendants' persistence in their use of the design after notice proves little or nothing against them."

(240 U. S. 179)

(Holmes concurred in an opinion vindicating a music-roll house, sued by music publishers. It was 1907, and the copyright law had not been modernized in conformity with mechanical progress.)

"ON PRINCIPLE anything that mechanically reproduces that collocation of sounds ought to be held a copy, or if the statute is too narrow ought to be made so by a further Act, except so far as some extraneous consideration of policy may oppose."

(209 U. S. 1, 18)

(In 1911 a motion picture was made of *Ben Hur*, violating the exclusive right of authors to dramatize their works. Harper Bros. said this was a dramatization. The Kalem Co. denied it and added that a monopoly cannot be extended to an author's ideas.)

"WE ARE OF OPINION that *Ben Hur* was dramatized by what was done. Whether we consider the purpose of this clause of the statute, or the etymological history and present usages of language, drama may be achieved by action as well as by speech. Action can tell a story, display all the most vivid relations between men, and depict every kind of human emotion, without the aid of a word. It would be impossible to deny the title of drama to pantomime as played by masters of the art. But if a pantomime of *Ben Hur* would be a dramatizing of *Ben Hur*, it would be none the less so that it was exhibited to the audience by reflection from a glass and not by direct vision of the figures—as sometimes has been done in order to produce ghostly or inexplicable effects.

"The essence of the matter in the case last supposed is not the mechanism employed but that we see the event or story lived. The moving pictures are only less vivid than reflections from a mirror. With the former as with the latter our visual impression—what we see—is caused by the real pantomime of real men, through the medium of natural forces, although the machinery is different and more complex. How it would be if the illusion of motion were produced from paintings instead of from photographs of the real thing may be left open until the question shall arise.

"It is said that the pictures of scenes in a novel may be made and exhibited without infringing the copyright and that they may be copyrighted themselves. Indeed, it was conceded by the Circuit Court of Appeals that these films could be copyrighted and, we may assume, could be exhibited as photographs. Whether this concession is correct or not, in view of the fact that they are photographs of an unlawful dramatization of the novel, we need not decide. We will assume that it is. But it does not follow that the use of them in motion does not infringe the author's rights. The most innocent objects, such as the mirror in the other case that we have supposed, may be used for unlawful purposes. And if, as we have tried to show, moving pictures may be used for dramatizing a novel, when the photographs are used in that way they are used to infringe a right which the statute reserves.***

"It is argued that the law construed as we have construed it goes beyond the power conferred upon Congress by the Constitution, to secure to authors for a limited time the exclusive right to their writings. (Art. I, § 8, cl.8.) It is suggested that to extend the copyright to a case like this is to extend it to the ideas as distinguished from the words in which those ideas are clothed. But there is no attempt to make a monopoly of the ideas expressed. The law confines itself to a particular, cognate and well-known form of reproduction. If to that extent a grant of monopoly is thought a proper way to secure the right to the writings this Court cannot say that Congress was wrong."

(222 U. S. 55)

"A WORD IS NOT a crystal, transparent and unchanged; it is the skin of a living thought and may vary greatly in color and content according to the circumstances and the time in which it is used."

(245 U. S. 418)

(The International News Service was enjoined from filching news from the bulletins sent by the Associated Press to its members "until its commercial value *** has passed away." Mr. Justice Pitney wrote the opinion that news articles may be copyrighted; that the special interest of uncopyrighted news matter is lost upon first publication but the appropriation of the result of news-gathering activity is unfair competition. Holmes wrote a separate opinion and proposed a way out, while Brandeis dissented from the majority, saying that it was for legislatures, not for courts, to specify the regulations.)

"WHEN AN uncopyrighted combination of words is published there is no general right to forbid other people repeating them—in other words there is no property in the combination or in the thoughts or facts that the words express. Property, a creation of the law, does not arise from value, although exchangeable—a matter of fact. Many exchangeable values may be destroyed intentionally without compensation. Property depends upon exclusion by law from interference, and a person is not excluded from using any combination of words merely because someone had used it before, even if it took labor and genius to make it. If a given person is to be prohibited from making the use of words that his neighbors are free to make, some other ground must be found.

"One such ground is vaguely expressed in the phrase unfair trade. This means that the words are repeated by a competitor in business in such a way as to convey a misrepresentation that materially injures the person who first used them, by appropriating credit of some kind which the first user has earned. The ordinary case is a representation by device, appearance, or other indirection that the defendant's goods come from the plaintiff. But the only reason why it is actionable to make such a representation is that it tends to give the defendant an advantage in his competition with the plaintiff and that it is thought undesirable that an advantage should be gained in that way. Apart from that the defendant may use such unpatented devices and uncopyrighted combinations of words as he likes. The ordinary case, I say, is palming off the defendant's product as the plaintiff's, but the same evil may follow from the opposite falsehood —from saying, whether in words or by implication, that the plaintiff's product is the defendant's, and that, it seems to me, is what has happened here.

"Fresh news is got only by enterprise and expense. To produce such news as it is produced by the defendant represents by implication that it has been acquired by the defendant's enterprise and at its expense. When it comes from one of the great news-collecting agencies like the Associated Press, the source generally is indicated, plainly importing that credit; and that such a representation is implied may be inferred with some confidence from the unwillingness of the defendant to give the credit and to tell the truth. If the plaintiff produces the news at the same time that the defendant does, the defendant's presentation impliedly denies to the plaintiff the credit of collecting the facts and assumes that credit to the defendant. If the plaintiff is later in Western cities it naturally will be supposed to have obtained its information from the defendant. The falsehood is a little more subtle, the injury a little more indirect, than in ordinary cases of unfair trade, but I think that the principle that condemns the one condemns the other.

"It is a question of how strong an infusion of fraud is necessary to turn a flavor into a poison. The dose seems to me strong enough here to need a remedy from the law. But as, in my view, the only ground of complaint that can be recognized without legislation is the implied misstatement, it can be corrected by stating the truth; and a suitable acknowledgment of the source is all that the plaintiff can require. I think that within the limits recognized by the decision of the Court the defendant should be enjoined from publishing news obtained from the Associated Press for—hours after publication by the plaintiff unless it gives express credit to the Associated Press; the number of hours and the form of acknowledgment to be settled by the District Court."

(248 U. S. 215, 246)

(An excuse for copying pictures from a billposter was that they were not art. Justice Holmes rejected it and at the same time extended the scope of copyright. But Justices Harlan and McKenna maintained that the Constitution did not permit protection to "embrace a mere advertisement of a circus.")

"OTHERS ARE FREE to copy the original. They are not free to copy the copy. . . . The copy is the personal reaction of an individual upon nature. Personality always contains something unique. It expresses its singularity even in handwriting, and a very modest grade of art has in it something irreducible, which is one man's alone. That something he may copyright unless there is a restriction in the words of the Act.

"If there is a restriction it is not to be found in the limited pretentions of these particular works. The least pretentious picture has more originality in it than directories and the like, which may be copyrighted.*** These chromolithographs are 'pictorial illustrations.' The word 'illustrations' does not mean that they must illustrate the text of a book, and that the etchings of Rembrandt or Steinla's engraving of the Madonna di San Sisto could not be protected today if any man were able to produce them.

"Again, the Act, however construed, does not mean that ordinary posters are not good enough to be considered within its scope. The antithesis to 'illustrations or works connected with the fine arts' [quoted from the copyright law] is not works of little merit or of humble degree, or illustrations addressed to the less educated classes; it is 'prints or labels designed to be used for any other articles of manufacture' [quoted from the patent law]. Certainly works are not the less connected with the fine arts because their pictorial quality attracts the crowd and therefore gives them a real use—if use means to increase trade and to help to make money. A picture is none the less a picture and none the less a subject of copyright that it is used for an advertisement. And if pictures may be used to advertise soap, or the theater, or monthly magazines, as they are, they may be used to advertise a circus. Of course, the ballet is as legitimate a subject for illustration as any other. A rule cannot be laid down that would excommunicate the paintings of Degas.***

"It would be a dangerous undertaking for persons trained only to the law to constitute themselves final judges of the worth of pictorial illustrations, outside of the narrowest and most obvious limits. At one extreme some works of genius would be sure to miss appreciation. Their very novelty would make them repulsive until the public had learned the new language in which their author spoke. It may be more than doubted, for instance, whether the etchings of Goya or the paintings of Manet would have been sure of protection when seen for the first time. At the other end, copyright would be denied to pictures which appealed to a public less educated than the judge. Yet if they command the interest of any public they have a commercial value—it would be bold to say that they have not an aesthetic and educational value—and the taste of any public is not to be treated with contempt. It is an ultimate fact for the moment, whatever may be our hopes for a change. That these pictures had their worth and their success is sufficiently shown by the desire to reproduce them without regard to the plaintiffs' rights. We are of opinion that there was evidence that the plaintiffs have rights entitled to the protection of the law."

(188 U. S. 239)

"BUT WHATEVER the consequences we must accept the plain meaning of plain words."

(206 U. S. 240)

[311]

INDEX